CYNEFIN®

weaving sense-making
into the fabric of
our world

DAVE SNOWDEN & FRIENDS

Edited by Riva Greenberg and Boudewijn Bertsch
Commissioned by Sonja Blignaut and Zhen Goh | Illustrated by Sue Borchardt
Contributions by:

Milica Begovic

Elmi Bester

Sonja Blignaut

Chris Bolton

Mary E. Boone

Greg Brougham

Anne Caspari & Johann Entz-
von Zerssen

Chris Corrigan

Jennifer Garvey-Berger, Carolyn
Coughlin, Keith Johnston &
Jim Wicks

Zhen Goh

Friso Gosliga

Riva Greenberg & Boudewijn
Bertsch

Lou Hayes Jr.

Steve Holt

Trent Hone

Harold Jarche

Iwan Jenkins

Alicia Juarrero

Gabriel Jurj

Liz Keogh

Marion Kiely & Ellie Snowden

Robert Koch

Steve McCrone & Ian Snape

Anne McMurray

Anna Panagiotou

Ann Pendleton-Jullian

Vivienne (Viv) Read

Kendra Rosencrans

Dave Snowden

Peter Stanbridge

John Turner & Nigel Thurlow

Jesko von den Steinen

Juanita Uribe & Andrés Jiménez

Simon Wardley

Gary Wong & Michael Cheveldave

Jules Yim

ACCLAIM FOR CYNEFIN®

"For many years I have been asking Dave to write a book to explain the Cynefin Framework. A book would allow many of us to benefit from concepts such as distributed cognition, exaptation, and contextual coherence. It gives me enormous pleasure that this day has arrived. You are reading the "Cynefin" book. I fully expect it will establish the Framework far beyond Dave's loyal network of followers whom he has managed to grow around him and his ideas, with his passion, endless generosity, and openness."

- *Andrea Tomasini: CEO, agile42*

"We have all moved from the age of enlightenment to the age of entanglement where sense-making aided by imagination is now more critical than ever. This book on the 21st anniversary of Cognitive Edge helps re-orient us to Dave's critical insights on complexity theory beautifully framed by his Cynefin Framework. It also highlights the community that has been built off of his thinking – on the ground wrestling with the ideas and practice that have been evolving over the past two continually disruptive decades. Dave is an edge-thinker and this is an edge community in the best sense – one that is deeply inspiring. I look forward to reading all of the pieces and continuing to follow the work being done at a moment when this thinking and practice are more critical than ever."

- *John Seely Brown: Former Chief Scientist Xerox Corporation and Director of Xerox Palo Alto Research Center (PARC)*

"The Cynefin Framework has been highly influential for planners and decision makers. Also impressive is the range of interventions crafted by the Cynefin community. In addition, I frequently refer back to the research project on team sense-making that I did with Dave Snowden and Chew Lock Pin."

- *Gary Klein: International expert on psychology and cognition. Author of Sources of Power, and Founder of Klein Associates and Shadowbox LLC*

"Knowledge of Cynefin should be required by leaders and decision makers in all organizations. I was trained as an engineer and led to believe there is only one way to approach a project; analyze and plan, resource and cost, implement, and finally operate and maintain. Good for building bridges as well as IT systems. But then why do large multi-stakeholders IT projects and attempts to transfer best practice from one organization to another often appear as wicked problems? Cynefin provides the answer – context determines the approach and choosing the wrong option often leads to unintended consequences. Dave's insights on the complex domain are especially relevant as more and more of the challenges we face in a hyper-connected digital world will fall into this category."

- Les Hales M.A.(Cantab): Chair, Innovation and Technology Committee, British Chamber of Commerce Hong Kong

"I am an engineering scientist and I study and co-create engineering designers, design thinkers, and innovation ecosystems in my practice. Cynefin has been a useful navigational tool for me, especially in terms of the symbol systems narrative and administrative aspects of design in contrast to the physical, energy, and thermodynamic aspects. In addition, Dave has been a wonderful and engaged collaborator, as well as an excellent educator. This latter role has been well captured and preserved in Dave's generosity in maintaining a living history of the development of Cynefin seen through various lenses - Dave (Physics, Theology), Cynthia Kurtz (Biology, Ecology), Max Boissot (Architecture, Information), Ikejuro Nonaka (Administrative Thinking, Information Flow) to name a few. This has allowed me to use Cynefin as a conceptual translational instrument between and within several disciplines. In a parallel manner, I have interacted with other members of his team at Cognitive Edge, in particular Zhen Goh, and I have seen how SenseMaker complements Cynefin, and can be used as a pragmatic translational tool to shift beliefs between and within different anthropologically defined populations. This combination of a deep scientific instrument and a generative technological tool, coming from the same person and organization is a rare occurrence, and I must tip my hat to Dave's integrity in keeping the instrument, the tool, and the people together this long, in short, for his sacrifice and perseverance."

- Ade Mabogunje: Center for Design Research, Stanford University

"This book makes a contribution to close the gap between theory and practice. It represents a valuable contribution to making the science of complexity more accessible for business practitioners. It is filled with rich text from different application situations to share with readers more about "how to" work with and through complexity to reach well grounded insights."

Prof Marius Ungerer: Professor, Strategy, Change & Leadership

Cynefin®: weaving sense-making into the fabric of our world

The Cynefin® sense-making Framework, brainchild of innovative thinker Dave Snowden, has never been more needed. The Framework empowers leaders across organizations, governments, and local communities, to work with uncertainty – to navigate complexity, create resilience, and thrive. As Snowden says, "The Framework guides us to make sense of the world, so that we can skillfully act in it." Come with us on the remarkable 21-year journey of Cynefin, a framework that enables people from all walks of life to improve – their situation, their work, their business, their relationships, and their environment. Cynefin practitioners share their wisdom, applications, and experiences using the Framework, across healthcare, leadership facilitation, organizational behavior, safety, software development, strategy, and well-being. You'll discover how to not only 'ride the rapids of complexity,' but find in so doing, grace, power, and inexplicable opportunity.

By Dave Snowden and Friends
Editors: Riva Greenberg and Boudewijn Bertsch
Commissioning Editors: Zhen Goh and Sonja Blignaut
Illustrator: Sue Borchardt
Production Editor: Gustav Rischmüller
Published by Cognitive Edge Pte Ltd

Regus One Raffles Place, Level 24, Tower 1, Singapore, 048616
www.cognitive-edge.com

Wayfinding icons designed by Freepik (freepik.com)

ISBN 978-1-7353799-0-6

To everyone navigating uncertainty

TABLE OF CONTENTS

NOTE FROM THE EDITORS

Boudewijn discovered Dave Snowden's work through an article in the IBM Systems Journal in 2003, and was captivated. In February 2007 he attended a workshop with Dave Snowden and Michael Cheveldave in Calgary, Canada. He then had his moment of discovery, while we were dining in a restaurant, that managing type 1 diabetes lives mostly in the Complex domain. It was life-changing for both of us and we write about that incident in this book. In 2010 we presented the Cynefin Framework together at the American Association of Diabetes Educators' annual conference. Our audience was intrigued. The Framework has accompanied and informed our work in diabetes and Boudewijn's leadership development work since 2007.

So how did we become the editors of this book? We call Zhen Goh to the witness stand. She visited New York and had dinner with each of us on separate occasions. The relationship grew. Impressed that Riva had written three books, and knowing Boudewijn was a Snowden disciple, she asked if we would edit this book you're holding.

We are delighted to contribute to Cynefin's celebratory moment, but please do cut us a little slack as we are not professional editors. Like everyone who has contributed to this book, it was an act of love – and we gave it our best go. We have also done our best to honor the original voices of the authors herein, and their passion and largesse.

To the Cognitive Edge team, we express our sincere gratitude for letting us walk with you in the Complex domain birthing this book – while yes, even taking an occasional dip into the Chaotic and Confused domains.

To the reader we say: "Dip in wherever you like in this book." Make this book that celebrates the 21st year of the Cynefin Framework, our birthday gift to Dave, a gift also to yourself. Trust us, you will be rewarded.

Riva Greenberg and Boudewijn Bertsch

Brooklyn, NY

INTRODUCTION

SONJA BLIGNAUT

I vividly remember the first time I was introduced to Dave and his weird swoopy lined framework. It was 2002, the terrible events of 9/11 were still fresh in everyone's mind. United States Secretary of Defense, Donald Rumsfeld, famously stated in a news briefing, "As we know, there are known knowns, there are things we know we know. We also know there are known unknowns, that is to say, we know there are some things we do not know. But there are also unknown unknowns – the ones we don't know we don't know." And if one looks throughout the history of the U.S. and other free countries, it is the latter category that tends to be the hardest. [1] Those of us who knew Dave, and who had seen Cynefin domains described with similar phrases, often wondered if maybe Rumsfeld overheard one of Dave's talks at the Pentagon. But whether there was a connection or not, Cynefin provided a framework that situated the distinction Rumsfeld popularized.

I was a consultant, working for IBM and even then, I was increasingly disillusioned by what I considered to be the exploitative nature of big five consulting with it's focus on selling best practices regardless of context or need. When Dave spoke about complexity, the centrality of context and 'chefs not recipes,' I felt an immediate resonance with the integrity of the approach, perhaps because of my background as a meteorologist. Thankfully, South Africa was deemed a geography that was 'safe-to-fail,' so along with one or two other nations, Dave was allowed to experiment here.

At the time, Cynefin was the new shiny object and it was a huge challenge to get involved in a linked project. Only the politically connected were chosen. Somehow, I managed to maneuver my way onto one of the more obscure projects at one of South Africa's large banks. However, it soon became apparent that the inherent integrity of seeing every context as unique, did not fit well within the business model of a traditional consulting firm. Cynefin's honeymoon period at IBM did not last very long. A few years later, Dave and I both left IBM at more or less the same time.

Since that time, the Cynefin Framework and its ecosystem of methods, including SenseMaker later on, has gifted me with a global network of like-minded people, opportunities to speak on international stages, and friendships with Dave and others that I value enormously. Had I not gone to listen to the irascible Welshman that day, I doubt my life would be as rich as it is today, a theme you will see repeated often throughout this book. For that reason, we could not let this 21st birthday go by without celebrating and paying homage.

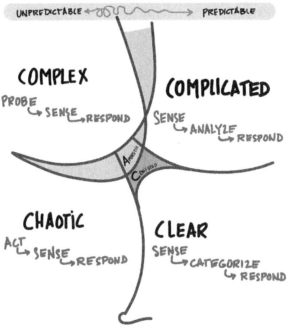

Figure 1. The Cynefin Framework version 2020

WHAT IS IN A NAME?

Cynefin. When Dave Snowden impulsively decided to use this name for his fledgling Framework, he couldn't have known just how apt it would turn out to be. The way he tells the story, Cynefin was chosen while he was preparing for a debate with Ikujiro Nonaka. When Dave heard that Nonaka would be using a Japanese word with spiritual significance (Ba), he decided he needed a Welsh one to level the debating field. The rest, as they say, is history.

Cynefin is an enigmatic word with a meaning that is both broad and deep. It is a dynamic word that speaks of flow through time and space; a multiplicity of tangled connections; of community. It may be hard to pronounce, but once understood, it is equally hard to forget. [2]

Dave describes how "Cynefin is a Welsh word with no direct equivalent in English. As a noun, it is translated as habitat, as an adjective familiar, but dictionary definitions fail to do it justice. A better, and more poetic definition comes from the introduction to a collection of paintings by Kyffin Williams." The meaning I prefer is a shortened, and possibly more poetic version that I have loved since the first time I heard it: "Place of Your Multiple Belongings." The Framework that inspired this book certainly lives up to its name. It means different things to different people, but at its core is a set of principles that I will expand on in a later chapter. There are two that I'd like to highlight here: Bounded Applicability (most things have value if we understand the boundaries within which they are valid) and Coherent Heterogeneity (embracing as much diversity as we can without fragmenting or becoming incoherent). These two principles enable anyone to locate themselves and their unique contexts in the Framework. Cynefin is by its very nature inclusive. As my colleague Zhen Goh writes in her chapter where she reflects on Cynefin and Daoism, it is like an empty vessel that we can pour our contexts into. It is like water that can take many forms.

Indeed, as you will see in this book, Cynefin is a meta-framework that can be applied in almost any context. It is a sense-making framework that helps us untangle our intractable problems in an actionable way. At its most basic, Cynefin allows us to distinguish between three different kinds of systems: ordered systems that are governed and constrained in such a way that cause and effect relationships are either clear or discoverable through analysis; complex systems where causal relationships are entangled and dynamic and the only way to understand the system is to interact; and chaotic systems where there are no effective constraints, turbulence prevails and immediate stabilizing action is required.

Cynefin acknowledges that these different systemic contexts exist in parallel, and in that way avoids creating false dichotomies and polarization. Unlike other frameworks, Cynefin has undergone multiple evolutions over the years, detailed in the chronicle of the 'three ages of Cynefin' in this book. As Dave's thinking evolves, so does the Framework. Some may find it frustrating, but the vitality of the Framework ensures its relevance and longevity. It may be because of this that it makes such an impact on those who engage with it. Many of the authors describe how their work, and sometimes their lives, were completely transformed by Cynefin. It may sound trite, but for me, at least, it is true.

THE STORY OF THIS BOOK

It is ironic that this book is coming into being, and that the Framework is coming of age in 2020, a year when it seems the world has never been in more dire need of sense-making. The COVID-19 pandemic was already well underway in the early part of May this year when I realized that Cynefin is turning 21 in October. Even with everything going on, it seemed an occasion that was too momentous to let pass without a celebration. I contacted my colleague Zhen Goh with a harebrained idea... Why not 'crowd-source' a book as a surprise gift for Dave?

I don't think either of us really knew what we were letting ourselves in for when she enthusiastically agreed! This book you are reading now is a testament to the incredible global community that has formed around the attractor that is Cynefin. Almost every person we approached to author a chapter said yes. Everyone, including our long-suffering editors, Boudewijn Bertsch and Riva Greenberg, and our wonderfully talented illustrator, Sue Borchardt, donated their time and generously shared their wisdom. In the midst of a global pandemic, with socio-political instability all around, climate change a growing concern, and every one of us dealing with the impact of a sudden shift to doing everything virtually, the community rallied to create, in a mere six months, what I believe is an important book for this time we are in.

HOW TO READ THIS BOOK

To an extent, Cynefin resists hard definitions and prescriptive categories, so we chose not to provide a linear, categorized Table of Contents for this book. Instead, we decided to offer you multiple ways to find your way and interact with the content. The book starts off with an intimate autobiography of not only Cynefin but also the man who created it, Dave Snowden. Dave has authored a delightful piece chronicling the birth and evolution of Cynefin. It provides a rare glimpse into the life experiences, influences and context that shaped Dave's thinking and led to its creation.

If you are new to Cynefin, you may want to start with Dave's short description of Cynefin, and then read Dave's origin story, my chapter on Cynefin principles, and Zhen Goh's chapter, Cynefin & ... Otherwise, you can choose a temporal lens and explore the chapters based on how long the authors have been in this community. Or, you can follow your curiosity and explore how the chapters are tangled in interesting ways, whether via authors that are from the same geographies, or perhaps chapters that share similar principles. How you read this book is up to you. However, no matter how you navigate your way, you are sure to encounter unexpected insights and connections.

You will find 20 chapters mostly about the practical application of Cynefin in fields as diverse as healthcare, safety, strategy, facilitation and software development. Woven throughout these chapters, you will find poignant shorter Vignettes where each author shares delightful stories of the impact the Framework has had on their work, as well as their personal encounters with Cynefin and its creator.

ACKNOWLEDGMENTS

There are so many people that deserve our appreciation and thanks for making this book a reality. This was a herculean, communal effort. A special thank you to:

- Boudewijn and Riva, without your generosity and fine editing skills, we would not have been able to create a book that we could be proud of, and that does Cynefin justice.

- Sue Borchardt, I almost couldn't believe it when you agreed to illustrate this book for us. More than just our illustrator, you were the glue that kept us together. Thank you for your generosity, energy and creativity.

- Marion Kiely, you are a cat herder of note! Thank you for helping us make our incredibly tight deadlines and for keeping everyone on track.

- Gustav Rischmüller, our intrepid designer. Thank you for putting up with us and for bringing your design brilliance to our buoyant, sometimes weird, ideas.

- To every one of our authors, there would not be a book without your contributions. Thank you for sharing your insight, putting up with our nagging, and above all, for helping take this work into the world.

- And finally to Dave, thank you for creating this body of knowledge and sharing yourself and your thinking so generously with the world.

Here's to the next 21 years!

References

1. "Defense.gov News Transcript: DoD News Briefing – Secretary Rumsfeld and Gen. Myers, United States Department of Defense (defense.gov)".
2. https://www.cognitive-edge.com/blog/origins-of-cynefin-by-any-other-name-would-it-smell-as-sweet/

FINDING YOUR WAY AROUND THIS BOOK

A CELEBRATION OF BEAUTIFULLY ENTANGLED COMPLEXITY

This isn't the type of book you should read from front to back. Although you could, and it'll be great. You could also read it from back to front, or just dip in anywhere your finger falls. Or browse the Table of Contents on page 9 and flick to something that sounds interesting to you today.

Like Dave's fabled analogy of bramble bushes in a thicket to explain complexity-theory, every part of this book is connected to and affected by many other parts. View the book like the illustration on the next page, the berries as chapters, and the entangled branches as pathways to other berries. Follow a random twig to find a juicy piece. Trace a path to the next fruit. Discover that this inter-weaved reading contains berries of all sorts, and even allows you to change your mind at the end of a chapter, and pull on a different sprig to see what shakes out.

Get lost. Get found.

Enjoy!

WAYFINDING GUIDE (IF YOU WANT)

- If you are new to the Cynefin Framework or you just need some honing, read the first four chapters starting on page 31, then navigate back to this page to plan your journey if you so choose. Otherwise, just read on - the chapters are ordered alphabetically by author's surname.

- **Chronological**: Read the chapters (*raspberry icon*) and vignettes (*blueberry icon*) in descending order of the length of time the author (*clock icon*) has been involved with Cynefin.

- **Type of article**: Follow articles that are theoretical (typically a case study, description, or an application of a method – *thought bubble icon*) or narrative (a recollection or story about applying or learning Cynefin – *open book icon*).

- **Cynefin principles:** For more information, see the chapter on page 62 (*Cynefin Framework icon*):

Principle 1: Embrace messy coherence		Principle 2: Descriptive self-awareness & self-discovery		Principle 3. Timing and Flow	
1.1.	Playing in tension	2.1.	Beware of unintended consequences	3.1.	Time and cadence
1.2.	Heuristics not rules	2.2.	Be a mirror not an expert	3.2.	Flow and patterns
1.3.	Bounded applicability			3.3.	Liminality

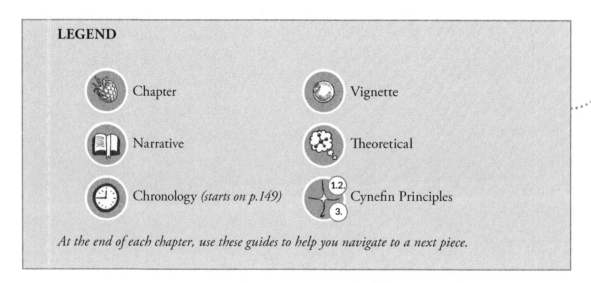

LEGEND

Chapter

Vignette

Narrative

Theoretical

Chronology (*starts on p.149*)

Cynefin Principles

At the end of each chapter, use these guides to help you navigate to a next piece.

START ANYWHERE

GO ANYWHERE

A VIGNETTE

A CHAPTER

ANOTHER CHAPTER

ANOTHER VIGNETTE

A TIME-LINE OF CYNEFIN

A LOOK AT 21 YEARS OF EVOLUTION

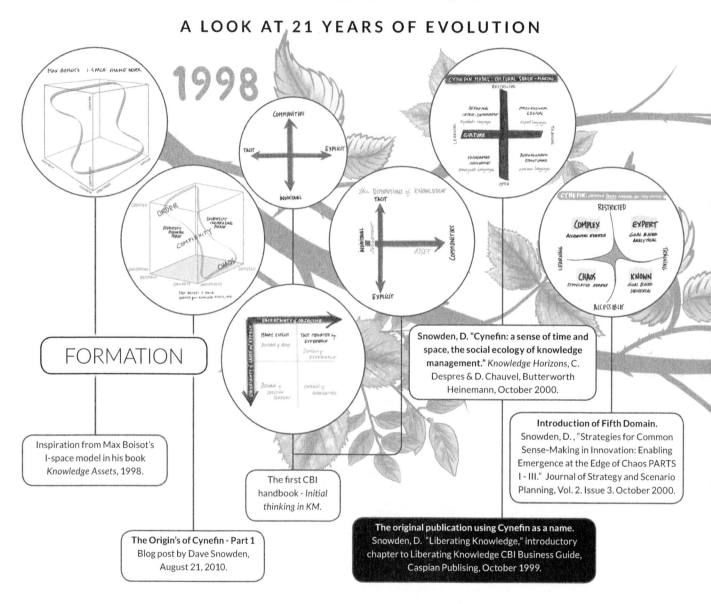

1998

FORMATION

Snowden, D. "Cynefin: a sense of time and space, the social ecology of knowledge management." *Knowledge Horizons*, C. Despres & D. Chauvel, Butterworth Heinemann, October 2000.

Introduction of Fifth Domain.
Snowden, D. , "Strategies for Common Sense-Making in Innovation: Enabling Emergence at the Edge of Chaos PARTS I - III." Journal of Strategy and Scenario Planning, Vol. 2. Issue 3. October 2000.

Inspiration from Max Boisot's I-space model in his book *Knowledge Assets*, 1998.

The first CBI handbook - *Initial thinking in KM.*

The original publication using Cynefin as a name.
Snowden, D. "Liberating Knowledge," introductory chapter to Liberating Knowledge CBI Business Guide, Caspian Publising, October 1999.

The Origin's of Cynefin - Part 1
Blog post by Dave Snowden, August 21, 2010.

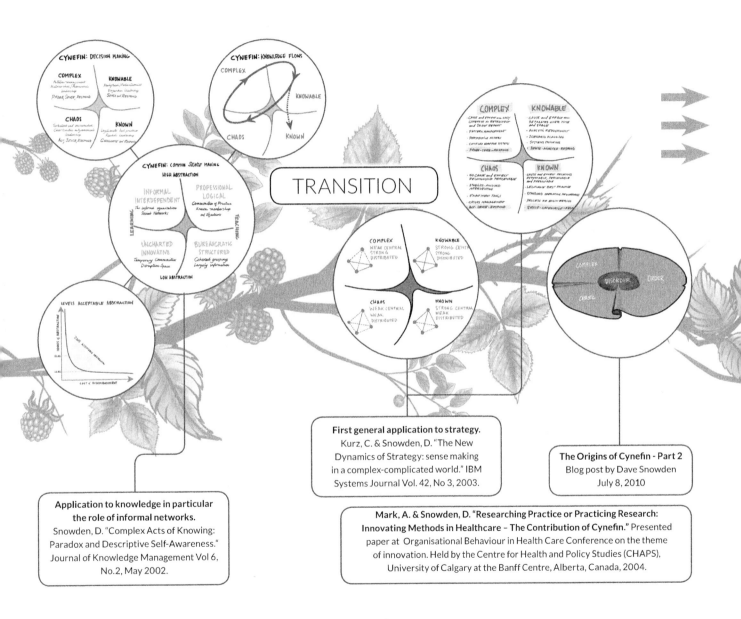

TRANSITION

First general application to strategy.
Kurz, C. & Snowden, D. "The New Dynamics of Strategy: sense making in a complex-complicated world." IBM Systems Journal Vol. 42, No 3, 2003.

The Origins of Cynefin - Part 2
Blog post by Dave Snowden
July 8, 2010

Application to knowledge in particular the role of informal networks.
Snowden, D. "Complex Acts of Knowing: Paradox and Descriptive Self-Awareness." Journal of Knowledge Management Vol 6, No.2, May 2002.

Mark, A. & Snowden, D. "Researching Practice or Practicing Research: Innovating Methods in Healthcare – The Contribution of Cynefin." Presented paper at Organisational Behaviour in Health Care Conference on the theme of innovation. Held by the Centre for Health and Policy Studies (CHAPS), University of Calgary at the Banff Centre, Alberta, Canada, 2004.

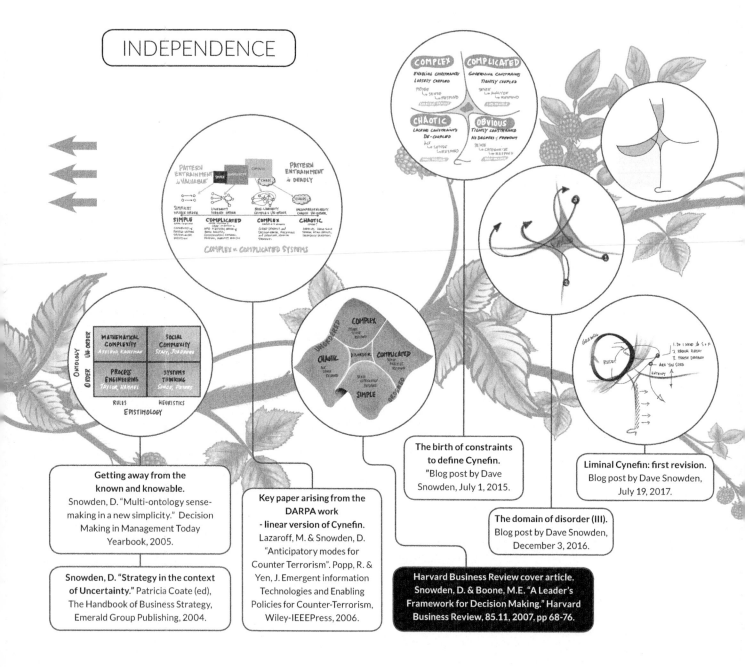

INDEPENDENCE

Getting away from the known and knowable.
Snowden, D. "Multi-ontology sense-making in a new simplicity." Decision Making in Management Today Yearbook, 2005.

Snowden, D. "Strategy in the context of Uncertainty." Patricia Coate (ed), The Handbook of Business Strategy, Emerald Group Publishing, 2004.

Key paper arising from the DARPA work - linear version of Cynefin.
Lazaroff, M. & Snowden, D. "Anticipatory modes for Counter Terrorism". Popp, R. & Yen, J. Emergent information Technologies and Enabling Policies for Counter-Terrorism, Wiley-IEEEPress, 2006.

The birth of constraints to define Cynefin.
"Blog post by Dave Snowden, July 1, 2015.

The domain of disorder (III).
Blog post by Dave Snowden, December 3, 2016.

Liminal Cynefin: first revision.
Blog post by Dave Snowden, July 19, 2017.

Harvard Business Review cover article.
Snowden, D. & Boone, M.E. "A Leader's Framework for Decision Making." Harvard Business Review, 85.11, 2007, pp 68-76.

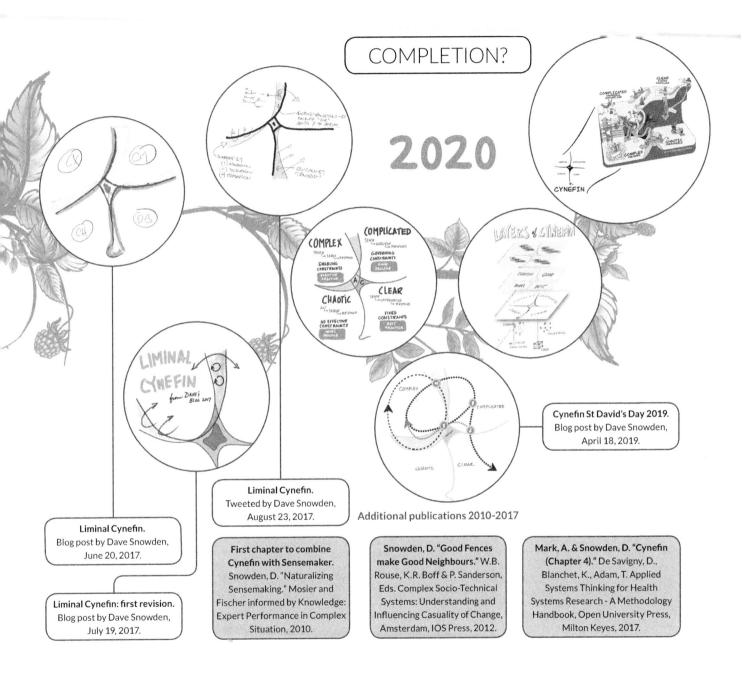

COMPLETION?

2020

Cynefin St David's Day 2019.
Blog post by Dave Snowden,
April 18, 2019.

Liminal Cynefin.
Tweeted by Dave Snowden,
August 23, 2017.

Additional publications 2010-2017

Liminal Cynefin.
Blog post by Dave Snowden,
June 20, 2017.

Liminal Cynefin: first revision.
Blog post by Dave Snowden,
July 19, 2017.

First chapter to combine
Cynefin with Sensemaker.
Snowden, D. "Naturalizing
Sensemaking." Mosier and
Fischer informed by Knowledge:
Expert Performance in Complex
Situation, 2010.

Snowden, D. "Good Fences
make Good Neighbours." W.B.
Rouse, K.R. Boff & P. Sanderson,
Eds. Complex Socio-Technical
Systems: Understanding and
Influencing Casuality of Change,
Amsterdam, IOS Press, 2012.

Mark, A. & Snowden, D. "Cynefin
(Chapter 4)." De Savigny, D.,
Blanchet, K., Adam, T. Applied
Systems Thinking for Health
Systems Research - A Methodology
Handbook, Open University Press,
Milton Keyes, 2017.

GLOSSARY

BRUSH UP ON SOME TERMINOLOGY

Abduction (Referring to "abductive reasoning")

The logic of hunches, involving inferring from available patterns and information. In abductive reasoning, we accept that all findings are "best explanations" rather than absolute truths, and that uncertainty is an inherent element. Findings are derived from a sense of plausibility. Abductive reasoning is often compared with deductive reasoning, which is seen as a "top-down logic," where conclusions are reached by applying rules in a reductive manner until the logic becomes necessarily true. Here findings are derived from probability. Abductive reasoning is also compared with inductive reasoning, which is seen as a "bottom-up logic," where hypotheses are tested against evidence. Here findings are derived from a sense of possibility.

Anthro-complexity

The study of complexity as it is experienced in human systems, rather than mechanistic or natural (animal and geological) systems. Human systems have a higher degree of complexity for many reasons, including, for instance, the different behavioral patterns that identity-structures create and how they act within different contexts.

Aporia (Aporetic)

The Oxford English Dictionary defines the adjective 'aporetic,' as "to be at a loss," "impassable," and "inclined to doubt, or to raise objections." It defines the noun form 'aporia,' as the "state of the aporetic" and "a perplexity or difficulty." In philosophy, an aporia is a philosophical puzzle or a seemingly impasse in an inquiry, often arising as a result of equally plausible, yet inconsistent, premises (i.e., a paradox).

Coherence

Something that appears to make sense as a whole, and in relation to available patterns.

Constraint

In plain English, a constraint is often thought of as a limitation or restriction. However, in the Cynefin use of the term, a constraint refers to how we contain, couple, and link things. A constraint can therefore also be enabling, as much as limiting.

Complex facilitation

An approach to facilitation designed to encourage emergence and allow for diversity. In contrast, more traditional rules of facilitation create planned activities with no variability in mind. In complex facilitation, we disrupt regular group dynamics, and facilitate through encouraging emergence and flow.

Cynefin

A sense-making framework. See the *What Cynefin is in Brief* chapter on page 58 for a more comprehensive explanation.

Disintermediation

Reducing intermediary interpretation of data and information to put decision-makers in contact with raw data, rather than pre-analyzed insights.

Epistemic justice

Fairness in knowledge and how knowledge is produced. This draws on British philosopher Miranda Fricker's identification of the unfairness built into systems of knowledge production (epistemic injustice), where certain viewpoints and personas are more represented and hold more power. Epistemic justice is the practice of correcting such imbalances.

Epistemology

The philosophical study of the nature, origin, and limits of human knowledge. In other words, how we know what we know.

Exaptive

The utilisation of an evolutionary feature for a use other than it was initially designed or developed for. Or, radical repurposing.

Exaptive practice

The practice of applying exaptive principles. This is typically utilized for radical repurposing and innovation.

Feedforward

Learning from the future, or information regarding how things can potentially evolve or shift in the future. (Contrast with feedback which learns from the past). "Feedforwards" are useful for on-going adjustments ahead of time.

Hermeneutic (in the context of hermeneutical injustice)

A methodology of interpretation and interpretive meaning. Hermeneutical injustice refers to the challenges that disadvantaged groups face when trying to understand and communicate their experiences to others; there is a lack of concepts that resonates with their own sense of meaning. These experiences of injustice are usually embedded within a culture's shared meaning structure and reflective of the dominant members of the culture.

Heuristics

The term comes from Ancient Greek to mean "I discover." Heuristics refer to strategies for problem solving that derive from learned patterns and previous experiences. Heuristics can also be referred to as "rules of thumb." They are mental shortcuts that ease the cognitive load making a decision.

Liminality

"Liminal" comes from the Latin root, limen or limin, meaning 'threshold.' A liminal space is an 'in-between' space, where you have left something behind, but what is emerging has not yet formed." In anthropology, this is the stage between phases, where agents are between a pre-ritual and post-ritual transition, and their sense of identity/status is suspended in-between. Within Cynefin, this refers to the liminal zones where things are transitioning between domains.

Ontology, Ontological

Related to the philosophical study of being (existence, reality, becoming and being). Or, the study of "what is."

Phenomenology

The philosophical study of consciousness and experiences from the first person perspective.

Polymorphic

The ability of a thing to take on multiple forms and uses.

Premature convergence

Reaching a consensus too early, or before a problem space has been properly explored.

Psychosocial work environment

Aspects that influence psychological safety and the well-being of employees while at work.

Scaffolding

A temporary support, or design structure, that is used to support the construction or maintenance of a system. In physical construction, for example, constructing buildings, these take on the form of temporary physical structures. However, in human systems, scaffolding is used more broadly and includes social supports. An example is the scaffolding of learners inspired by developmental psychologist Lev Vygotsky: when teachers scaffold learners by providing support and encouragement, learners can perform beyond their current abilities. These supports are gradually reduced as learners become more adept and self-sufficient.

Sense-making

Defined by Cognitive Edge as the way in which we make sense of the world in order for us to act in it. Sense-making, as Dave Snowden uses the term, differs slightly from sensemaking as situated in other schools. Snowden takes a more evolutionary approach (than Brenda Dervin's hermeneutic approach, Karl Weick's collective approach and Gary Klein's mental model approach) and considers sense-making a knowledge production activity: using data toward a shared understanding of problem areas so as to generate the right action.

CYNEFIN: A TALE THAT GREW IN THE TELLING

DAVE SNOWDEN

ABOUT THE AUTHOR

Dave Snowden is a Welshman, known for his curmudgeonly style and his love for opera, rugby and mountain walks. He is the originator of the Cynefin Framework. His article with Mary E. Boone on leadership was featured on the cover of the *Harvard Business Review* in November 2007 and also won the Academy of Management award for the best practitioner paper in the same year. Dave divides his time between two roles: Founder Director and Chief Scientific Officer of Cognitive Edge, and the Founder and Head of the Cynefin Centre. His work is international in nature and covers government and industry looking at complex issues relating to organizational design and decision making. He has pioneered a science-based approach to organizations drawing on anthropology neuroscience and complex adaptive systems theory.

CYNEFIN: A TALE THAT GREW IN THE TELLING

DAVE SNOWDEN

THE SHORT ANECDOTAL ACCOUNT OF THE HISTORY OF THE CYNEFIN FRAMEWORK RECOUNTED BY ITS CREATOR

Cynefin (pronounced kun-ev-in) is a Welsh word with no direct equivalent in English. As a noun it is translated as habitat, as an adjective acquainted or familiar, but dictionary definitions fail to do it justice. A better, and more poetic, definition comes from the introduction to a collection of paintings by Kyffin Williams, an artist whose use of oils creates a new awareness of the mountains of his native land and their relationship to the spirituality of its people: "It describes that relationship as the place of your birth and of your upbringing, the environment in which you live, and to which you are naturally acclimatised." [1] It differs from the Japanese concept of 'Ba', which is a "shared space for emerging relationships" in that it links a community, into its shared history – or histories – in a way that paradoxically both limits the perception of that community while enabling an instinctive and intuitive ability to adapt to conditions of profound uncertainty. [2] In general, if a community is not physically, temporally, and spiritually rooted, then it is alienated from its environment, and will focus on survival rather than creativity and collaboration.

Opening paragraph of the first Cynefin article "The Social Ecology of Knowledge Management" published in Despres & Chauvel, Knowledge Horizons, 2000. [3]

J.R.R. Tolkien starts his foreword to the second edition of *The Lord of the Rings* with the phrase, "This tale grew in the telling." [4] He continues to explain that something that started as a sequel to the children's book *The Hobbit* "was drawn irresistibly towards the older world" by which he means the mythology and legends of the Elder Days. As such, it developed "glimpses that had arisen unbidden of things higher or deeper or darker than its surface." [5]

For my generation, *The Lord of the Rings* was a defining experience that opened up the whole genre of fantasy through which much inspiration can be gleaned. I find it very difficult not to make literary (and frequently fantasy) references when I deliver a keynote or have everyday conversation, as the richer meaning of such texts enhances any exchange. Over the decades, very few years have passed where I have not returned to Tolkien's three novel series in one form or another. My hardback, sixth impression of the second edition, is still with me from its original purchase in 1971, when I was in the Sixth Form of what is now the Alun School in Mold, or in Welsh, 'Yr Wyddgrug,' which means the prominent hill. That is a reference to Bailey Hill, which dominates the landscape of the market town where I grew up from the age of four.

I was able to buy the book thanks to a £60 book token, the tangible result of winning the Hayden Williams Prize for contributions to the broader community. My parents were probably happier with the kudos of the award ceremony in County Hall, as all pupils in Flintshire Schools were eligible for the one annual award. Still, for me, this was a once in a lifetime opportunity. Armed with what in current day purchasing power is over £800, I got my father to drive me to the nearest large bookshop. It happened to be just over the border in Liverpool. I loaded up the boot of his car with paperback Penguin classics and some mainly dystopian novels. Each book cost 0.40p, and my three hardback volumes of *The Lord of the Rings* (replacing a much thumbed single-volume paperback borrowed from my cousins in Cardiff) cost only £2.25 each. Overnight I acquired a library of well over a hundred books, and by the time I went to University less than a year later, I had read them all (frequently without understanding.) That was the start of a life-long love of Philosophy and History.

By now, the casual reader may be wondering what this has to do with creating a sense-making framework of some twenty plus years standing? Well, the most obvious link is that Cynefin, as a framework, has been itself a two decade plus emergent and evolutionary process of development that grew in the telling, literally, through workshops and conference keynotes, all informed by reading and thinking. In this telling I will also draw out and elaborate on five, sometimes tangential connections, some looser than others, and finish with the three ages of Cynefin and its future trajectory.

CYNEFIN IS AN ENTANGLEMENT OF THEORY & PRACTICE

When I put the first versions of the Framework together, I had no real idea what I was getting into. It was in the early days of knowledge management, and I was laying the foundations for what became known as Organic Knowledge Management. What now has become a much-cited framework used in a broad range of fields was then an outcome well beyond my imaginings. The Framework grew and developed through a complex mix of reading combined with practice. A significant strength of Cynefin is that it was not created, and then propagated, from a single based study or process. It evolved through a fluid entanglement of *sophia* and *phronesis* to reference Aristotle. The latter is a type of practical wisdom, translated by the Romans as *prudentia*, which comes from *providentia*, meaning foresight and sagacity. Sophia is a combination of *nous*, which has a sense of discernment and *epistēmē*, which in the modern day would be science: knowledge that is teachable and built through logic.

For Aristotle, both are associated with virtue, "Although the young may be experts in geometry and mathematics and similar branches of knowledge (*sophoi*), we do not consider that a young man can have Prudence (*phronimos*). The reason is that Prudence (*phronesis*) includes a knowledge of particular facts, derived from experience, which a young man does not possess, for experience is the fruit of years." *Nous*, by the way, is one of those curious words; for Aristotle it was the ability to think rationally, but in collegial English, it often means *common-sense*, and both meanings are central to Cynefin.

Phronesis also links to the definition of sense-making, or *naturalising sense-making,* that I have developed over the years, namely: *How do we make sense of the world so that we can act in it?* With that definition comes the concept of sufficiency, how do we know that we know enough to determine the type of action we can take? After all, that is the primary function of Cynefin; at its heart, it is a decision support framework. I am using a hyphen in sense-making rather than the neologism created by Karl Weick. Weick, Dervin, Klein, Russel and myself are now identified in the literature as five distinct schools of sense-making/sensemaking and I've had the privilege of working with both Brenda Dervin and Gary Klein and can call them friends. [6]

CYNEFIN AROSE AND DEVELOPED THROUGH TEACHING

The process of Cynefin's creation, I'm sure you realize by now, is a story of some magnitude. Much of the critical work was done on flip charts with groups of people in various states of bemusement as ideas came to me. I never understood why many academics do not want to teach. For me, teaching is a vital part of research; it is where ideas come together. Those flip charts may have seemed messy, but the mess was coherent and the process was not nearly as ad hoc as it may have looked at times. I've always used frameworks to force insight. It is an old trick of rhetoric, start in front of a large audience with the phrase, "There are three key aspects to [name subject]..." and even if you can only think of one as you begin, the other two will always come to what I call the prepared mind. My flip charts were all about forcing my mind (and often a part of the audience) to think differently and critically synthesize whatever emerged.

To this day, I frequently accept invitations to present at conferences or deliver a lecture on a subject or idea that is in an early stage of exploration. I do this knowing that the live audience, and consequent adrenaline surge, will create new insight. To be clear, that only works with preparation, if you have both read up on the subjects and practiced the material you are teaching. Experience counts over a significant length of time.

Of course, there were often catalyst points along the way. I remember one in particular, when the chaos fold or cliff at the base of Cynefin, manifested itself during an extended conversation with Max Boisot in Washington. I had played with, and talked about, the different types of boundaries with colleagues for some time before then, and there were lots of sketches in various notebooks. However, the critical moment of creation was when Max's, "What you are really talking about is..." exposition of René Thom's 1972 book, *Structural stability and morphogenesis*, validated and informed what I knew in practice: namely, that the boundary between order and chaos is materially different from the others. [7] That conversation happened to come after a harrowing session I had had at the Academy of Management in 2001. The price to me for receiving an award for original contributions to the field of Knowledge Management (KM) was to present the Cynefin Framework to a highly knowledgeable audience and then handle formal responses from Max and J. C. Spender.

One of the things that J.C. said at the time was that just as organizational theorist, Ikujiro Nonaka, had made the word *knowledge* problematic, I was making the word *meaning* problematic. For J.C. this was a good thing. It meant that a concept we thought was familiar was now being explored in novel ways. That proved significant in directing my own thinking, and the idea that we take the meaning of *meaning* for granted, and this directed much of the development of Cynefin.

CYNEFIN REFLECTS MY TRANS-DISCIPLINARY UPBRINGING & READING

There is no single academic discipline behind Cynefin - it interweaves the sciences and the humanities. Cynefin was brought up and cultured by generalist thinking, just was I. Science and humanities interacted in my family life and daily discourse, and I doubt anyone without an upbringing in generalist thinking could have created it. My impulse to buy over a hundred books in a day came from being in a family and school that treasured learning and sought to avoid the narrow confines of specialization. My father was a veterinary surgeon, my mother, a linguist and teacher. Both were from working-class backgrounds and had fought in various ways for the right to a University Education. They were well-read in literature, and my mother was a political activist of the first order. I was on an Aldermaston March in a pram, and there is a picture somewhere of me as a baby on Bertrand Russell's knee. Family meals were not places for the faint-hearted or naive arguments. That also translated into school.

I still remember in 1965 at the age of eleven, walking to the front of the class wearing long trousers at school for the first time (only shorts were permitted in primary school regardless of the weather) to be handed a record card on which was printed "You support capital punishment," and told to speak on the subject for seven minutes, without preparation and with penalties for under- or overshooting.

Capital punishment was something I loathed even then. While it was only abolished in 1969, it was suspended in England and Wales that year, so it was a hot topic. The school I went to fostered a tradition of impromptu debate: debating either side of a contentious issue was something we did every week from the ages of eleven to eighteen. Today we see how debate without rancor is rare, and in a modern environment challenging. But for me I carried on in the House of Debates at Lancaster University, where I rose to the rank of Convenor. That simple process meant voraciously reading everything you could as you never knew what would come up. A good and steady habit that has served me well.

While I focused on science in the sixth form, I was as well-read as anyone studying English Literature and was still in love with History as a subject before moving on to Poetry. To this day, I am still reading in both the humanities and sciences regularly, using two fountain pens and different colored inks to mark passages and add comments. Much of Cynefin has come from me synthesizing knowledge, while thinking on my feet in front of a flip chart responding to questions. When I am working on something new, I often set myself up. I write a title and an abstract, which I know will (one) force me to complete some reading before the time and (two) create a situation that will force the synthesis of that material while I am in front of a live audience. A lot of that ability harks back to the confidence I developed during those years of debate in its many manifestations.

MY ENGAGEMENT WITH THE ARTS WAS KEY TO CYNEFIN

I'm not sure that Cynefin would have ever happened if I hadn't fallen in love with Robert Frost's poem "Mending Wall" when I had to learn it by heart in the Third Form. [8] For anyone who walks the mountains of Wales its opening is all too familiar:

Something there is that doesn't love a wall,
That sends the frozen-ground-swell under it,
And spills the upper boulders in the sun;
And makes gaps even two can pass abreast.

The poem is about boundaries and their need for renewal. As the author meets his neighbor for the annual cycle of repair they 'set the wall between us once again,' and in an evocative statement introduce the key message of the poem:

One on a side. It comes to little more:
There where it is we do not need the wall:
He is all pine and I am apple orchard.
My apple trees will never get across
And eat the cones under his pines, I tell him.
He only says, 'Good fences make good neighbors.'

That final phrase stayed with me from the day I first read it and perhaps remarkable to say it informed the creation of Cynefin in ways I probably still don't fully comprehend. The body of Anglo-Welsh poetry has always been a part of my life, from the production of Dylan Thomas' "Under Milk Wood" that I directed at school to another Thomas, the ever dark fierce R.S. Thomas, whose "The Bright Field" has always been key for me to Cynefin. [9] I quote in full:

I have seen the sun break through
to illuminate a small field
for a while, and gone my way
and forgotten it. But that was the
pearl of great price, the one field that had
treasure in it. I realise now
that I must give all that I have
to possess it. Life is not hurrying

on to a receding future, nor hankering after
an imagined past. It is the turning
aside like Moses to the miracle
of the lit bush, to a brightness
that seemed as transitory as your youth
once, but is the eternity that awaits you.

The idea of turning aside, of serendipitous encounters, and being open to those pearls, is critical to discovery and creation. In that context, another quote from Dylan Thomas comes to mind: "When one burns one's bridges, what a very nice fire it makes." I've never been afraid to burn the odd bridge, or for that matter, a boat or two. Mind you, the association with Cortés in 1519 is not one I desire!

I was an enthusiastic poet when at school, and I still remember my submission for the annual school Eisteddfod (an essential aspect of Welsh Culture), which started thus:

The craggy two toothed martinet,
pretending love while meaning hate

and carried on in the same vein. The Head of History, a good friend and teacher, was the judge that year and gave me the second prize. He said he would have given me first but felt I would understand why that was not possible. He was suppressing laughter all the while, as were most of the staff; he had realized that it was a direct attack on the Head of English at the time with whom I had had several run-ins. She resented my winning election as Secretary of the School Literary and Debating Society over her manageable favorite. Fortunately, she didn't realize she was the target, although most of her colleagues did. It is a tactic of rhetoric that, if I am honest, I can't resist. That desire to provoke, to use another metaphor, upset the apple cart, has been with me all my life, and without it, you would not have Cynefin.

Opera and Fine Art, along with Poetry, has also been a part of the creation of Cynefin. I've had some of my best ideas sitting in the Amphitheatre at the Royal Opera House. The whole concept of liminality in Cynefin crystallized while standing in awe in front of Caravaggio's *The Seven Works of Mercy* on a visit to Naples. Think of the use of light to represent grace if you want to get a sense of why. The naturalistic intensity of that painting, its use of *chiaroscuro*, is vital, and that contrast of light and shadow gives you a final clue.

CYNEFIN IS, AND ALWAYS HAS BEEN, ABOUT COMMUNITY

Broader community engagement has been key to the development and use of Cynefin. The Framework is fractal in nature, it is self-similar at different levels of understanding so you can understand it simply and quickly, but as you use it more and go deeper, more and more is revealed. At its simplest, the Framework distinguishes order from complexity from chaos. Its most sophisticated version has five domains, four liminal areas and a host of overlays for different functions and types. I remember sitting in Helsinki, listening to a group of community activists tell me how Cynefin (without any involvement from me) had transformed their work. I've seen multiple YouTube recordings and slide sets in which ordinary, and extraordinary, people can use the Framework without expert coaching or, God preserve us, certification. The primary definition of Cynefin, is at its heart, about a flow of engagement over time with things known, unknown and unknowable, loved, and unloved all, of which entangle our lives and create meaning. It may now be the best known Welsh word outside of Wales and Patagonia, and for that, I feel some pride.

The story of Cynefin has had both heroes and villains over the years, some of whom I will mention in this discourse. The story has held both tragedy and comedy elements, but the arc of Cynefin's story has maintained coherence over the years, which was a bit of a surprise for me when I reviewed all the sequence of articles through which it was created. The basic themes have been there since the start, but the articulation and the representation have changed. That might help explain why it has been used as widely and as for as long as it has.

THE THREE AGES OF CYNEFIN

Another connection here to *The Lord of the Rings* is each has three distinct stages in the arc of its story. In Cynefin we see a similar progression with its direct equivalent to the naïveté of *The Fellowship of the Ring*, then through the various types of sundering in *The Two Towers* to the resolutions of *The Return of the King*. The section that follows chronicles this three-part story arc.

1. FORMATION

I'd spent several years designing and coding decision support systems for corporate executives in the early days of the commercial use of computers. That was a fascinating education. I spent time with Financial Directors and CEOs of companies such as Guinness and Thorn EMI, who were engaging with information processing opportunities beyond their previous dreams. I remember running two-day courses on how to use VisiCalc for nothing more than the reconciliation of accounts. My early days as a Development Accountant involved days of using calculating machines to handle tasks that these days are fully automated. I built two software businesses arising from that work as a General Manager and then moved onto Corporate Strategy.

A significant achievement was to string together Object Orientation with legacy systems management and Rapid Application Development/Joint Application Development (RAD/JAD) methods for software design. This later became the GENUS program with which we beat Microsoft's launch of the latest Windows platform to win the British Computing Association's marketing awards. The RAD/JAD work was the foundation of what became the Dynamic Systems Development Method (DSDM) consortium, set up by myself and two competitors based on a dinner in a pub in Cheltenham. DSDM was a crucial feeder into the Agile Manifesto, which was primarily U.S.-based and needed a week in a ski resort in contrast!

All of that was in DataSciences, and I'd been part of the management buy out from Thorn EMI, so when IBM bought the company in 1996, I had mixed feelings. On the one hand, the profit arising from the sale solved some financial issues and built an extension on the house. Still, it also meant that my plans to set up a European-wide consortium of Software Services companies around the theme of "many cultures, one method," with me running the method centre, was lost overnight. I designed that slogan to take on the big consultancies whose services were designed as "any old method, one culture." Either way, we were now being assimilated (I use the word deliberately) into what I considered the enemy.

Eventually, it worked out well for me, but there is still a side of me that wonders what might have been. Given that we had been mainly acquired for, and as a result of, Genus I had some prominence and was moved into a new strategic function to develop methods and market positioning. I had to fight to report at the right level, which prompted one of the two occasions I resigned from IBM (it is regrettably often the only way to get attention). But I got the free floating role I wanted and the chance to create something new. My first pick was the then-emerging field of knowledge management. Ikujiro Nonaka and Hirotaka Takeuchi's book, *The Knowledge-Creating Company*, had been published five years earlier and was now gaining traction. [10]

I profoundly disagreed with the authors on the subject of tacit to explicit knowledge conversion. I was not too fond of the whole Socialization, Externalization, Combination and Internalization (SECI) thing, and the opening chapter that stereotyped Western and Eastern philosophy, but I could see the potential. To cut a long story short, I got Philip (one of the many brilliant bosses I have had over the years) to give me the budget to create a Confederation of British Industry (CBI) handbook on knowledge management, a portable facilitation centre (lots of stickies, butcher paper, and large display boards that flipped over) and a first KM conference. It was held at the new Hilton Hotel at Heathrow and I was a keynote speaker by default. That was the big break in thought leadership, as people talked about what I had done (attack orthodoxy with metaphor and irony). Subsequently, I began getting many invitations to speak and I started to form academic connections, the most important of which (and one that has lasted to this day) was with Yasmin Merali, who was then at Warwick University. It was Yasmin who introduced me to Max Boisot by organising a seminar for us both at the University in 1998, and that was the event at which Cynefin was conceived, with its baptism coming the following year.

The relationship with Max has been fundamental to my own development, and to providing academic rigour and stimulation in the development of Cynefin. We spoke almost weekly, from our first meeting until his untimely death from cancer in 2011. I'd happily be talking about some new idea and he would interrupt me with a phrase I learnt to dread, but always loved: "You can't talk about this until you have read..." That statement led to the population of a large part of my library.

People used to sell tickets when Max and I got together. We both came from a similar tradition and were happy to ferociously argue a position that we didn't, or only might wish to believe, in order to better explore the space. Max was generous to a fault with his time, treating venerable professors, less venerable senior business executives, and young students as equals. But if you failed to respond in kind or advocate an idea twice without first researching it, the relationship was probably over.

I remember once asking Max a question about demands to dumb down language. His view was simple: "If you need to use language, do, but not unnecessarily, and if people can't live with that, move on." I am paraphrasing here by the way. Along with Yasmin, Alicia Juarrero, Peter Allen, Bill McKelvey and Pierpaolo Andreotti, we had formed a powerful group, working on the development of complexity as a field in a different way from the then dominant work of Ralph Stacey. In those days the University at Lecce in Southern Italy was a common meeting ground and I have fond memories of several key events.

One session I organised at IBM Bedfont Lakes with Yasmin's help included Jack Cohen (scientific advisor to Terry Pratchett) and Brian Goodwin, who was associated with The Schumacher Institute at the time. At that event Mike Lissack ran up to me and handed over a handwritten note that read, "You must read Alicia Juarrero's *Dynamics in Action*." [11] That in turn led to another evening in Maryland where I still remember Bill (who is more irascible than I) saying of Cynefin that "while he didn't normally find this sort of thing useful he quite liked this one." That was high praise indeed and propelled me to the winter conference of Organizational Science where Max saved me from an overconfident attack on hypotheses!

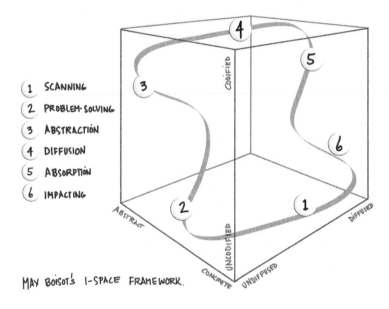

1 SCANNING
2 PROBLEM-SOLVING
3 ABSTRACTION
4 DIFFUSION
5 ABSORPTION
6 IMPACTING

MAX BOISOT'S I-SPACE FRAMEWORK.

Figure 1. Max Boisot's I-Space Framework from his book, Knowledge Assets, 1998

But to return to the story. I had read Max's seminal book *Knowledge Assets* and was familiar with the I-Space, but it came alive when he presented it. [12] At that time, and based on the first CBI handbook, I was arguing against the famous Data - Information - Knowledge - Wisdom (DIKW) pyramid. My position was that knowledge is the means by which data becomes information and knowledge exists on a spectrum between tacit and explicit. But, in contrast with Nonaka, I was also arguing strongly (with Polanyi) that all explicit knowledge has a tacit element and that the cost of codification of tacit knowledge exceeds any benefit (assuming it was possible, which other than in limited circumstances it is not). The I-space gave me a better way of understanding this. I took two dimensions of the I-space, namely Abstraction and Codification, and used them to create a simple diagram which showed that cost curve. At the highest level of abstraction I am making notes to remind myself of what I know, at the lowest level of abstraction I am trying to codify everything to create independence from people. Between the two there is a limited zone of acceptable cost of codification where formal knowledge management makes any sense (and it is more limited than people realize.)

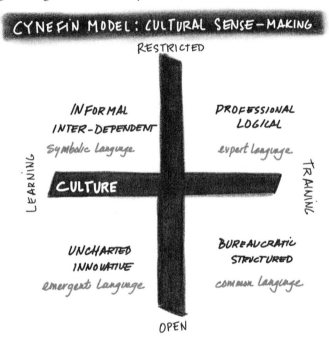

Figure 2. First published version of the framework with the name Cynefin, 1999

Over the next year that model morphed into a two by two, showing abstraction on the vertical and the nature of knowledge on the horizontal. This was published several times, especially in the Knowledge Management year book and came to the attention of the editors of *Knowledge Horizons*. I was commissioned to write a chapter, which I am still proud of, although I believe it needs to be resurrected and updated for current work in organizational design. I called that framework Cynefin, in part due to the stimulus of my parents' Christmas gift of the Kyffin Williams' book, where the opening quote of this article comes from. The rest was to have something to compete with Nonaka, who I was engaged to debate with in Lyon. If a Japanese framework can have a name with spiritual significance (Ba) then so too can a Welsh one. The first technical publication was in a supplement to the second CBI handbook, *Liberating Knowledge*, which came out in 1999 with the *Knowledge Horizons* book published in 2000. [13] Cynefin had been born, in its early inception, as a straight-lined cross. Still, true to how I always saw it – as open, not closed and with the concept of dynamics firmly embedded in the *Knowledge Horizons* book chapter.

2. TRANSITION

The CBI books and growing recognition were all good news, but then we arrived at a period I term 'The Knowledge Wars.' One day I was told that IBM Consulting in the U.S. had hired Larry Prussack, an early thought leader. He was to lead their KM efforts. I booked myself in to meet him when he came to London. Although I was forbidden access to the day long training he was conducting, I was allowed to appear at its

end. Naively, I had assumed that my consulting colleagues and I were all interested in the field, but it turned out many were not especially happy, about a maverick with top cover in marketing, who had brought in the big guns, and were about to develop 'The Method.' Larry had been briefed that I was a troublemaker and that first meeting was more like a catechism class. The last thing the UK consultants wanted was someone in the room who had knowledge of the field. That was when I realized the full nature of IBM politics and felt somewhat like Mole in *The Wind in the Willows*: [14]

"And as he lay there panting and trembling, and listened to the whistlings and the patterings outside, he knew it at last, in all its fullness, that dread thing which other little dwellers in field and hedgerow had encountered here, and known as their darkest moment – that thing which the Rat had vainly tried to shield him from – the Terror of the Wild Wood!"

Adapted from the original illustration by Paul Bransom published in the 1913 book The Wind in the Willows by Kenneth Grahame

Larry and I later became good friends, after the UK team's attempt to attack my group's work had failed, and a negotiated peace settlement took place in Nice at the Institute for Knowledge Management meeting. That process was helped by the appointment of a new head of IBM's global KM function, Scott Smith. I met him in the Tarrytown Hilton and he greeted me with, "Where are the horns and tail?"

My position was now strengthened by strong allies in IBM and key public events which were increasing my profile. As Cynefin was shifting from a KM to a general theory of management focus, three of these events were critical.

1. At a KM conference, at the Hotel Dell in San Diego, I preceded the late and great Peter Drucker onto the stage and made the mistake of belittling Frederick Taylor. Having reduced me to a puddle of humiliation, Drucker decided I might be redeemable and took me out for dinner. After that we ran leadership seminars together. Since that date, and after the discussion with Peter, I advocated that Scientific Management and Complexity Thinking have more in common with each other than the popular, cybernetics-based approaches to Systems Thinking. The reason is that they both leave a role for human judgment. Scientific Management maintained an apprentice scheme for management, for example Taylor wanting to improve conditions for workers. In contrast, the referenced approaches to Systems Thinking have, in practice, resulted in management by spreadsheet, platitudinous mission statements and the tyranny of targets all of which depersonalize the workplace.

2. I'd been to Singapore to speak at events and was largely ignored by IBM until Jimmy Kwang, an account manager in the government group interested in KM, introduced me to the IBM Country General Manager, Janet Ong. After an hour she said, "I don't understand a word you are saying, but I don't understand you the way I don't understand Peter Ho so I will introduce you." Peter was the Permanent Secretary at the Ministry of Defence. Our fifteen minute meeting lasted an hour, and after a series of dinners and meetings, I became an advisor to the Ministry. That was only the beginning of a significant relationship. Peter became a good friend, and after leaving IBM, we were invited to put in a tender for complexity aspects of a risk assessment and horizon scanning project for Singapore; by that time he was the Head of the Civil Service and a fierce advocate of the Civil Service College where I taught. I share more on this later.

3. One day I was happily working in the Lotus offices, across the river from Boston, when I got a summons to Washington D.C. to summarize my work on narrative and complexity. I met an oldish guy who was not immediately familiar to me. I spotted Patrick O'Brian's books on his shelf and we

fell into an animated conversation about what would have happened after the publication of *Blue at the Mizzen* if only the author had lived a few more years. At that moment I spotted a picture of my host with Ronald Reagan and realized I was talking to Admiral John Poindexter.

My political background didn't prepare me for the affection and respect I came to garner for John (and my mother being a good Welsh socialist never understood). He had what I would call command presence and a sharp intelligence like numerous submariners I have met over the years. As the meeting progressed, I drew Cynefin on a sheet of paper and his response was, "that explains fifty years of failure in American Foreign Policy." That meeting led to work with the Defense Advanced Research Projects Agency (DARPA) before and after 9/11. The Genoa II project was led by myself for IBM with Cynthia Kurtz along with Sharon Darwent and others from the team and we pulled in Max and Yasmin. John Lawrence and Tom Boyce of Stanford Research Institute (SRI) in Menlo Park were the other major partners, and the whole initiative was led by Mark Lazaroff (who kindly introduced me to American Civil War Battlefields), Dennis Gormley and Stephen Sickels.

I wrote an important book chapter with Laz. Genoa II paralleled Total Information Awareness (TIA) which unfortunately got John into trouble with the Congress, but we provided its corollary, human intelligence, sense-making and human terrain mapping. [15] This was formative for both the theory that surrounded Cynefin and the ideas that, post IBM, would result in the development of the SenseMaker® tool. We also won the main contract against bids from IBM research which, as you might imagine, created some downstream tension. But what I will always remember is that we finished the first successful pilot project in Arlington the day before 9/11. I flew back to the UK that night and heard the news the next day, while driving to Warwick University to deliver a RA-RA speech to IBM Sales Executives. As I was asked to go on stage, I could see the towers falling down on CNN. It would be a few weeks before I knew all my team were still alive. Afterward the work progressed swiftly under a wonderful program manager from DARPA, Tom Armour, who sadly died tragically in February 2007. Things were never the same after Tom's passing but we began some serious work with some major players. I spent months staying in Club Quarters near the White House, developing a love of gin and tonics with my team at the Arlington Marriott bar, where John always stayed and had an expense account rife for abuse!

Cynefin had come a long way from its origins in Knowledge Management in a relatively short period of time. The lines of the cross were now wavy and the central domain had emerged. I think this evolution happened at a Lotus event at La Hulpe, where I also met Friso Gosliga for the first time. Earlier in the year, I discovered that it was first published in that form in a series of three articles I wrote on innovation for a management journal. That was about a year prior to its more cited use in the peer-reviewed "Complex Acts of Knowing," now one of the most cited papers of all time in the KM field. [16] As a result of this, I was approached by the editors of the *IBM Systems Journal* and asked to write an article on strategy. Cynthia had just come to work for me at the IKM so I suggested we jointly author what became "The New Dynamics of Strategy." [17] This article is often wrongly attributed as being the origin of Cynefin in its five domain form, but in fact it was the fourth paper to use it.

Cynthia had originally been a part of the IBM Story group. It included Wendy Kellog and her husband John C. Thomas and architect turned UX designer, Tracee Wolf, who were all part of the Knowledge Socialization Group at IBM's Hawthorn Research facility. This informal group also included people from Lotus and one of IBM's speech writers. I vividly remember at our first meeting discussing a key scene from the movie *Jaws* in which the three main characters (if we ignore the shark) are alone on a boat at night comparing scars. It is a key transition scene for the whole film, and no matter how many times I use it in training, I discover deeper layers of meaning. My introduction to *Story* by Robert McKee also helped me understand the fractal nature of good sense-making. [18]

The Story group survived for a few years but then fell victim to an IBM process or two. But as stated by then, Cynthia was a part of the IKM and eventually she was joined by the UK group (Sharon, Fiona and the two Nicks) and I finally had some resources. Cynthia and I went on to write two papers together and she came to Cognitive Edge as a contractor when I left IBM a few years later. It was, shall we say, an interesting relationship. In her own words:

"My collaboration with Dave was a paradox: the best of times and the worst of times. Some of our work together was the finest I've ever done (with any-one other than my husband; he gets first place of course), and some of the disappointments were my worst as well." [19]

We have different memories of key events and I suspect we were at times told different things about each other in multiple one-to-one conversations! Not everyone could work with Cynthia's directness and refusal to compromise. Several times I was asked in Washington and Somers why I insisted on her being a part of the various programs I was running, to which my response was, "Why would I want otherwise?" The last thing anyone wants is to be supported by sycophants. It was not without difficulty however; somewhere on my IBM personal record there is at least one, if not two formal warnings for some of the politics I played to keep her engaged and as importantly paid. All in all the disagreements with Cynthia were as productive, if not more so than the agreements!

Now I was moving towards Simple and Complicated along with Chaos and Complexity. They were ontological (the nature of things) terms, while other labels confused ontology with epistemology (the theory of knowledge.) Cynthia liked the mix. *New Dynamics*, which elaborated on disorder as the central domain and a series of dynamic movements, was the last publication to use known and knowable for the ordered domains. We also included some network diagrams that Cynthia subsequently morphed into her Confluence Framework. I fell in and out with these over the years finally abandoning them as people were misinterpreting them as categories of organization. Another aspect of this article I regret (but only after a decade of thinking about it) is classifying Chaos and Complexity as both being un-ordered. In fact, they are as different from each other as each is from order i.e., they cannot be grouped together the way that the ordered domains can.

At this point things were going well. I had sufficient resources and was able to task Cynthia, Sharon, Fiona and others to create methods to operationalize Cynefin. That took place at an IKM meeting working with members. Thankfully Cynthia was there to document and provide additional rigor to these methods. Our contract with DARPA provided funding to IKM to cover costs and I was spending a week every month in Washington D.C. An interesting tidbit: It turned out later that the car park under the office block where we were working was where the Deep Throat meetings took place during the Watergate affair.

Around 2001 all hell broke loose. IBM went through one of its near annual re-organizations and the IKM was collapsed into a new entity called the Institute for Business Value. It was part of the Consultancy Group, which had very different performance measurement systems. Larry was offered an early retirement deal, and while many of us in the IKM wanted to fight, there was little point and I found myself unexpectedly without a home. Fortunately, by then, the wider application beyond KM was being recognized and my original UK sponsor, Philip Oliver, (another one of those brilliant bosses whom I have been blessed with over the years) was now based in the U.S. and had the right connections.

I received funding to set up the Cynefin Centre for Organizational Complexity (at one stage it was called CAROC but I can't even remember what that stood for)! I had staff and a business manager in Mike Stephenson. We were allowed to launch a world wide training program which brought in Kevin McCaffrey from New Zealand, who had just been acquired with the PWC purchase, and with him Mark Anderson, who was appointed as my minder, a role he has attempted to occupy from time to time ever since! South Africa was another focus area and a training program in Gold Reef City brought Sonja Blignaut into the core network. I had a great new manager in Christian Noll and was about to be promoted to a Director role (important in terms of securing share options etc). I had even been allocated a company car at that grade and all was looking good. We were an emergent business unit (a program I had partially designed) and in the first full year we were the only ones to achieve our business goals – and the only ones to be terminated!

So all hell broke loose, again. We had been allocated $5M in funding for 2004 in the budget round and all looked good. Then late in 2003, while I was in transit at Vancouver airport to teach a five day masterclass, an email came in. It said that our funding had been withdrawn. The 'Spectre" at the feast was a V.P. in research who thought everything was about semantic analysis. Technically he was to be our host. Worse, when our funding had been reduced earlier that year, I was not aware that my knuckles were being rapped and that if I had apologized, the money would have been restored. I had simply said "Okay" and got funding directly from our clients.

By this time the body of methods around Cynefin was well developed and we had a lot of brilliant supporting material. Yet despite that, seemingly overnight, it was over. My staff was reallocated and my friends at high levels within IBM didn't have the time to deal with it before the year end cut off. I, and they, had been politically outmaneuvered by the "Spectre." I believe that the timing was deliberate. Withdrawing $5M of funding at the last minute seems it can't be other than political. Cynefin simply did not fit with a research community heavily into algorithms and physics. Once again, I was homeless.

It was a miserable Christmas. Then in January, en route to a client meeting in the Midlands, I got a phone call from my mother. She'd had an X-Ray and a diagnosis of possible lung cancer. I canceled my meeting and commenced a nightmare three months, in which I saw my father die ten days before my mother. IBM was very good about this, there was no expectation that I would do any work during this time. Returning to work that March, I had trips to South Africa and Australia planned and committed but I was now a problem – a resource owned, but not wanted by the UK.

Ironically, I had just been featured in a world wide advertising campaign as one of six IBM 'on demand thinkers' in an advert run in the Financial Times, the Economist and other leading journals. Subsequently, I received an email from the IBM General Manager for Government Business world-wide congratulating me. We had met the previous year in Sydney where I had told him, in no uncertain terms, and to the horror of his executive assistant, that I would not follow his advice regarding what to say in my keynote. Admittedly I was heavily jet lagged at the time and in no mood to moderate my language. To his credit he came to the presentation and afterwards told me I had been right to reject his advice. He was one, along with Philip and others, who were part of what made IBM great. Still, I was being forced out of IBM. He then did his level best to keep me, but the UK Consultants did not want me. When a forged email emerged suggesting I had disobeyed a direct order, I realized it was over.

A few phone calls later and I had an early retirement package. I turned 50 exactly one month after my mother's untimely death. Now I was out on my own, and a new transition, both for Cynefin and my own life, was about to begin. IBM was, to paraphrase Dickens: The... best of times and the worst of times. Without IBM, Cynefin would never have scaled. One thing the experience taught me was that if you start out with an idealistic set of ideas, you are unlikely to stay engaged as a consultant.

3. INDEPENDENCE AND COMPLETION?

The post IBM period runs from mid 2004 to the current day, a broader span of time than the previous two periods. After I left the DARPA, the work that came with me was near to ending. John Poindexter's issues with the Congress resulted in us being transferred from the DARPA to Intelligence Advanced Research Projects Activity (IARPA). Laz moved on and the whole effort lost momentum. But in parallel, the work with the Singapore Government was developing fast.

Following my encounters with Peter Ho, we had been commissioned to run a major workshop on complexity and I managed to have Cynthia and Alicia help. It was in that workshop that I invented the four points and linear methods for creating Cynefin. I've always done that; Future Backwards was developed live in a workshop for the Singapore Police and Ritual Dissent in a strategy and communication session for Canadian Pacific in Kananaskis. It's not improv, but rather informed- and adrenaline-driven creativity. Most methods I've developed that way have had little need for further enhancement. The IBM account team were amazed when the Ministry of Defense phoned the next day to ask how they wanted to be paid. That was without precedent in government work, and positioned us well with IBM in Singapore, as a part of the campaign to keep me.

But this is about work post IBM, along with a major think tank on futures work organized by Peter Ho in Singapore, that generated the 'Risk Assessment' and 'Horizon System' (RAHS) requirements. Max was present at the workshop where I first met Peter Schwartz, pioneer of scenario planning. I have since spoken at all the IRAHS conferences and I was proud last year when Peter and I were acknowledged at the opening dinner as the original inspiration for the program.

To cut a long story short we were aware of the tender for the RAHS contract coming and were awaiting details from our prime contractor, The Arlington Institute. It was important as Steve Bealing (who had left IBM for this) and I had founded Cognitive Edge Pte Ltd in Singapore on the basis of it. I was in

The Ministry of Defence one day when Patrick Nathan (a good friend and program manager designate for RAHS) asked why we had not bid for RAHS. I was shocked and said we hadn't been told about it. A few hours later the CEO of the Arlington Institute called and apologized for his error failing to let us know. I found this hard to believe as I knew he didn't want to work with us, but it gave me three days to write, cost, and risk assess a $1.3M bid. I achieved this working with Peter Stanbridge, who has long shared my vision for SenseMaker. It wasn't a bottom-up bid but an activity + team + time bid on a single spreadsheet, and I'm pleased to say it came in on budget. Steve and I later estimated that had we used IBM costing processes it would have come in at over $5M. I learned a lot on that project and also spent three months on a sabbatical at Nanyang University in 2006 where two habits started: blogging and editing Wikipedia. I was meant to write the book but got caught up in the politics of the project. All in all it was a good period.

We finally completed the project and it was launched at the first IRAHS event in Singapore on March 19, 2007, the day after England was due to play Wales at the Millennium Stadium. I couldn't miss the game, so I ended up watching the match (which thank God we won), then breaking various speed limits to get to Heathrow, and fly overnight to deliver an opening keynote at the launch. I stayed up all night preparing for it, showered, and then went on stage to find my 15 minute slot extended to 45 minutes. I'd received five minutes notice and last-minute whispered instructions from the Chairman. I'd been given the time to dig the previous speaker out of a hole. Luckily, it all worked out, and critically it delivered the first version of SenseMaker thanks to Peter, Cynthia and Paul (her husband) along with Ken McHugh. Ken, after a brief absence is still with us and is directing the creation of the next generation of the software.

All in all, Singapore has been a good home to Cognitive Edge and to Cynefin. It has been taught to the next generation of Singapore civil servants in their college, something that continues today to filter out which trainees move into senior positions. Few other civil servants would have created the space for experimentation with novel ideas; Peter Ho was, and is, unique in that respect.

That year (2007) was also significant for Cynefin as a framework. Tom Steward, then editor of the *Harvard Business Review* (HBR) and a good friend from my Knowledge Management days, had not only commissioned the HBR article, but also put me together with Mary Boone as co-author. I already knew her from IBM, where she had interviewed me for a book she was writing on narrative. The relationship worked from day one, and she also rescued me from a pack of 'Appreciative Inquiry' fanatics on the West Coast of Ireland, as part of her research when she was finalizing the book. The article took several years, some in gestation, some while navigating the aftermath of the death of my parents and Mary surviving cancer, but we finally got it done with the help of Bronwyn. I still remember sitting in Liverpool airport when the email came saying it had been selected as the cover article for the November 2007 edition. We subsequently got some of their best copy editors to work on it. I couldn't imagine but they took out 1000 words, and improved it! [20] That article was key to the growth of Cynefin and it went on to win two separate awards at the Academy of Management.

In parallel, I had presented Cynefin at an XP (Extreme Programming) event in London in 2004, and a group of people from that event attended a Cynefin training course in London the following year. Now I had been involved in software most of my adult life, and had been a part of founding DSDM which, like XP, was one of the established bodies of methods that became part of the Agile Manifesto. Interestingly, the Agile Manifesto is roughly the same age as Cynefin; though they evolved separately, by 2008 they started to come together, and the interaction has been a rich source of ideas and practice ever since. Scrum (the dominant method within the Agile movement) had in part grown up around the Stacey Matrix, which uses some of the same language, but is different in nature. Cynefin is about how things are, how we know them and how we perceive them, while Stacey focuses more on perception. I think one of the reasons Cynefin took off in the Agile community was its both/and nature. Cynefin says that there is nothing wrong with order, if you can achieve it. This is the principle of 'bounded applicability,' different things work or don't work in different domains.

Over the next few years I was increasingly engaged with the Agile community, and while the XP event was key, so was a conference in Limerick in June 2008 from which many invitations to speak at Agile events spawned. Agile is interesting in that its growth and nature, in some ways, is very much like Knowledge Management. Most management movements start with a single guru and book, but both KM and Agile had multiple sources and were more resilient as a result. Both unfortunately generated multiple conferences and events, as well as certification scams and schemes. While KM is more or less dead strategically (although the practices remain) Agile, if anything, is attempting to shift from software development to wider applications. My suspicion is that this will succeed, but like KM, it will possibly morph a new name, or a new way linked to its origin.

Cynefin was originally developed, in part, because I tired of management fads, each trying to sweep away what had come before. One of the main functions of Cynefin is to make practical the idea that the last thing we did had value, we just may have tokenized it and tried to make it universal. Most things have value, within boundaries, and Cynefin tries to establish what they are and gain an understanding of what it takes to move between domains – something which has historically been called Cynefin dynamics. They were around before New Dynamics, but were more fully elaborated within that. I still remember when Cynthia and I were looking for a name for one of the dynamics and we came up with The Masada Gambit for throwing things into chaos for its own sake because all else has failed. There were a lot of aha movements like that over the years.

Speaking of dynamics brings me to a personal note. In 2013 I was diagnosed with Type 2 diabetes. By my 60th birthday the following year I had lost 35kg and reversed my diabetes. I celebrated with a week-long walking holiday in Snowdonia. I did a solo walk from the Ogwen Valley to Aber Falls returning to the mountains from which I had been too long absent. The next year my daughter and I went on the Annapurna Sanctuary Walk and I also managed to walk all the way 'round Wales and back, through the middle, in 67 days, spread over four years.

On the business front during this time, Steve Bealing left the company and after a long period in which I had to act as CEO, including one failed merger, Marion Eickman and Andrea Tomasini, long term friends from Agile42, stepped in as investors to support the company during a difficult time. Despite the various vicissitudes, Cynefin continued to develop. One of the ongoing problems with 'dynamics' was that people found it difficult to cope with two classification systems - domains and dynamics. Two things then happened that changed things dramatically. First, I was working on domain models, three by three matrices to elaborate each of the four Cynefin domains (excluding what was then un-order). My original intent was to work out a way to create a version of SenseMaker which could auto-generate Cynefin, still an ongoing project. Second, I was doing a lot of reading and thinking about boundary states and understanding when to cross and when to suspend crossing them, all of which brought me to the idea of liminality. Using the blog (a constant source of innovation as it allows me to explore ideas without commitment) I experimented with some ideas.

Then one day on a whiteboard I drew a green line which was open at the top, it intersected disorder but closed the boundary between Chaotic and Complex. With that simple line the liminal version of Cynefin with four new sub domains was born. Dynamics are still drawn, but the liminal version carries with it the concept of movement and it allows a more nuanced way to classify methods. It also recognizes the value of methods which focus specifically on the Complex to Complicated transition. It resolved the issue with disorder, which at one time had been drawn like an open pit mine – illegitimate in the middle and better when transitioning around the edge. Now we had a more legitimate, liminal aspect, and an illegitimate aspect, representing confusion on the edge of chaos.

At a long meeting in Boston with Mary Boone and other members of the team, we settled on Clear instead of Obvious for what had been Known and then Simple. That made for four Cs, as it wasn't a big step to rename disorder as confused, which is more descriptive. Earlier this year (2020) John van Breda reminded me of the idea of Aporia, deliberate puzzlement through paradox and other techniques. That resolved itself as we now had a liminal area in Confused where you focus on creating Aporia. What had been an accidental drawing of the green line to keep a small liminal space in Complicated, post COVID-19, became critical as it represented the domain of competing expertise – something for which I had earlier created the Triopticon technique.

IN PHILOSOPHY, an APORIA is a PHILOSOPHICAL PUZZLE or a SEEMINGLY INSOLUBLE IMPASSE in an INQUIRY, OFTEN ARISING as a RESULT of EQUALLY PLAUSIBLE YET INCONSISTENT PREMISES, I.E. a PARADOX.

Cynefin now had a reasonable degree of symmetry and coherence without being too neat and tidy. I suspect its current form is near final. Perhaps at 21 it's time to grow up! Currently I'm working on my next major sense-making project, the development of Apex Predator theory for strategy. It is roughly in the same position Cynefin was in a decade ago: it has my focus and I want to complete it.

SO WHAT HAS THIS ALL MEANT?

I'd like to come back to J.C. Spender's original comment about "Making meaning problematic" which has stayed with me for years. Looking back over two decades, I didn't set out to create Cynefin. It emerged as various things became problematic for me and were resolved in different ways, or in some cases not fully resolved. Cynefin was not a framework created from a single study and then published in a book. It emerged through flip chart drawings, and as I read more and explored new areas, more ideas were incorporated. It was, to return to the title, "A tale that grew in the telling."

After I finished my degree, I worked internationally for the student branch of the World Council of Churches. My ambition was to be a worker priest within the tradition of Liberation Theology. For various reasons that didn't work out and I moved from managing student services, through HR and Training to

Finance, to building and designing decision support systems. From there I moved to general management with a career path that looked conventional. Then the IBM acquisition threw me back into academic life. The one thing I have never regretted is returning to that arena, after several decades, with a greater wisdom of how things work. I never stopped reading and thinking. That said, I've never regretted not doing a PhD although people often assume I have. If I had followed that route immediately after University I would not be what I am today. Cynefin means the place of your multiple belongings, a multi-threaded and entangled path that makes you what you are, and continues to change over time. Learning to live with that and to work with it is key to maturity and impact. I haven't always been successful but I have tried.

Three things I am most proud of in this work:

1. Cynefin is fractal, it is self similar at multiple levels but can be understood simply, or on further investigation in more complex ways. Like a good book, revisiting it does not involve repetition but new and deeper insight.

2. Many, many people have taken up and applied Cynefin without the need for me to be involved and they have used it in ways coherent to the original, but with fascinating variations. Cynefin can stand on its own without expert facilitation and it can be drawn on the back of a napkin from memory.

3. Cynefin has made a difference to people's lives ranging from minor interest to transformation. I've tried not to be precious as to its use, correcting only blatant falsehoods or deviations, and that has built a community of practice which continues to grow.

I could add to this list that more people have become aware of a small nation of three million people with a unique language and a unique culture. Then of course, aside from the community of Cynefin, there are the staff of Cognitive Edge (present and past) not already mentioned along with the Cynefin Centre Coven and the SenseMaker team, without whom none of this would have been possible and without whom there would be no future.

Elmi Bester, Sonja Blignaut, Michael Cheveldave, Cory Costanzo, Zhen Goh, Warwick Holder, Dawn Lincoln, Ian Macdonald, Ranjini Mei Hua, Meg Odling-Smee, Tony Quinlan, Angelina Seah, Julia and Peter Stanbridge, Jules Yim, Emma Jones, Anna Panagiotou, Poppaea Roberts, Beth Smith, Natalie Smith, Eleanor Snowden, Nia Angharad Williams, Vinodhini Anand, Tengku Asyraf, Christine Dorothy, Amaljith Indrajith, Harshadi Khare, Manami Majamdar, Ken McHugh, Saranya Ranganathan, and Ramya Ramatha.

At the start of this chapter I quoted from Tolkien who said *The Lord of the Rings* enabled "glimpses that had arisen unbidden of things higher or deeper or darker than its surface." I think Cynefin has allowed that process of discovery and will continue to do so, but it is incomplete. [21] Here, I and the whole community, are one with St Paul in one of my favourite quotes from *the Bible*, "For now we see through a glass darkly (1 Cor 13:12)." My definition of sense-making is, how do we make sense of the world so that we can act in it. Cynefin is a key part of that body of work. It makes no absolute claim, but it helps us make sense and act accordingly.

References

1. Sinclair, N. in his preface to Williams, Kyffin. The Land & the Sea. Llandysul: Gwasg Gomer, 2004. Print.

2. Nonaka, Ikujiro, and Noboru Konno. "The Concept of "ba": Building a Foundation for Knowledge Creation." California Management Review. 40.3 (1998): pp. 40-54.

3. Snowden, D. "The Social Ecology of Knowledge Management." (2000): 237-265. In Chauvel, Daniele, and Charles Despres. Knowledge Horizons: The Present and the Promise of Knowledge Management. Boston: Butterworth-Heinemann, 2000.

4. Tolkien, J.R. R, The Lord of the Rings. London: HarperCollins, 2007. p.5

5. Tolkien, J.R. R, The Lord of the Rings. London: HarperCollins, 2007. p.5

6. https://www.oxfordbibliographies.com/view/document/obo-9780199756841/obo-9780199756841-0112.xml

7. Thom, Rene, Structural Stability and Morphogenesis: An Outline of General Theory of Models. Redwood, Calif. [u.a.: Addison-Wesley, 1989. p.33

8. Frost, Robert, and Edward C. Lathem. The Poetry of Robert Frost: the Collected Poems, Complete and Unabridged. New York: Holt, Rinehart and Winston, 1975. p.33

9. Thomas, R.S., Collected Poems 1945-1990 Phoenix 2000 p.302

10. Nonaka, I., & Takeuchi, H. (1995). The knowledge-creating company: How Japanese companies create the dynamics of innovation. Oxford university press.

11. Juarrero, A. (1999). Dynamics in action: intentional behavior as a complex system. Cambridge, Mass.; London: MIT Press.

12. Boisot, M. (1998). Knowledge assets: securing competitive advantage in the information economy. Oxford: Oxford University Press.

13.   Snowden, D. (1999) "Liberating Knowledge" Introductory chapter to Liberating Knowledge CBI Business Guide, Caspian Publishing October 1999 pp.9-19

14.   Grahame, K. (1910). The wind in the willows (5th ed. ed.). London: Methuen.

15.   Lazaroff, M & Snowden, D "Anticipatory modes for Counter Terrorism" in Popp, R & Yen, J, Emergent Information Technologies and Enabling Policies for Counter-Terrorism Wiley-IEEE Press 2006

16.   Snowden, D. (2002), "Complex acts of knowing: paradox and descriptive self-awareness," Journal of Knowledge Management, Vol. 6 No. 2, pp. 100-111. https://doi.org/10.1108/13673270210424639

17.   Kurtz, C F, and D J. Snowden. "The New Dynamics of Strategy: Sense-Making in a Complex and Complicated World." Ibm Systems Journal. 42.3 (2003) pp.462-483

18.   McKee, R. (1998). Story: substance, structure, style and the principles of screenwriting. London: Methuen.

19.   Kurtz, C. F. (2014). Working with Stories in Your Community Or Organization. Kurtz-Fernhout Publishing. p.634

20.   Snowden, D.J, and M.E Boone. "A Leader's Framework for Decision Making. a Leader's Framework for Decision Making." Harvard Business Review. 85.11 (2007) pp. 69-76

21.   Tolkien, J.R. R, The Lord of the Rings. London: HarperCollins, 2007. p.5

WHAT CYNEFIN IS IN BRIEF

DAVE SNOWDEN

So what is Cynefin? Cynefin is a key framework in what is known as Naturalizing sense-making. The term *naturalizing* relates to the use of natural science, and sense-making (with a hyphen) is defined as, "How do we make sense of the world so that we can act in it?" Cynefin is also part of a body of work looking at the dynamic interplay between deductive, inductive, and abductive sense-making. At the time of this writing, the Framework looks as shown in Figure 1.

Figure 1. Visual of Cynefin in 2020

We also share a humorous 3D representation at the end of this chapter (Figure 4.)

The essence of the Framework can be summarized as follows:

1. **Domains** – Cynefin is a typology that describes three primary types of systems: Ordered, Complex, and Chaotic, each defined by the type of constraint, or absence thereof. Order is constrained and future outcomes are predictable as long as the constraints can be sustained. The Complex domain has enabling constraints, and many levels of entanglement that make it dispositional in nature, with no linear material causality. Chaos is the absence of effective constraints. The shifts between the primary domains are all phase shifts for which the best metaphor is latent heat – energy is required to achieve the phase shift from liquid to gas even though the temperature does not change, similarly phasing from liquid to solid gives off energy.

   The early historical use of Unorder, as a collective name for Complex and Chaotic, has been dropped because Complexity and Chaos are as different from each other as they are from Order. Further, we have the Confused domain, formerly known as Disorder. This is the state of not knowing which domain you are in. It is frequently, but wrongly (sic) confused with Chaos. The Confused domain is appreciated as A/C (Aporia/Confused). More about this in point 3., the Liminal Line.

2. **Order** – To accommodate the disconnect between reality (ontology: how things are), perception (epistemology: how we perceive things), and knowledge (phenomenology: how we know things) in human systems, Order in Cynefin divides into two domains: 1) Clear (constraints are rigid or fixed and the relationship between cause and effect is self-evident and clear to any reasonable person) and 2) Complicated (causal relationships exist but require expertise or analysis to discover them. Constraints are governing, providing confidence in the boundary of expertise).

3. **Liminal Line** – Cynefin is a dynamic framework; things transition between domains. The liminal zones in Cynefin are demarcated by the intersections between the liminal lines. These liminal zones provide a space to accommodate significant transitions between domains. The liminal line is open at the top (Figure 2), closed at the bottom, and intersects all domains except Clear. Liminality in the Clear domain is not visible, making the boundary between Clear and Chaotic a cliff or catastrophic fold. It is easy to walk blindly off this cliff through excessive confidence in the context-free applicability of rigid constraints.

   The liminal line creates liminal states in Complex (still uncertain but transiting to Complicated), Chaos (the deliberate removal of effective constraints for decision support and/or innovation),

Complicated (where the analysis method or type of expertise is in question) and Confusion where the liminal area is one of aporia, a state of authentic confusion i.e., being confused and aware. To be unknowingly in the Confused domain is not advisable, and it is adjacent to the catastrophic fold for a reason. Aporia is also something that can be intentionally created to stimulate pathways into any of the domains other than Clear.

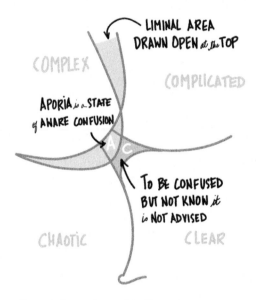

Figure 2. Liminality in Cynefin

4. **Practice** – There are different types of practice in each of the Cynefin domains including the liminal areas. In the Complex domain practice is 'exaptive,' or focused on radical re-purposing of existing capability. In the Complicated domain we apply 'good practice,' in Clear we have the only legitimate application of 'best practice,' In the liminal area between Complex and Complicated, practice is iterative in nature. Transitions into Clear should be done only when the practice has truly been established as best practice. The energy it requires to shift something into Clear, with 100% best practice is high. This shift should be done only when you are confident that change will not be needed for some time. In Chaos, practice is generally novel, either by accident or, in the liminal area, by design. In the liminal area of Confused, practice is aporetic – the deliberate creation of paradox and puzzlement to get people thinking differently.

5. **Framework** (not method) – Cynefin is at its heart a decision support framework, not a method or model. It is based on the principle of 'bounded applicability'; there are few if any context-free solutions, but many valid context-specific ones. The Framework is a way of determining what methods or approaches you should adopt, and when you should change them. Movement between domains can take many forms, which have been represented in the past as 'dynamics.' The most stable pattern of movement is a constant iteration between Complex and Complicated, with things being consigned to Clear when there is sufficient stability to warrant and the risk of getting it wrong is low (black dotted line paths in Figure 3).

Occasionally there is a need to dip into the 'aporetic liminal' area from Complicated, to disrupt entrained expert thinking (grey dotted path in figure 3 formerly known as a shallow dive into the Chaos domain). The 'aporetic liminal' area is the normal target for an exit from involuntary Chaos. There is also a dynamic that constantly moves from Complexity through all liminal zones and then back again (dashed line path in figure 3). This means stability of any type is not possible and you are, in effect, to quote one of my favorite authors and interlocutors, Anne Pendleton-Julian, living in a "white water world." If you can't navigate the flow, you drown. If you can, you emerge from the rapids, changed. The α β γ & δ points are key monitoring points where you have to make decisions.

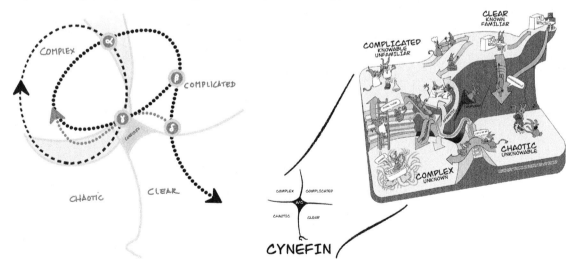

Figure 3. Dynamics and decision points in Cynefin

Figure 4. Martin Berg's Vige cartoon of Cynefin adapted with permission from the 3D version by Rob England in collaboration with Chris Bramley

ORGANIZING PRINCIPLES: THE SPIRIT OF CYNEFIN

SONJA BLIGNAUT

ABOUT THE AUTHOR

Sonja Blignaut is a thinking and sense-making partner for leaders and change-makers who need to better navigate uncertainty. She is based in South Africa and has a background in the natural sciences. She is a sought after speaker and recognized authority in Complexity, Cynefin and Organization Development. Sonja has almost two decades of consulting experience and is certified in various individual and systemic coaching methods. She looks after the commercial business of Cognitive Edge and is also Founder and Managing Director of More Beyond in South Africa.

ORGANIZING PRINCIPLES: THE SPIRIT OF CYNEFIN

SONJA BLIGNAUT

When I first encountered Cynefin in 2002, it wasn't only the Framework that intrigued me but the entire ecology. Sure there was the Framework and the ever-evolving suite of methods and tools that support it, but there was also a set of organizing principles woven through it all. These principles provide guidance and safety guardrails, if you will, to practitioners as they apply methods that in many contexts are counter to the norm. They describe the 'stance' we need to adopt, or in other words, how to show up in a way that is congruent with the spirit of Cynefin i.e., how we inhabit and embody the 'place of our multiple belongings.'

While the Framework and some of the methods may seem deceptively simple, if used without applying these principles, they easily lose their transformative value and we may not get the hoped-for results.

The original set of organizing principles or heuristics, dating back to 2003, consisted of 13 heuristics roughly grouped into four broad themes. Our thinking has evolved a lot since 2003, so Dave and I revisited these principles and brought them up to date. The new set has three main organizing principles, each with a few precepts below it.

I will attempt to describe the essence of each of the updated principles in this chapter. I will also provide my interpretation drawn from nearly two decades of practice as a consultant and thinking partner. This chapter aims to help users of Cynefin understand the principles behind it, and the context we need to create to get the most out of the Framework and the methods.

(To enrich the reader's understanding of these principles, we are using symbols to indicate throughout the book which of these principles are relevant to each of the chapters. You can use the Wayfinding section of the book, or you can simply note the symbols as you are exploring the chapters themselves).

PRINCIPLE 1: WE EMBRACE MESSY COHERENCE

EMBRACE MESSY COHERENCE

"Physics is really nothing more than a search for ultimate simplicity, but so far all we have is a kind of elegant messiness." – Bill Bryson [1]

Most of us seem to have an innate sense of when something is coherent, and when it isn't. However, articulating this isn't easy. I find it challenging to explain coherence, and often resort to giving examples of incoherence instead. We recognize incoherence easily, such as someone's speech after a brain injury, or when they've had a little too much to drink.

Constraints or boundaries create coherence. A sentence makes sense when it exhibits the structure of a particular language (i.e., I am able to determine if it is English or Russian) and roughly follows grammatical rules. However, when these constraints are lacking, it becomes noise, a jumble of words or sounds that make no sense.

Language requires diversity – if the alphabet had only one letter, or only vowels and no consonants, it would be hard to form words. Similarly, if we only had a fixed set of words with prescribed meanings, we would not be able to express new concepts or ideas, and language would be purely functional, not a form of creative expression. When the need arises, new words are invented spontaneously, sometimes old words are repurposed (for example Brexit – itself a new word – gave us 'remoaners,' Covid-19 gave us 'quaranteams' and 'Zoombombing'). And yet, with all of this flux, language remains understandable to us. It remains coherent as long as the messiness is bounded by the rules or principles of grammar. In this way, language is an excellent example of messy coherence, or in other words coherent heterogeneity. We can accommodate differences within boundaries that ensure coherence. (For another perspective on constraints, read Steve Holt's chapter that contrasts Cynefin to Goldratt's Theory of Constraints.)

Cynefin is all about boundaries. In that way, it reflects human systems such that knowing where the boundaries are between specific contexts are critical to our meaning-making, identity structures, and ability to relate to each other. Cynefin's boundaries help us to know what kind of systemic context we find ourselves in, and when we are transitioning from one to another. Being able to locate ourselves also helps us determine the appropriate actions to take, and the methods and tools that are fit for that particular systemic context.

Methods, tools, and frameworks, however, are not universally applicable; there are no silver bullets. We articulate this in Cynefin with the term 'bounded applicability' i.e., we believe that most things are useful within certain boundaries. I find this notion particularly helpful when introducing decision-makers to something new or novel. It is extremely off-putting when someone tries to sell you on a new way of thinking by devaluing everything that you have used, or believed, in the past. By applying this principle, we can help decision-makers locate the methods and tools that they have found valuable thus far, validate their usefulness within certain boundaries, and show them how they are unhelpful in others. It is a much less triggering and arrogant approach.

So this principle of messy coherence enables us to accommodate much diversity of approaches, methods, and tools within Cynefin. Coherence comes from understanding the boundaries of their applicability.

PLAYING IN THE TENSION

Cynefin values coherence and difference, even though they are in tension. Too much difference and things become incoherent. Too much coherence and things become too homogeneous.

For example, in large organizations there is often a drive to align the entire workforce behind a particular goal and create a singular culture. This singular alignment, one could argue, is an extreme form of coherence. It strips away the diversity of a system to a point where its resilience is compromised. On the other hand, too many subcultures and conflicting goals in an organization will become incoherent and lead to fragmentation. Applying the principle of coherent heterogeneity, we can accept and value the diversity of localized sub-cultures, as long as they are coherent with the identity of the whole. The key here is that the difference is bounded or contained in such a way that it does not become incoherent or fragmented. (Jennifer Garvey-Berger and team's chapter explores how they applied this approach in their company.)

Cynefin uses this inherent tension as generative, creating a space for the novelty to emerge. Most of our methods work to generate this space by embracing and sometimes intentionally creating ambiguity, paradox, and aporia. (For more on Aporia, read Zhen Goh's chapter.)

"Conflict and paradox are critical to the advancement of understanding. Aside from verbal paradox, Cynefin methods often deliberately introduce conflict and ambiguity into group interactions to gain this higher level of understanding. Introducing a state of Aporia, or deliberate puzzlement, allows us to present seemingly contradictory and competing understandings as valid and useful pieces of the bigger picture." – Dave Snowden

The world abounds with false dichotomies: management vs. leadership; agile vs. waterfall; purpose vs. profit; theory vs. practice... The list goes on and on. We embrace – And-And rather than Either-Or – which means we seek out, or play in tension, rather than creating binary options or false dichotomies. Cynefin values ambiguity, dialectic, and even paradox. We attempt to avoid prematurely converging to one particular idea or solution, and we try to play in ambiguity and a broad option field for as long as we can. Keeping our options open as long as possible creates a liminal space. Liminality is a key concept that was introduced into the Framework a few years ago. Liminality is about transitions, about being in the 'in-between.' When we find ourselves in the in-between spaces, the liminal space, our task is to be mindful of suspending judgment, keeping our options open and enabling action that allows novelty to emerge and patterns to stabilize.

"The issue is not to swing to either extreme but to increase diversity (and thereby conflict, discontinuity, and paradox) when it is necessary and reduce it through alignment when the situation demands. The attempt to remove (or require) conflict, in many idealistic approaches that value stability or turbulence but ignore context, is the worst of all possible worlds. By always choosing one option or another, we can get the worst of both." – Dave Snowden

HEURISTICS

"Designing rules assumes an ordered universe in which we can predict the outcome of a defined action and in which we can know the range of possible circumstances. Heuristics, on the other hand, provide more general guidance; they have a level of ambiguity which makes them more adaptable.

Heuristics are not the same thing as value or principle statements that are vague enough to be selectively interpreted, or rationalized, to justify different and contradictory actions. Heuristics within the bounds of common sense are not that ambiguous; i.e., we can objectively determine whether or not they were followed. Heuristics are often associated with delegation of authority, while rules are about control. Both are right, and both are wrong – it depends on the context." – Dave Snowden

Military contexts, perhaps because they have long struggled with the need for distributed authority and responsiveness, abound with examples of heuristics. Napoleon, for example, told his armies to 'march to the sound of the guns' instead of waiting for orders. Another example: when the battle plan falls apart – capture the high ground, stay in touch, keep moving. In both these examples, the heuristic is ambiguous enough to apply in different contexts, yet specific enough to know if someone followed them or not. This is explored in greater detail in Trent Hone's chapter.

PRINCIPLE 2: ENABLE DESCRIPTIVE SELF-AWARENESS AND SELF-DISCOVERY

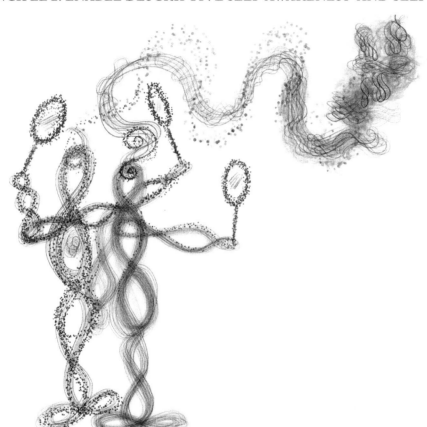

ENABLE DESCRIPTIVE SELF-AWARENESS

"People are generally better persuaded by the reasons which they have themselves discovered than by those which have come into the mind of others." – Blaise Pascal

Cynefin is about proactive meaning-making and sense-making. We seek to understand the evolutionary potential in the present and discover how to enable novel connections and act appropriately. We are making sense in order to act, not to gain reflective insight only. Attaining a state of descriptive self-awareness, where individuals or systems 'see' themselves and their context differently, often leads immediately to actionable insight. A Cynefin-informed approach, therefore, entails creating the conditions that enable such awareness. When we tell or advise, we are undermining this process. (Read more about this in the chapter by Riva Greenberg and Boudewijn Bertsch.)

If, like me, you are a consultant, you likely resist the urge to analyze or prescribe. Instead, you focus on creating the conditions where the client becomes able to see and describe their current state differently and potentially know how to act. This principle is held in a deep belief that we need to address epistemic injustice, i.e., mitigate the power imbalances and the unfairness that accompany knowledge. Our processes and tools are designed so that every voice is valued equally, and that participants interpret their data. Facilitators, consultants, and experts are not privileged to hold interpretive power the way most other methods work. We create a context where voices are heard, and hold up a mirror so that the 'system can see itself' in different and potentially possibly transformative ways. (For more on this, read the chapters by Viv Read and Chris Corrigan).

There is a broad range of Cynefin methods that facilitate this 'holding of the mirror.' For example, we create two contrasting sets of emergent archetypes from the same narrative material, to show how two different groups, say customers view themselves and product developers see them. The contrast between the two perspectives makes things (often unpalatable things, or 'elephants in the room') visible in a way that cannot be ignored. Because they were part of the creation of the data, without anyone guiding or advising them, they cannot reject the unpalatable conclusion in the way that they can deny conclusions intermediated by an expert or analyst's interpretation of the data. This disintermediation between decision-makers and data or insight is a key aspect of most of our methods and tools, and foundational to our SenseMaker software tool.

While easy to accept in theory, this can be problematic in practice, especially for experts, consultants, or those in leadership roles. It is hard not to intervene, advise, or apply expertise when that is what you have valued in other contexts. It is also difficult not to 'rescue,' which is a normal empathetic response when we see others struggle. When you find yourself tempted in these ways, consider a time in your own life when you discovered something, about yourself for yourself, compared to when someone gave you advice: What do you remember best, and which changed your mind the most? Which of those effects will be most useful and sustainable for the other person?

"It sometimes takes patience and confidence to communicate to clients the value of emergent methods; this gets much easier as one sees the methods working in practice and can compare the efficiency and effectiveness of these fine tools with the blunt edges of recipes." – Dave Snowden

ON UNINTENDED CONSEQUENCES

We can also never forget that complex systems are open systems; whenever we interact with them, we become part of that system. The systems we deal with are typically complex socio-technical systems, and in these systems, there is no such thing as an independent or neutral observer or consultant. When we enter a system, we become part of it; its dynamics influence us, and in turn, it changes in response to our presence. A team is not the same once a coach arrives, even if all that person does is observe. When a consultant turns up, the system changes. New connections and meanings form that change prevailing systemic patterns in unpredictable ways. Because of this, every diagnostic is an intervention, and every intervention is a diagnostic (if we are situationally aware).

In complex systems as well, despite our best efforts, there will be unintended consequences flowing from our interactions with the system. We mitigate these by keeping our interventions small and safe-to-fail, and ensuring that we have dampening strategies in place should unintended negative consequences arise. Sometimes these may be 'helpful accidents,' and when these happen, we embrace serendipity and attempt to amplify them. The fundamental principle here is to understand that there will be consequences, because we know that they are our responsibility to manage.

People in a particular system generally have in-depth contextual knowledge, but they may have been part of the system for so long that they no longer see what's right in front of them. Leaders often got to be in their influential positions because they were the best competitors in the old paradigm. It is hard for people to face the idea that the knowledge and skills that brought them this far in their careers may have become detrimental. When we enter these systems as change agents, it is best to cultivate a thick skin as we will encounter defensiveness when we challenge customers' long-held beliefs and 'best practices.'

I've learned to be wary of the subtle, and not-so-subtle, ways the system often attempts to seduce me into colluding with some of its dysfunctional dynamics. This is where it can be beneficial to have a thinking partner or coach, or even to be part of a professional reflection group that can help keep us honest and force us to look in the mirror ourselves. One of the critical things to remember here is that we cannot force another person or a system to change. Our role is to help people see and think differently, be a mirror, challenge, and sometimes teach, mentor, and introduce new tools and methods. But in the end, we can't control what happens regarding their gains in the process. The famous Biblical parable of the sower applies here. We sow seeds, some fall on fertile ground, others on impenetrable soil, and yet others sprout but get overgrown by weeds. Our responsibility is to keep sowing the seeds, that is all we have control over.

PRINCIPLE 3: ATTUNE TO TIMING AND FLOW

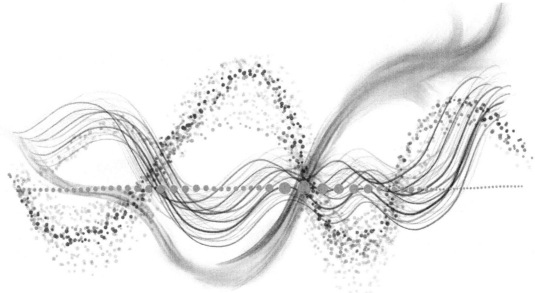

ATTUNE TO TIMING & FLOW

"An important aspect of complex systems, one that certainly complicates our understanding and modeling of such systems, is their temporal nature. Complex systems unfold in time, they have a history that co-determines present behavior and they anticipate the future. Moreover, as we know at least since the work of Prigogine, the behavior of complex systems is not symmetrical in time. They have a past and a future that are not interchangeable. This being 'situated in time' does not always receive adequate attention in our analysis of complexity.

The central notion at stake when we talk of time and complexity is that of 'memory.' Memory is the persistence of certain states of the system, of carrying something from the past over into the future. It is not merely the remembering of something in the past, as if belonging to that past, it is the past being active in the present." – Paul Cilliers [2]

Time matters in human systems. The patterns we can observe today were shaped by the initial starting conditions of the system and many years of evolutionary change.

This means that while complex systems are inherently unpredictable and non-causal, they have dispositional states i.e., they are predisposed towards certain behaviors. If we understand these dispositions and follow those 'natural contours,' the energy gradient for change is lessened.

An analogy I often use is elephant paths. There are two ways to design a garden or park. There is the ordered systems approach where we spend a lot of time and money up-front in the design: we survey the soil, observe the light, and design aesthetically pleasing vistas. When we finally open the gates to let in the first visitors, they almost immediately proceed to mar our beautifully designed gardens with elephant paths. Elephant paths, or desire lines, are informal paths that pedestrians prefer to take from one location to another rather than using a sidewalk or, in our case, the paved garden paths.

A more effective way to determine where our paths should go is to lay the lawn and then let people in and see where they naturally walk. We can then use those naturally emergent paths to guide us on where to put ours. Similarly, we can only really know how to intervene in a system once we understand the structure and dynamics of that particular system. That enables us to expend less energy in our attempts to create conditions for change. In contrast, recipe-based approaches waste much energy forcing solutions onto the system regardless of whether they fit the context.

ON TIME AND CADENCE

Alicia Juarerro, during a talk in Washington DC in November 2019, reminded me that we often under-estimate the importance of time and timing in human complex systems. We also forget that there are different ways to perceive time. There is Chronos (chronological or sequential) and Kairos (opportune) time. Chronological time is agnostic of context as it inexorably moves along. Kairos time, defined as right, critical, or opportune moments, is inherently linked to context. For each unique context, there will be unique Kairos moments. [3]

We are used to being in Chronos time. Cynefin seeks to engage with Kairos time, time entangled with context. When we understand the dispositional state of a system, we can also recognize Kairos moments, opportune times when the system is poised for change. Cynefin is about embracing the here and now; we learn from the past, but we don't rely on it to predict a future; we are evolving into a future, but we are not aiming at an idealized future state. We search for the evolutionary potential in the present, and when Kairos moments arise, we take them.

Many of our methods are scaffolds, they create temporary structures within which new meanings can emerge. (For more on scaffolds, read Ann Pendleton-Jullian's chapter.)

ON FLOW AND PATTERNS

Cynefin is a flow concept. It recognizes a continuous dynamic flow of many entangled patterns through time. Meaning is something that emerges from tangled connections over time. Our meaning-making is active and "in the moment." The narrative becomes important here as it is a primary human meaning-making mechanism. It is how we make sense of our experience over time. As Dave said regarding this flow and pattern making:

"Human decision-making and interactions are determined to some extent by patterns of prior experience. Some of that experience is direct; some is gained through commonly heard (and told) stories. The patterns of acceptable cultural and political diversity range widely among countries – think of the differences between acceptable political opinion in the U.S. and Europe. These differences are not about right or wrong, or empirical truth or falsity, but arise from stories told and retold within families and the culture as a whole. The same is true in organizations, where both formal and informal stories define acceptable ranges of behavior and provide a regulatory structure that determines the possible. The use of narrative to reveal patterns, and to pattern in its turn, is central to Cynefin methods.

Sometimes our meaning-making patterns become traps. They become like biased lenses through which we view the world that lock us into a particular perspective. We call this phenomenon 'pattern entrainment.'

To counter this entrainment, we need multiple perspectives and disruption. It is not enough to ask for people to be more objective, or to rise above local prejudice or the patterns of past success. Even if they manage to do so, it will be impossible to sustain. Cynefin methods focus on disruption through descriptive self-awareness, and creating contexts where people can see things from different or new perspectives." – Dave Snowden

You can better see now that the typical (and usually linear) problem-solving orientation that dominates many workshops and projects is not helpful in complex socio-technical systems. In ordered contexts, we are dealing with solvable problems; in complex ones, we are dealing with emergent and entangled patterns. Cynefin methods propel us to see and approach them as such.

ON LIMINALITY

"In the universe, there are things that are known, and things that are unknown, and between them, there are doors." – William Blake

Liminality is a key concept that was introduced into the Framework a few years ago. Liminality, from the Latin word līmen, meaning 'a threshold,' is about transitions, about being in the 'in-between' and crossing thresholds. Being in an ambiguous liminal state can be disorienting and anxiety-provoking, yet it is also a place of emerging opportunity and many options. People often forget that Cynefin is a dynamic framework, and that the system states in Cynefin are dynamic and things move between them. The liminal zones between domains are transformational. Here we are able to suspend judgment, keep our options open, and enable the emergence of novelty. We remain in a state of constant awareness so that we don't miss those Kairos moments. (This links to the notion of Wu-Wei, which you can read more about in Zhen Goh's and Jules Yim's chapters.)

CONCLUSION

In short, Cynefin methods are based on finding the evolutionary potential in the present, setting a broad future direction, and moving towards 'adjacent possibles.' The best way to describe this is by crossing a river by feeling the stones. The intent or direction is to cross the river. We are not aiming for a particular spot (in contrast to the idealist approach of engineering a bridge to a specific point on the opposite river bank.) We start from a place on the near side where there are reachable stepping stones (adjacent possible), and every time we take a step, new options become visible that we couldn't see from the starting position. Sometimes we need to take a chance and take a step without seeing the next stone; we sense or feel our way forward. It is a purposeful and emergent and evolutionary journey firmly rooted in the present, not an engineered approach rooted in an idealized future that may never come about.

In closing, the Cynefin Framework's ecosystem, methods and tools are powerful when used in ways coherent with the 'spirit of Cynefin' as articulated in the heuristics above. Conversely, when we apply them with mechanical and linear mindsets, they lose their power. I end with one of Dave's favorite Mulla Nasrudin stories that serves as a parable for Cynefin practitioners:

Nasrudin found a weary falcon sitting one day on his window-sill.
He had never seen a bird like this before.
"You poor thing," he said, "how ever were you allowed to get into this state?"
He clipped the falcon's talons and cut its beak straight, and trimmed its feathers.
"Now you look more like a bird," said Nasrudin [4]

References

1. Bill Bryson (2014). "A Short History of Nearly Everything", p.154, Lulu Press, Inc.

2. Cilliers, F. P. 2006. On the importance of a certain slowness. Emergence: Complexity and Understanding 8, pp.106-113.

3. https://medium.com/@sonjablignaut/flowing-through-time-the-need-for-a-certain-slowness-76fa6321bb0b

4. Shah, Idries (1985) The exploits of the Incomparable Mulla Nasrudin & The subtleties of the Inimitable Mulla Nasrudin. London: Octagon Press.

Please note: Quotes by Dave Snowden are snippets taken or paraphrased from the original principles document.

CYNEFIN & ...

ZHEN GOH

ABOUT THE AUTHOR

Zhen Goh is an active proponent of: "knowledge is a martial art." She is currently a Senior Consultant with Cognitive Edge, and enjoys working in the fringes between the commercial and non-profit lines of Cognitive Edge. Her work is transdiscplinary in nature. Zhen believes that responsible business and research has to advance societal improvement. She is a Social Anthropologist by training, and has co-authored a book on Cynefin for the Japanese market. She is currently preoccupied with exploring the intersectionality of ancient Asian philosophy and Western philosophy.

CYNEFIN & ...

ZHEN GOH

"Thirty spokes share the hub of a wheel;
yet it is its center that makes it useful.
You can mold clay into a vessel;
yet, it is its emptiness that makes it useful.
Cut doors and windows from the walls of a house;
but the ultimate use of the house
will depend on that part where nothing exists.
Therefore, something is shaped into what is;
but its usefulness comes from what is not."
- Dao de jing, Lao Tzu (Verse 11) [1]

INTRODUCTION

I close my eyes and inhale deeply. Hold for ten seconds. I breathe out. Hold for ten seconds.

This is a sequence I repeat whenever I start to feel anxious or tense - emotions I experience much too often for my liking these days. It has almost become trite to say that the world is increasingly uncertain and complex. In a 2020 that has been uprooted by the COVID-19 pandemic and more, that reality is now impossible to ignore.

I vacillate in my response to this uncertainty. When I feel particularly tense, I cast around for answers, and certainty. I am aware that these answers will change; they are illusions of control at best. While I can enjoy the creature comforts of being swaddled in known boundaries, I am painfully aware that they do nothing to insulate us from the seismic undercurrents of the change we are experiencing.

How do we move forward with an acute awareness that the ground is shifting as we go? The breathing exercises come in here. As does my well-worn copy of the Dao De Jing (akin to the bible of the Dao), that reminds me of the wisdom of remaining in the question and allowing for emergence.

Dave Snowden and I have long discussed the complementarity between Complexity and Daoism (the Dao, or "the way"). In both, there is a focus on understanding things as they are. There is a need to dance a subtle sidestep - the dance between holding the space open to allow for emergence, whilst responding in a manner coherent to the issues at hand. Both Complexity and Daoism are Naturalistic approaches that seek to explore and uncover the ontology of things, and to work with the system as it is, rather than to impose rigid and unnatural constraints.

Our discussions always take my mind back to the Lao Tzu phrase quoted in the opening of this chapter. Just as complexity has similarities with the Dao, Cynefin acts almost as a manifestation of the Dao. Its value primarily derives from the fact that it is a heuristic-based framework, empty of data. It is not a model and is therefore not bound to any industry or sector. With that agnosticism, Cynefin can morph into countless forms depending on the context in which it is used. Its use is that it is an empty vessel. We need merely have an awareness of the principles that underlie the Framework's domains. With that, we can pour personal context into the vessel that is Cynefin, which then provides form and texture that enable us to "get a grip" on our problems and make decisions. This chapter is named precisely for this polymorphism. As is evidenced in this volume, the use of Cynefin is legion because we can talk about Cynefin in multiple ways, and across infinite contexts:

Cynefin as _____.

Cynefin and _____.

I have long been drawn to the domain of Disorder (now Aporetic/Confused) in Cynefin. To me, that domain resembles the hollow center in the hub of a wheel - the central emptiness, which makes the wheel useful.

Figure 1. The update of the domain of Disorder to A/C makes the "empty center" of the Framework resemble the yin-yang symbol. On the right of Figure 1, we see the "empty center" overlaid to resemble the center of a wheel with spokes, allowing the wheel to spin and do its job.

When Dave made the update from Disorder to Aporetic/Confused (or A/C), it even began to visually resemble a little bit, the yin/yang symbol that people commonly associate with Daoism. The yin/yang symbol is popularly used to symbolize the importance of harmony and coherence of seemingly opposing influences. It serves as a reminder to consider how every action we take has ripple effects and affects other things in non-linear ways. The Dao suggests that the world is inherently entangled, and this interconnectivity means that everything we do will have consequences, often in unknown, and even unknowable ways. All of this should sound familiar to complexity practitioners.

In this chapter, I explore the Dao of Cynefin. I also look at why the inclusion of the Aporetic/Confused domain further emphasizes coherence with the Dao and completes the Framework. The Aporetic refers to an awareness of an irresolvable internal contradiction or logical disjunction. In Cynefin, we encounter this as a domain, but here we explore it as a method with implications on decision-making and Cynefin dynamics. We will also explore the Daoist concept of Wu Wei (Chinese: 無爲; pinyin: wú wéi) or actionless action. Whilst we typically seek to remove ourselves from confusion as soon as possible, the Aporetic encourages us to remain in the question. It facilitates Wu Wei, offering a contemplative space where we can remain suitably undecided and meditate on difficult situations.

Before we delve into the Aporetic, let us explore the complementary nature of Dao and Complexity.

THE DAO OF COMPLEXITY

There is a historical Chinese legend dating back to 2000 BC, depicting two lords who spent their lives attempting to tame the waters of the Yellow River. Archaeological evidence indicates that during this time, floods plagued the Chinese heartland through which the Yellow River runs. Floods prevented economic and social development. [2] At the time, the emperor assigned an official, Gun, to devise a system for controlling the floods. Gun spent a decade constructing an elaborate system of dams along the river. Gun's approach was described as Confucian, emphasizing control, governance and order. However, all the barriers failed as the current of the Yellow River refused to be controlled.

Gun's son, Yu the Great, was assigned to take over the task when he became an adult and adopted a markedly different approach. Instead of dams which seek to control the flow of water by applying a rigid boundary, Yu decided to "follow the water as his master... and followed the way of the water." [3] He worked with agriculture masters, slept, and ate with common folk and sought to understand the context and landscape. Yu worked with them to construct an intricate system of irrigation canals. This system consisted of many dikes that ran parallel to the Yellow River and relieved flood water into agricultural fields. The overflow fed rice paddies and aquaculture. Working with the natural energy of the river's current, he solved a flooding problem and created a surplus!

Yu's approach echoes the naturalism of Daoism. A softer and more organic complex adaptive approach: meeting the system where it was, he followed the energy instead of seeking to control its flow. This system of irrigation can still be found across the world, spanning regions from the Yellow River to the Mekong, to the Nile.

Figure 2. Dujiangyan Irrigation System. An illustration of the aerial view of the irrigation system, and the agricultural fields it feeds into together with pressure relieving river inlets. The oldest and only surviving no-dam irrigation system in the world. The irrigation system drains off floodwater, irrigates farms and provides water to more than 50 cities in the Sichuan province. This irrigation system was built for the Ming Jiang, by Li Bing in 3rd Century BC. Li has been compared to Yu the Great as he is seen to have followed in his approach of following the water. The Daoist style of irrigation canals, and enabling flow has allowed the system to evolve with new challenges, maintaining a similar pattern of flow channels since its initial build in 300 BC.

The contrast between the approaches taken by Gun (control and govern through rigid constraints that prevent flow) and Yu (modulate through permeable boundaries that encourage flow) represent interesting parallels for the Complicated and Clear (Ordered) and Complex domains, respectively.

APORETIC MEDITATIONS

Now, just as Yu's dredging cut canals along the river to enable new flow, so the pen-strokes that cut the Cynefin domain of Disorder into A/C enabled new sense-making.

The development of the A/C domain took place over two years. Two St David's Days marked iterations of Cynefin – first, in 2019, where Dave introduced the liminal domain, [4] then in 2020, when he renamed Disorder – the often overlooked domain in the center of the Framework – "Confused." [5]

Confused, this seemingly empty center of the framework, overlaid with liminal allowed for A/C to emerge. [5]

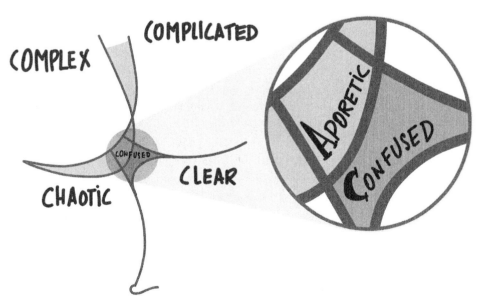

Figure 3. In Dave Snowden's annual St David's Day series in 2019, he introduced the update of Cynefin with liminal (to the left), and in his 2020 iteration, Dave introduced the update with A/C (to the right).

When we look at these two iterations side-by-side, the evolution of the Framework becomes clearer. When we are in any of the four domains of either Clear, Complicated, Complex or Chaotic, there are appropriate actions that can be taken. The Confused domain refers to a state of not knowing where to situate ourselves in the rest of Cynefin. It is, therefore, challenging to make decisions or take appropriate action.

The carving out of A/C introduces nuance to the state of confusion. In Confusion alone we might be unaware that we are confused and choose to proceed with familiar actions and solutions without much thought. We tend to be led by yesterday's "knowns" even though the situation has evolved. This is a dangerous state of ignorant confusion that may cause us to take a not so shallow dive into Chaos.

The Aporetic domain highlights the importance of reflexivity and awareness of one's state of confusion. In the Aporetic domain, we are well aware that we are confused and we know that we need to adopt different ways of learning, perceiving, interpreting, and exploring to work our way out. Aporia was introduced by Aristotle to describe a state of impasse in our thinking. Translating from the Greek root of the word, "'a' not + 'poros', path or passage", aporia means no way through. [6]

"The aporia of our thinking points to a knot in the object; for in so far as our thoughts are in aporia… it is impossible to go forward." [7] Aristotle also emphasized that the undoing of this "knot" can only be done by those who are aware of this impasse. In the Aporetic/Confused domain, we place importance on our awareness of being in a new type of confusion. This awareness is what shifts the Aporetic from domain to method.

The Aporetic turn refers to the method of intentionally creating doubt and paradox, so we may explore the many contrasting truths present in this space. We may be concerned with a lack of, or contradictory information, differing perceptions, ethical dilemmas, resource constraints – and how all these concerns impact each other. There are also unknown unknowns and questions we haven't thought to ask yet. The Aporetic method facilitates discussion across the many interconnected parts of the problem.

ACTIONLESS ACTION: WU WEI (CHINESE: 無爲; PINYIN: WÚ WÉI)

When we first introduced the Aporetic concept and its implication on decision-making, we had some people ask us what this means for decisions in the Ordered domains of Clear and Complicated. In the Clear domain, we state that we can simply know a problem, categorize it, and respond. There is clear programming. In the Complicated domain, while lay people might not have the answers, the right expert would be able to sense and analyze the problem and develop the correct response. Does the Aporetic then have little implication for someone who works generally in the Ordered domains?

Systems often present as Russian Dolls, i.e., there are systems nested within systems. Cynefin helps with making sense of this nestedness. More or less complexity reveals itself as we explore and experience different parts and layers of the system. The Aporetic grazes the Complicated, Complex, and Chaos domains. The Confused grazes Clear. In today's hyper interconnected world, where systems are entangled and layered like meshwork, there is constant grazing against Complexity and even Chaos. This might occur less frequently in Clear systems, but under special circumstances, it might be prudent to pull things into the Aporetic. Crises, or situations where we are experiencing disruption and novelty might be examples of when such a move might be necessary.

A Daoist concept that I have found useful in thinking about the Aporetic is Wu Wei. Loosely translated, it means "actionless action," "action in inaction," or "effortless action." These might sound like oxy-morons, but the ambiguity encourages a state of seeking the most energy flow-coherent approach. It goes back again to the naturalistic approach of "following the way of the water," rather than attempting to control its flow. Wu wei implies conscious inaction so we can allow the most natural, effortless action to emerge. In complex situations, any diagnosis or action is an intervention and small changes can produce significant effects, intended or unintended. The concept of small, safe-to-fail experiments is coherent with wu wei. We direct energy where the system is receptive. We seek parallel approaches rather than direct responses.

To quote the Dao De Jing again, "the Way never acts, yet, nothing is left undone," and "the Way acts, it does not contend." This is the paradox of Wu Wei. We might be engaged in the most frantic tasks, but we must seek to do so at peace. We seek mastery through small, incremental actions. Yu the Great, who calmed the floods, did so by becoming familiar with the common folk, living and working among them. The work was hectic and required exertion, but the solution was one that emphasized effortless action by following the nature of the water. With Wu Wei, we allow the Way (the Dao) to emerge; a quiessence between yin and yang.

"BE WATER, MY FRIEND."

I have developed a penchant for thinking about water - the nature of water, and its management - when considering Complexity and the Dao. I find it apt, and Dave has also used the different states of water to illustrate the difference between domains. In the Complex domain, which is the most energy-efficient, water is liquid and fluid. We have to exert energy to either cool it into a solid-state (Ordered) or heat it into a gaseous state (Chaos). [8, 9]

We have discussed the example of the different approaches that Gun and Yu took to calm the Yellow River floodwaters. Floods continue to be a threat to our living environments. Rapid urbanization, global warming, and rising sea levels compound to make water management more pertinent than it was in 2000 BC. Let's have a look at two contrasting approaches to contemporary water management before I close:

1. Three Gorges Dam, Yangtze River, China

The dam was first envisioned by Sun Yat-sen in 1919, and the ambition transferred from government to government over the years that lapsed till 2003. Constructed over nine years, from 2003 to 2012, the Three Gorges Dam was developed to control flooding and harness the river's current for hydro-electricity. Adopting an approach similar to Gun's of seeking to control water flow, the dam is a modern engineering feat: made of concrete and steel, and costing U.S. $32 billion. The dam has met the initial goal of producing pollution-free electricity. However, the rigid constraint imposed by the dam holds the mass and pressure of a 410-mile long reservoir of moving water. This added pressure has increased the danger of earthquakes and landslides in the region. It has also caused residents in a downstream province to lose access to drinking water. [10] The dam solved a resource problem but created geological and ecosystem challenges. In early July 2020, officials had to open their discharging outlets to ease pressure, contributing to one of three floods that plagued the Yangtze River and surrounding regions.

Just as we observed with Gun, the dams did not work.

2. Sponge Cities, China

All coastal cities are facing sea-level rise. Asian cities are in for a particularly rough ride... populations of coastal cities are bulging: about four out of every five people impacted by sea-level rise by the middle of this century will live in East or South-East Asia." [11] To tackle the issue of rising sea levels, select Chinese cities have started investing in the development of "sponge cities." They have recognized that hard engineering alone is not enough. Strategies have to involve environmental and people-based approaches. The goal is to distribute absorption capacity across targeted areas. They are covering roofs with plants, and cultivating wetlands along coasts. Reconstruction of pavements with permeable materials is underway. This will allow the storage of excess water, and allow for evaporation, which will moderate temperatures. It means 70% to 80% of the wastewater will also be reusable.

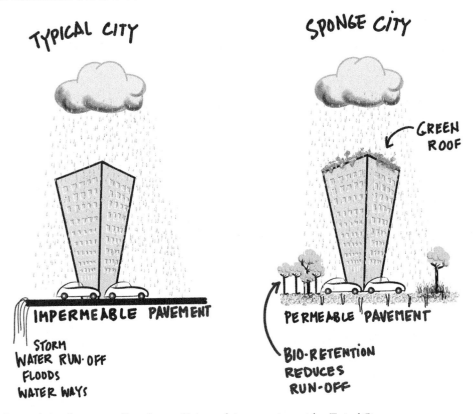

Figure 4. An illustration of how Sponge Cities work in comparison with a Typical City.

This approach is much more complex-adaptive and Daoist. It is holistic and will require on-going sustained efforts. However, sustainability, by its very nature and as suggested in its name, requires sustained and sustainable approaches.

CONCLUSION

When brainstorming this chapter with my friend and fellow author in this series, Sonja Blignaut, I discussed my desire to write something on Daoism. Seemingly disjointed ideas at the time, I explained how this links with Cynefin, energy flow, and water management. She joked that I would become the Bruce Lee of Cynefin.

"Be water, my friend," Lee was famous for saying. Celebrating the "wateristic" and flow-minded philosophy of Daoism that permeated his approach to life, and influenced his unique style of martial art. "You put water into a bottle, and it becomes the bottle. Water can flow, or it can crash."

Now, to add a Cynefin lens to this, I would reiterate the importance of how Cynefin acts as a useful vessel into which we can pour the fluidity of our contexts:

Cynefin as _____.

Cynefin and _____.

We can use it to understand how to make decisions and take action. However, when you are not sure of the way forward, make quick friends with not-knowing. Utilize the Aporetic method, rather than be incapacitated. We will be served by becoming comfortable with not knowing, and adopting an Aporetic mode as we co-exist with higher levels of uncertainty. It will improve our fluency with paradox and dialectics. As you operationalize and take action through each of the Cynefin domains recognize when and how to practice Wu Wei so you allow the Way forward to emerge.

References

1. Over the course of this article, I make reference to the Dao De Jing by Lao Tzu. Behind the Bible, the Dao De Jing is the second-most translated book in the world. Each translation is slightly different, and will present unique nuances. In this article, I quote the Dao as it was taught to me: in phrases, each contextualized and bound by specific lessons of the moment. The translation from Chinese to English means we lose and gain meaning in the process. For those seeking a more comprehensive reference, I recommend Jonathan Star's translation: Star, J. Tao Te Jing: The Definitive Edition. Tarcher Cornerstone Edition; 2008.

2. Lewis M.E., The Flood Myths of Early China. State University of New York Press, 2012.

3. Allen B. Vanishing into Things: Knowledge in Chinese Tradition. Harvard University Press, 2015.

4. Snowden D. Cognitive Edge. Cynefin St David's Day 2019 (2 of 5). Published April 16, 2019. Accessed July 5, 2020. https://www.cognitive-edge.com/blog/cynefin-st-davids-day-2019-2-of-5/

5. Snowden D. Cynefin St David's Day 2020 (1 of 5). Published March 1, 2020. Accessed July 5, 2020. https://cognitive-edge.com/blog/cynefin-st-davids-day-2020-1-of-n/

6. Bunnin N, Yu J. The Blackwell Dictionary of Western Philosophy. In: Aporia. Blackwell Publishing, 2004:39.

7. Arthur Madigan S. Aristotle Metaphysics : Books B and K 1-2. Oxford University Press; 1999: Chapter 2.

8. The phase changes between domains require threshold states and is indicative of the liminal zones between phase changes. "Think here of latent heat; if I heat water to 100ºC it doesn't immediately become steam. I have to continue to apply heat before this happens. When water becomes ice, it drops to 0ºC. But then more heat has to be thrown out before the transition happens." From Snowden D. Cognitive Edge. Cynefin St David's Day 2019 (3 of 5). Published April 17, 2019. Accessed July 6, 2020. https://cognitive-edge.com/blog/cynefin-st-davids-day-2019-3-of-5/

9. Just as this constraint applies to natural systems, so does it apply to human systems. Thresholds in human systems could, for example, take the form of ritual transitions between one's work, home, and party personas.

10. Wines M. China Admits Problems with Three Gorges Dam. The New York Times. https://www.nytimes.com/2011/05/20/world/asia/20gorges.html. Published May 19, 2011. Accessed July 6, 2020.

11. Muggah R. How China's sponge cities are preparing for sea-level rise. World Economic Forum. https://www.weforum.org/agenda/2019/06/how-china-s-sponge-cities-are-preparing-for-sea-level-rise. Published June 28, 2019. Accessed July 6, 2020.

HOW THE CYNEFIN FRAMEWORK CHANGED MY TAKE ON RESEARCH

MILICA BEGOVIC

ABOUT THE AUTHOR

Milica Begovic works as a part-time senior manager at UNDP (United Nations Development Programme) Montenegro. In charge of the Economy and Environment program, she oversees programs focused on low emissions economy and increasing resilience of communities and ecosystems. Milica is engaged part-time as a knowledge and innovation specialist at UNDP Regional Center for Europe and CIS, where she is experimenting with using alternative methods for policy making, project management and research, including the use of big data and challenges in development, and application of complexity theory to development.

ABOUT THIS CHAPTER

 Vignette   Narrative

 Chronology: Piece 16 of 33

HOW THE CYNEFIN FRAMEWORK CHANGED MY TAKE ON RESEARCH

MILICA BEGOVIC

During my first corporate assignment on innovation, my boss asked me the question, "If you could talk to one person on how to resolve complex issues, who would that be?" My immediate response was, "Dave Snowden." The Cynefin Framework continually came up during my PhD studies. To my surprise my boss said matter of factly, "Well, OK then, speak to him and see whether there are opportunities to bring his work into our organization."

My first conversation with Dave kicked off a decade-long learning process that would change how I do research and cultivated an ongoing friendship. Working with the Cynefin Framework, and its survey methodology SenseMaker, helped me to 'see' non-obvious linkages and early signals of change that no mainstream method had done up to that point (Translation: You don't get answers to the questions you don't ask). [1] It helped turn me into a more curious researcher, obsessing far more about system dynamics and ways of resolving uncertainty than prematurely converging on solutions. It also made me more humble, appreciating far more the importance of agency when faced with wicked policy problems and a need to generate more (as opposed to less) policy options when dealing with complex issues.

The latter was evident in a case I was involved in several years ago when a partner asked, "What do I do when someone tells me that on a scale from 1-5, they are at 3 when it comes to the likelihood of investing in solar panels?" My colleagues were struggling to understand how best to improve the uptake of solar panels in their communities. Using a traditional linear Likert scale survey gave them some idea about the attitudes people had. Still, it remained a mystery as to what would lead to more actual investments in solar panels.

With the SenseMaker survey methodology's help, we could formulate nonlinear questions and invite more context-rich stories. The results allowed us to identify patterns from respondents' stories, which led to a discovery that people consider investing in solar panels for their homes after seeing their neighbors install the panels. Such is the nature of humans. Complex, adaptive, and relational, people react to each other. Our hypothesis about discretionary income levels turned out to be of secondary importance.

Many more mainstream monitoring and assessment tools had an over-reliance on surveys with linear causality built into the same design. Yet, in the messy field of citizens and community behaviors, we know that causality is hard to attribute. And while we also utilized focus groups to get deeper under the numbers, they were difficult to scale across large groups of citizens. The SenseMaker survey allowed us to capture close to real-time insights from communities; it addressed crucial blind spots.

We are now in a position to harness the value of disintermediated data more practically. The fragmented narratives from the field provide us with a degree of granularity that becomes actionable for us. Here, I use the royal "we" to include the community beneficiaries, development workers, and stakeholders. The method created the space for socialized sense-making and the process of inquiry, discovery, and design that ultimately shifts the power and agency to the citizen.

From that initial phone call ten years ago with Dave Snowden, I have walked many paths with this method. Viewing the world through the Cynefin Framework has made me much more sensitive to carefully choosing my arsenal of tools to address the problem space I find myself in. And I am no longer hesitant to address these complex problems that we find increasingly around us in the world. In SenseMaker, I have found a survey approach that makes complex problems accessible as an exciting opportunity to accommodate uncertainty, 'see' the system's dynamics, and discover multiple options for engaging with it.

It is said that in complex systems, unintended consequences are inevitable. For me, that initial phone call was an experiment that created serendipitous results. If anything, it has made me more confident as a researcher. That initial phone call translated into a friendship and life mentorship that is invaluable to me.

Happy birthday Cynefin - many many returns!

How the Cynefin Framework Changed my Take on Research

References

1. SenseMaker® is the world's first crowdsourcing method for human judgment, meaning, and feeling. Everyone's voice deserves to have an impact and SenseMaker® offers a science-based approach to guide collective impact and leverage the strengths of being human in uncertain times.

What to read next

 Next Vignette: Knowledge Management and Cynefin, Elmi Bester, p.94

 Next Chronological: Knowledge Management and Cynefin, Elmi Bester, p.94

 Next Narrative: Knowledge Management and Cynefin, Elmi Bester, p.94

KNOWLEDGE MANAGEMENT AND CYNEFIN

ELMI BESTER

ABOUT THE AUTHOR

Elmi Bester is passionate about new ways of conducting business, new forms of organization and new ways of working, relating & learning. Elmi was the founding Convenor of the Southern African Knowledge Management Summit. She is currently with Cognitive Edge and focuses on the growing network of Cynefin practitioners.

ABOUT THIS CHAPTER

 Vignette Narrative

 Chronology: Piece 17 of 33

KNOWLEDGE MANAGEMENT AND CYNEFIN

ELMI BESTER

As a knowledge management practitioner, I was privileged to be part of the beneficiaries of Cynefin-thinking in its first decade. Dave's now-familiar curmudgeonly objection to the engineering-based and Newtonian approaches that prevailed in knowledge management, was a steady voice at knowledge management conferences and gatherings.

I cherished his message - not to dismiss or celebrate one approach over another - but to approach knowledge management in a manner true to the context. Dave did not suggest that we should now abandon all best-practice programs and only do Organic Knowledge Management. [1] This was quite different from some other management movements that were in fashion championing one approach over others. Why would he? The very nature of Cynefin encourages us to leave either/or thinking and understand that different approaches work in different contexts, and why. The Cynefin-speak for this is 'bounded applicability.'

As Cynefin turns 21 years old, I reflect on the field of knowledge management and invite my fellow practitioners to reconsider our profession through the lens of Cynefin once more. How do we move beyond our demarcated knowledge management practice understanding that the perceived messiness in complexity and chaos is counter-intuitive for many of us? Especially when your training leads you to create functional order in knowledge and information systems, as Don Norman so aptly puts it: "[finding] a place for everything, and everything in its place." [2] How can practitioners develop comfort outside the realm of ordered systems and the domains of best practice and expert communities? What makes for knowledge management in complexity and uncertainty?

KNOWLEDGE MANAGEMENT AND CYNEFIN

Not so long ago, I settled in at a coffee shop hoping to make sense of the fresh flow of appeals for organizational learning and more specifically for Communities of Practice. This time the proponents were practitioners in Learning & Development (L&D) and Agile. I soon realized that I needed to draw the Cynefin Framework to get perspective. The L&D practitioners rightly proposed that the focus on training is no longer commensurate with a world that is continuously changing at rapid speed. The process of compiling practices in training courses is too slow.

With the Cynefin Framework, it is possible to begin mapping the shift away from a training focus on best practices in the Clear domain to Communities of Practice in the Complicated domain. The role of the Community of Practice then becomes the peer-to-peer sharing of good practices. This is still all in the ordered domain.

Expanding out further, when we want to foster innovation, adaptability, and the cultivation of emergent practices, the Cynefin Framework helps us see that we need to consider practices that are different from those we use in the ordered domains. In Cynefin's Complex domain, we need social processes of learning and knowing. Here, new competencies and insights emerge through experimentation and action. The questions then are: "How do we provide the necessary conditions for informal networks and communities to form and come to fruition? How do we monitor so that we can discover which practices stabilize? How do we decide when and how we formalize the networks and communities that have emerged?" This is one example of how the Cynefin Framework helps us with critical inquiry into this new landscape of possibilities.

For knowledge management practitioners, the Cynefin Framework helps us to formulate rich and incisive questions to reflect on our professions' future and relevance. When a new management package surfaces, for example Digital Business or Social Business, the Framework helps us discover why and where adopting and adapting existing practices makes sense, and where we need new practices. It also provides a common language so that different disciplines can have collaborative conversations and align perspectives, instead of wasting energy on turf wars for positioning on the organizational chart or the executive agenda.

One of the presumptions in knowledge management is that it should be embedded in organizations and just be the way we work, and that we can add to it by strategizing when and where necessary. With Cynefin, strategy emerges from an understanding of context. Respecting context, various knowledge management flavors can be discussed, and employed, in a shared language in tandem with IT, HR, Organizational Development, Strategy, and Innovation. Cynefin also opens up possibilities, and our abilities, to diversify our responses to key issues, such as the retention of critical knowledge or mobilizing knowledge in times of need. As Ludwig Wittgenstein puts it "the limits of my language are the limits of my world." [3]

Throughout the reflections in this book, knowledge management practitioners will notice many elements of knowledge management weaved into interventions for innovation, safety, health and leadership, just to name a few. I wholeheartedly recommend we join and embrace this new arena of possibilities so that we can contribute to our unfolding knowledge-driven organizations, economy, and knowledge society. And I encourage you to invite your fellow executives to sense and see the world through this magical framework.

References

1. Organic Knowledge Management is about utilizing narrative-based methods for knowledge elicitation, just-in-time transfer of knowledge into policies, procedures and best practices, informal communities and working with the natural flow of knowledge creation, disruption and utilization. Snowden, D. (2002), "Complex acts of knowing: paradox and descriptive self-awareness," Journal of Knowledge Management, Vol. 6 No. 2, pp. 100-111. https://doi.org/10.1108/13673270210424639.

2. Norman, Don. Things that make us smart: Defending human attributes in the age of the machine. Diversion Books, 2014.

3. Newman, Victor. The Knowledge Activist's Handbook: Adventures from the Knowledge Trenches. Capstone, 2003. p.59.

What to read next

 Next Vignette: A Short History of a Long Process..., Mary E. Boone, p.108

 Next Chronological: Cynefin and Strategy, Steve McCrone and Ian Snape, p.257

 Next Narrative: The story of Cynefin 'coming home' to Welsh Public Services..., Chris Bolton, p.98

THE STORY OF CYNEFIN 'COMING HOME' TO WELSH PUBLIC SERVICES: EXCITING AND TERRIFYING IN EQUAL MEASURE

CHRIS BOLTON

ABOUT THE AUTHOR

Chris Bolton has lead the Good Practice Team at Audit Wales for over ten years. This involves working with a wide range of people and Public Sector organizations to identify and share good practice to support improvement. Outside of work, Chris is a Board Member of two cooperative organizations that provide social care and social housing. These roles link his interests in delivering effective governance and audit that is innovative and socially sustainable. In 2018 Chris was awarded a Winston Churchill Memorial Trust Travelling Fellowship. Through his Fellowship he spent time in the Basque Country (NE Spain) and the North East of the USA studying the governance of cooperatives. Chris reflects on these, and other experiences, on his personal blog: www.whatsthepont.blog. Chris has a science background and before joining Audit he worked for many years in environmental improvement and regulation.

ABOUT THIS CHAPTER

 Full Chapter   Narrative

 Chronology: Piece 8 of 33   Cynefin Principles

THE STORY OF CYNEFIN 'COMING HOME' TO WELSH PUBLIC SERVICES: EXCITING AND TERRIFYING IN EQUAL MEASURE

CHRIS BOLTON

This chapter describes how the Cynefin Framework was gradually woven into the fabric of the Welsh Government's Public Services. While initial lectures from Dave stimulated early support and enthusiasm, they also terrified government employees wed to the 'one size fits all' approach. I'll take you on the 12 year journey that brought the Cynefin Framework, and understanding complexity, back home to Wales.

BANGOR UNIVERSITY, PRITCHARD JONES HALL, JUNE 2008

If you stand outside the Main Arts College at Bangor University, affectionately known as 'Hogwarts,' you can see Yr Wyddfa, Mount Snowdon. On a damp Thursday morning in June 2008, 250 of the 'future leaders' of Welsh Public Services gathered inside the Pritchard Jones Hall waiting for the other Snowden. Dave was headed our way to deliver a keynote on narrative, complex systems, and the Cynefin Framework.

What happened that day is part of the history of how the Cynefin Framework established itself in Welsh Public Services. From a novel, and for some, challenging concept, the Framework has since disrupted established thinking and become part of the language, landscape, and future of Wales and our public services. It's a journey I've been privileged to observe.

The mid-2000s were interesting times in the development of Public Service in Wales. Devolution and the transfer of powers from the UK Government were still relatively new and we were finding our feet. Public

Services Management Wales, who organized this 2008 Summer School that brought us together, aimed to disrupt our thinking to create a 'Public Services for the future.' Dave and Cynefin were part of the plan.

I'd been introduced to Dave a few years earlier by a Welsh Government friend, Mary Hughes. Thus I had a rough idea of what was coming. I remember positioning myself in the Hall so that I could see Dave's keynote, and at the same time, observe how it was landing with the audience. Dave did not disappoint.

TERROR AND EXCITEMENT IN EQUAL MEASURE

Dave used some great favorites in that keynote that always got people excited and interested in what he had to say. Things like the 'Gorilla playing basketball eye test' and the 'How to organize a party for teenagers' story. They went down like a storm. You knew, because people were frantically taking notes. In the post Summer School enthusiasm, Dave 're-presented' these at seminars and workshops held by Welsh Public Service Organisations for the next half a dozen years. All of a sudden it seemed like almost everyone in Wales had seen the Gorilla and basketball video; the excited contingent shared generously, including me.

However there was another contingent who were terrified. Dave's ideas didn't fit with much of the 'standard operating model' that existed at the time. Hierarchical structures were strongly valued and ideas like 'distributed leadership' were highly threatening. Senior officials' policies were based on cause and effect, linear relationships, and 'one size fits all.' We commonly heard "Develop best practices and spread them across Wales." No one questioned the idea that a policy developed in a Cardiff Headquarters building could be delivered with the same efficiency in a rural community in Welsh-speaking Snowdonia, and the post-industrial Valleys Towns like Pontypridd.

2008 was also the peak of Lean and Six Sigma. These popular approaches fit neatly with the 'one size fits all' ideology. Standardize, set targets, measure and quantify everything as part of a 'Deliverology' dogma was the norm. People had invested themselves in developing their careers in these areas, so it was no surprise that they were terrified by what Dave had to say. When they saw the Cynefin Framework, they saw only Complexity and Chaos. Management in Public Services was all about making things 'simple,' not making them more complex. Cognitive dissonance was ringing in people's heads.

When Dave said something akin to, "Management practices that have passed their sell-by date in the Private Sector get re-sold to the Public Sector by Consultants to maximize their value extraction. Usually this is about ten years after being introduced into the Private Sector," you could see half the audience nodding in agreement and the Six Sigma Green Belts shifting uncomfortably in their seats.

ONCE YOU HAVE SEEN IT, YOU CAN'T GO BACK

"I've seen it. I can't now unsee it." That summarizes the conversation among people who were excited by Cynefin. Many of these conversations were in the Belle Vue Hotel or The Greek Taverna in Bangor, so there was no guarantee they would survive until the next day of Summer School. But there were enough people in the 'excited' camp to make sure something happened.

This kind of activism by a band of the 'excited' may be how Cynefin spreads in small countries. Dave's interpretation of a small country, as far as I can work out, is any group of less than 5 million loosely connected people in a defined geographical area. Nova Scotia, New Zealand, Singapore (in 2008), the Nordic Countries, individual Australian States, and Wales are all on the Small Countries list.

Over the next few years, Dave's ideas, from the 'Gorilla Eye Test' to specific courses to teach the principles of Complex Adaptive Systems, the Cynefin Framework, and SenseMaker, surfaced in many spots within Welsh Public Services. For anyone unfamiliar with SenseMaker, it is the software developed by Cognitive Edge that allows you to collect and make sense of narratives, stories, and the fragmented pieces of information that reflect the reality of life. It's an essential tool for working with Cynefin, particularly in the Complex domain.

Within the Welsh National Health Service, enthusiasm from people like Matt Wyatt and Sion Charles led to several cohorts of people being trained and a raft of SenseMaker projects. In one 'crossover moment,' a representative from the Australian State of Victoria, John Wyn Owen of the Welsh Learned Society, came to speak at a major health conference in Wales about their use of SenseMaker in health promotion. It felt gloriously like the Small Countries around the world were connecting through Cynefin.

SAFE-TO-FAIL PROBES SLOWLY BECOMES AN OPTION

Dave often references the Apollo 13 film when he talks about innovation. The third Apollo mission to the moon failed due to technical problems and the Earth-based and Apollo-based crews had limited equipment to fix the situation. But Dave's reference to the film is also known for the famous quote 'failure is not an option.' So famous did it become that NASA even put it on T-Shirts and souvenir mugs. From my perspective, it matches my experiences of running multiple SenseMaker exercises in Welsh Public Services between 2009 and 2016.

One of my key challengers and learning experiences during this time was getting so far and then having the project stall. I would talk with a Snowden enthusiast (the man not the mountain) who had seen Dave speak and wanted to do more. Then there'd be a session with a group of middle/senior managers in the organization and the commitment to use SenseMaker. We'd develop a set of SenseMaker signifiers and suitable prompt questions to look at organizational culture, staff engagement, or how to use staff ideas for improvement.

The final SenseMaker survey would go to senior management for sign off and then – get shelved. I'd be at a loss to understand why? With a bit of digging and the passage of time, it became clear to me that senior leadership wasn't prepared to deal with what SenseMaker might tell them. Using SenseMaker, they were going to open the door to answers they would struggle to deal with. SenseMaker reveals stories that describe what is happening in an organization. It is an insight into our 'water cooler conversations.' Not really wanting to know would stall the project.

I remember a brief but peak conversation with Dave about things not working out. We were at a Cardiff Blues game, and I was agonizing about my failures. Dave said calmly and in a matter of fact way, "But things will fail. You are probing in a complex space. Not everything will work." And that was the end of that particular conversation. The recognition that some things will fail trying them out in a complex space seems obvious now. However at the time, working for the Wales Audit Office in Public Service Improvement, my world of Audit could not imagine failure as an option. We were only just entering a time when 'safe-to-fail probes' were a possibility. Slowly however 'safe to fail probes' became translated into 'audit speak,' and the Auditor-General for Wales started declaring, "I encourage Public Bodies to take well-managed risks." Small but significant changes for sure.

LAMPETER UNIVERSITY CYNEFIN, SUMMER SCHOOL 2016

Eight years after the Bangor Summer School, Dave was back on stage delivering another keynote to 250 Welsh Public Services leaders. The organizers had changed their name, Academi replaced Public Service Management Wales, and the venue had moved to Lampeter University. Lampeter is the fourth oldest University in the UK (after Oxbridge and Durham). It was also home of the famous Welsh writer Dylan Thomas. It was also warm and sunny.

The 2016 Public Service Leaders were different from the 2008 Bangor cohort. They had a greater awareness of complexity and the Cynefin Framework. Many had heard Dave speak, seen his videos, or read relevant materials. In the reception area I could overhear comments as people were filing in, "This is thought-provoking stuff, you'll enjoy it…". For the keynote, there was no more 'Gorilla Basketball Eye Test,' it was straight into an in-depth explanation of what it means to deliver public services in complex times.

But just like Bangor in 2008, some people were terrified. I remember the Myers-Briggs Type Indicator (MBTI) being lined up for a bit of rigorous scientific evaluation by Dave (he savaged it). Many people agreed vigorously, and a few might have even cheered. We had entered the world of social media in Welsh Public Services, and people were sharing their positive responses on Twitter. However, upon leaving that day, I did encounter several MBTI practitioners from an Organizational Development Team who were stunned; some of their deeply held views on how the world works had been blown apart.

Dave says one of his favorite events to speak at is Summer School. A Welsh audience understands exactly his cultural references – such as Cynefin, in the sense of the Welsh meaning of the word – the habitat where you come from. On this note, Dave's keynote video is worth watching if only as an example of how completely at home he is with the people and surroundings.

THE CYNEFIN CENTRE, BANGOR UNIVERSITY

The other major event of 2016 was Dave taking a Professorship at Bangor University to establish the Cynefin Centre. The Centre was part of the Psychology Department with links to the Wales Centre for Behaviour Change, the Department of Computing, and the Design and Innovation Department based at the new Pontio Arts Centre. A combination of interests that may only make sense to Dave and his deep love of diversity.

The awareness of Cynefin across Welsh Public Services had grown broadly. Senior leaders were actually talking about complexity. In particular, they spoke of the need to understand narrative – what people say at work or the 'chatter in the Post Office' or the stories people share in their communities. That had certainly been absent in 2008. Gathering narratives and making sense of them was seen as a key part of making sense of complex situations. In 2016 I was happily seconded from the Audit Office to work with Dave on managing change in complex environments. Two things stick in my mind from this period at Bangor. The engagement around SenseMaker and the famous 'Incident on Tryfan.'

Through my work with the Wales Centre for Behaviour Change, I met people from public services who felt the established change programs weren't working. Simultaneously Dave's concepts were gaining traction like gathering narratives. People were beginning to see the usefulness of understanding where people are, and then looking for a disposition for change. This enables developing appropriate behavioral 'nudges' to move things in the right direction. Story gathering was rising as an attractive alternative to the 'information deficit' as were communication/marketing-led programs common to behavioral changes.

Also that year sitting in the Pontio Arts Centre with a recently retired Unitary Authority Chief Executive, Directors of Public Sector Bodies, and University Professors to design a SenseMaker survey, I felt like the

Cynefin Framework and SenseMaker were now becoming mainstream. In addition, the development of the Valleys Project in South Wales, with the team of Beth Smith, Emma Jones, Jules Yim, and Ellie Snowdon, was a major project with the Welsh Government to engage with communities across the South Wales coalfield.

THE INCIDENT ON TRYFAN

As part of the secondment, we ran a "Behaviour Change Festival" at Bangor University. It was two weeks long and covered much, from small local projects to international research. The culmination was to be Dave delivering a keynote to close the event and send everyone away full of enthusiasm. This would cover Cynefin, the use of narrative in complex environments, disposition for change, and the use of behavioral nudges – all under the heading of 'Nudge not Yank.'

By this time I'd worked with Dave long enough not to get anxious if he wasn't visible just before his speaking slot. We'd once run a session with Public Service Chief Executives at the Audit Office when Dave's plane had landed late at Heathrow (7:30 a.m.), and he was due to speak in Cardiff at 10 a.m. It's at least a 2-hour 30 minute drive from Heathrow to Cardiff at that time in the morning. In walked Dave at five past 10 looking completely unflustered. What was even more impressive was that Dave had found the time to talk to the office receptionist on the way.

However, on the occasion of the Bangor University Behaviour Change Festival's finale, all was not well. Fifteen minutes before Dave's keynote, a text alerted me to the fact that he had slipped on Tryfan – a mountain in Wales – and cut his head quite badly. There was even a gruesome picture to prove it. When he should have been closing the festival, he was being x-rayed and sewn up at Ysbyty Gwynedd Hospital. We ended up showing a video of one of Dave's keynotes with me improvising alongside, but it's just not the same, is it?

NEVER WASTE A CRISIS

At the beginning of 2020, the Coronavirus crisis led us to use Cynefin and SenseMaker in Wales in ways that we hadn't previously. At Audit Wales, we stopped audit work, and using SenseMaker, focussed a large number of our staff to look for new and innovative practices across Public Services.

Dave's quote, "During a crisis you should be deploying Innovation Teams alongside the Business Recovery Teams, to capture the novel practice," fired people's imagination during this time. It's a quote I've heard from Dave on many occasions and, more recently, on a webinar with Robert Koch, the Head of Enterprise Resilience for Eskom, South Africa's electric public utility. The quote captured Welsh Public Services' imagination, and you could see people using variations of it in many places, quite often linked to their recovery planning processes.

Beyond Wales, I was asked to speak to academics at Northumbria about a webinar I'd done with Toby Law on our approach to Complexity, Learning, and Coronavirus. I mentioned this to Dave, and he signed up for the webinar to listen. This created great excitement and delight among the Northumbria University people. I was a bit more anxious, and my response was, "Great, it's like having your dad come to watch you play rugby." I told Dave, I think he laughed.

FUTURE GENERATIONS OF PUBLIC SERVICE AND WHAT COMES NEXT FOR CYNEFIN

Going back to something Dave said about small countries being capable of incredible things, Wales is the first country to have a legal requirement on public services to act sustainably and consider the impact of future generations' decisions. That was created through the 2015 Wellbeing of Future Generations Act.

In many ways, the Cynefin Framework and the Wellbeing of Future Generations Act are perfect partners. The Act requires that public bodies behave in certain ways. The Five Ways of Working are:

1. Collaboration
2. Long Term Thinking
3. Integration
4. Citizen Involvement
5. Prevention of all statutory requirements of the Act

The Act's architect, former Welsh Government Minister Jane Davidson, has been a faculty member at a Cynefin retreat so it's no surprise to find the Act and the Framework aligned. The Act's requirements, and the changes brought about by the Coronavirus pandemic, have in odd ways cemented the position of the Cynefin Framework. From a world of 'one size fits all' and 'failure is not an option,' we now talk of 'safe-to-fail probes' and small actions that reflect the local context. Things that come from communities themselves stand a far better chance of being sustainable for future generations.

The Cynefin Framework has been influencing the public service narrative in Wales since before 2008 and I am sure will continue to do so well beyond 2020. In a journey that has been exciting, unpredictable, and sometimes terrifying, Cynefin has come home to Wales and Welsh Public Services and I couldn't be happier. Happy 21st anniversary Dave!

What to read next

 Next Full Chapter: Cynefin and Delivery, Greg Brougham, p.113

 Next Chronological: Welcome to the Cynefinogi (The People of Cynefin), Iwan Jenkins, p.203

 Next Narrative: A Short History of a Long Process..., Mary E. Boone, p.108

 More on Cynefin Principle 1.3: Cynefin and Delivery, Greg Brougham, p.113

A SHORT HISTORY OF A LONG PROCESS: THE STORY OF "A LEADER'S FRAMEWORK FOR DECISION MAKING"

MARY E. BOONE

ABOUT THE AUTHOR

Mary E. Boone, president of Boone Associates located in Essex, CT, designs strategic, complexity-based approaches to communication, leadership and large-scale face-to-face, virtual and hybrid meetings. Boone and Dave Snowden received an Academy of Management award and an Emerald Citation of Excellence Award for their *Harvard Business Review* cover article "A Leader's Framework for Decision Making." Boone's books include *Managing Inter@ctively* (McGraw-Hill) and *The Information Edge* (co-authored with N. Dean Meyer, Dow Jones) and *Leadership and the Computer* (Prima Publishing), which was "required reading" for the U.S. Congress in 1994.

ABOUT THIS CHAPTER

 Vignette    Narrative

 Chronology: Piece 2 of 33

A SHORT HISTORY OF A LONG PROCESS: THE STORY OF "A LEADER'S FRAMEWORK FOR DECISION MAKING"[1]

MARY E. BOONE

I met Dave Snowden in 2000. It was the early stage of his development of the Cynefin Framework. At the time, I was working on my book entitled *Managing Interactively,* and I had successfully secured funding for the research from IBM, where Dave was working at the time. Mike Zisman, then VP of Strategy for IBM, was my sponsor for the research. He connected me to Tony DiMarco, then Lotus Director of Marketing Communications, who suggested I interview Dave for my book.

Our relationship started with that interview, on a Skype call scheduled for one hour. It ended up lasting two. At its conclusion, we vowed to stay in touch. The results of that interview are in the book that came out in 2001.

In 2002, I received a call from Tom Stewart, who had recently taken over as Editor of the Harvard Business Review (HBR). He said that Dave was on his shortlist for inclusion in an HBR issue. He believed that, for his readership, my pragmatic approach to writing about leadership would be the perfect match for Dave's more esoteric, academic approach. "I remember the first time I saw Dave speak," Stewart recently told me in a conversation. "It was at a conference in London. His slides weren't working, so he just started talking. I didn't understand a word, but I did get the basic concept of Cynefin – and was wowed by it. I constantly challenged him to be more understandable and less Snowdenesque." [2]

The three of us agreed that it was a good idea to combine forces for this article. We all figured it would take about a year to pull the article together, including the conscientious HBR editing process. (Remember, I had just written a 300-page book in about a year and a half. How long could it possibly take to write a 5,000-word article? You'll see.)

Shortly after, Dave came to the States and we had our first in-person meeting to start writing. We brainstormed furiously and then began exchanging a series of drafts. Our differences in that initial writing process became quickly apparent. Dave kept saying, "But we have to include this..." and "We can't oversimplify this..." and I kept saying, "We have a word count limit" and "No one will understand this unless..." It was also the inception of our perennial discussion about examples. Dave is wary of them, and I love them. Understandably, he doesn't want people to resort to "best practices" and copy others. Still, I push to make sure the theory is understandable – and in my opinion, that's a real challenge without clear examples. I also want to note here that it was during this initial in-person meeting that I first suggested changing the name of the "simple" domain to "clear." (That didn't end up happening for 20 years. I'm patient.)

I'll draw a curtain of charity over the comments we received about that first draft.

The upshot was that Tom assigned us one of the best primary editors on the HBR staff, Bronwyn Fryer. That was a game-changer for us. When I spoke with her recently about this vignette, she said her memory was a bit hazy but that one thing was crystal clear: "It was a f*ing bronco of an article. We struggled with the angle, the leadership question and we had to simplify it to bring a useful perspective to HBR readers. The concepts were so abstract we were going in circles. But finally, we got the right approach: Focus on how the Framework helps decision-making. What made it come to life were structure and story and picking out the examples was essential." (No comment on that last statement.) [3]

Each time we thought we were getting close to completion, there was more to do. We had to redo the framework graphic (with the help of my friend Deb Johnson). We had to add the table of potential leadership interventions (which turned out to be very useful but taxing). It was a monumental and seemingly endless editing process.

In 2007, we met our HBR manuscript editor, Lilith Fondulas, a woman I nicknamed "The Surgeon." She was phenomenal. I will never forget the final edit pass. I called Dave as soon as I received the edits,

"Do you want the bad news or the good news first?" I asked. Being Dave he said, "The bad." I said, "She cut out over 1,000 words." He groaned on the other side of the Atlantic, "And the good news?" he asked. "You can't tell," I laughed. He called me back later and said, "You're right!" It was indeed a remarkable job. I recently spoke with Fondulas, and with a precision that perfectly matches her work, within 24 hours she told me exactly how many words she had cut out of our article 13 years ago. "The original version I received for editing stood at 6,167 words, and the final version I sent into production was 5,042." [4]

The article came out in November of 2007, five years after that initial call with Tom Stewart. Recently Tom told me, "Some articles take off like a rocket and some never take off. This one had an accelerating pattern that started slowly and gathered steam. It was quiet. The immediate impact was soft, but I could feel it building over time." In 2008, it won an award from the Academy of Management as the Outstanding Practitioner-Oriented Publication in OB. Then, in 2011, it won an Emerald Citation, based on the number of citations it had received over the previous four years. In 2017, HBR republished it in a compilation of leadership articles. The article continues to be widely cited.

Stewart continued, "[This article] was important. It's abstract. There isn't immediate understanding the first time you read it but it's one of those remarkable pieces about how to think that changes how people think." Stewart includes himself in the group of people who have been influenced: "I use the Framework all the time in my everyday life. It's so practical." [5]

I, too, use the Framework all the time in my everyday life. It has shaped all my subsequent work and serves as a lens on my personal life. I'm happy to report that my health is good. I'm out of the Chaotic and into the Complex on that account. And the aforementioned "baby" is now a teenager, so I spend a lot of time viewing my interactions with him on the "unordered" side of the framework.

As I write this, we are all facing tremendous uncertainty related to environmental, social, financial, and health-related concerns. I hope that many people worldwide will continue to benefit from this simple framework that provides insight into how we can manage complexity both now and as we enter an increasingly unpredictable future.

References

1.   Snowden, David J. and Boone, Mary E., A Leader's Framework for Decision-making, Harvard Business Review, November 2007, 85(11), pp.68-76.

2.   Stewart, Thomas. Personal interview. 6 July, 2020.

3.   Fryer, Bronwyn. Personal interview. 7 July, 2020.

4.   Fondulas, Lilith. Personal interview. 8 July, 2020.

5.   Stewart, op. cit.

What to read next

 Next Vignette: With Cynefin we found our own ecology, Anne Caspari and Johann Entz-von Zerssen, p.124

 Next Chronological: Cultivating Leadership with Cynefin..., Jennifer Garvey-Berger..., p.139

 Next Narrative: Embodied Cynefin: Teaching with the body, Chris Corrigan, p.128

CYNEFIN AND DELIVERY

GREG BROUGHAM

ABOUT THE AUTHOR

Greg Brougham has a few decades experience building and delivering complex systems. He has nearly a decade of experience using Cynefin in delivery and has published a short book that provides an introduction to do so. More recently he spent a year as director of engineering for a blockchain startup and is currently helping one of the leading UK telecom vendors with their digital transformation. Greg has been speaking at lean agile conferences on architecture and delivery for a number of years.

ABOUT THIS CHAPTER

 Full Chapter

 Chronology: Piece 20 of 33

 Theoretical

 Cynefin Principles

CYNEFIN AND DELIVERY

GREG BROUGHAM

"Elite sport is a running machine: stop moving forward and you fly off." Dave Brailsford [1]

We submit that leaders and consultants cannot know the future in our fast-changing world. The conventional way consultants work, creating an idealized future and suggesting that leaders realize this future, is an illusion. Instead, we recommend that we need to involve the workforce more, use narratives, and work from the evolutionary potential of the present, using principles of complexity theory.

CONTEXT

In 2004, the economists Paul Ormerod and Bridgett Rosewell published a paper entitled, "How much can firms know?" It was about the evolution and extinction of firms. [2] The paper drew on research that showed that there are two stylized facts about firms' extinctions: 1) the probability of extinction is highest in a firm's early life and 2) there is an empirical relationship between the size and extinction of a firm that exhibits a power law. [3]

The paper drew on extensive research. One study looked at the analysis of a database of six million firms by state and industry in the United States between the 1980s and 1990. Another database had firms of eight OECD countries over the 1977-79 period, which showed a power law with an exponent of -2.

The authors concluded that executives could not know much about their competitors or the market, which is inconsistent with the stylized facts of the earlier studies. That means that planning made little difference, and that is consistent with complexity theory – if the environment is complex, which is the state of most markets, then we cannot predict the behavior of competitors or the market, and no amount of analysis will help. De Geus explores this theme in his book, *The Living Company*. [4]

The strategy community has largely ignored this research. They continue to focus on the development of strategic plans and initiatives, but if we can't predict how the market will react, it raises the question: Is there any value in such an approach? It is also noted in Christensen and Raynor's book, *The Innovator's Solution*, that most strategy is emergent and not deliberate. [5]

THE ROLE OF THE TRADITIONAL CONSULTANT

We established what we probably already knew, that we couldn't know much about the market. But this position is reflected by few consultancies. Let's look at the model of Checkland's Soft System Methodology to understand how consultants typically operate, as this provides a meta-model for a traditional consultancy engagement. [6]

Figure 1. How traditional consultants work to formulate strategy

The client engages the consultant to answer a question like, "How do we improve our operational performance?" or "What should the company's strategy be?" The consultant approaches this by modeling the company or area of interest to develop the 'as-is' model – this may be a simple spreadsheet of existing costs by area, a detailed value stream analysis of a business area, or a dynamic systems model of the company.

The consultant then uses this to drive the options analysis. Note, this is about options and not hypotheses based on their experience of the market (it may also include engagement of the organization's employees). These options help to determine the 'to-be' models that provide the desired benefit to the client's question. There may be some discussion of the options to ensure they result in an acceptable outcome from the client's perspective before proceeding to the next stage – mapping the 'to-be' model back into the real world to define the target end-state.

Finally, there's the definition of the roadmap, which moves us from the current 'as-is' to the future 'to-be.' This may be outlined as a five-year strategic roadmap (after all, this project was expensive, so you need to get value for your money). The plans are then developed. The leaders of the organization begin work to deliver on the strategic objectives, or engage another consultant to support implementation, someone who has a wonderful planning approach and great Project Management Office (PMO) capability that would be a great fit.

The problems start at the beginning. For one, the options outlined are only based on the experience and knowledge of the consultant. Even consultants who tout their expertise, once they undertake delivering the series of workshops, for instance, to engage the company's employees, the workshops are based on their existing thinking. They do not include the outliers or ideas that may lead to a revolution of the business. There may well be talk of embracing good or best practice, but that does not mean that they are current practices and there is a saying, 'best practices are someone's past practices.' Also the work is typically based on a small set of examples. Therefore, the applicability, in this context, is not tested; it is basically an inductive model.

The approach is fundamentally based on an idealized end-state model that assumes that we can second guess the market, that we have largely perfect knowledge, and that we can affect the market with the consultant's limited strategy. As Paul Ormerod and Bridgett Rosewell's paper indicates, this is inconsistent with reality. We need a new model that reflects the reality that we exist in today and allows us to discover, as Dave Snowden suggests, "The evolutionary potential of the present."

AN ALTERNATIVE DELIVERY MODEL

"Oral narrative is, and for a long time has been, the chief basis of culture itself." – John D. Niles [7]

We need to make sense of a current situation in order to act wisely. One approach is the use of narratives. It allows us to explore the current environment and include a wide and diverse set of people and views. This supports the emergence of ideas, and avoids making premature assumptions. We stress that this is not storytelling, but the use of narrative fragments to explore the current space. [8]

"Find the real experts so you can learn more quickly." – David Kelly, The Deep Dive

An example of this is how anecdote circles were used by Tony Quinlan and Ron Donaldson working with Pfizer. [9] The anecdote circles engaged employees to capture and signify narrative fragments. These are like water cooler conversations, those unguarded comments about what is going on and the real issues people face.

In an anecdote circle, someone tells a narrative about the work environment that they find significant, and others contribute theirs. This is an indirect way of engaging and is not hypothesis-driven. We are not seeking to confirm a particular individual's view of an issue, but looking at what emerges out of the narratives that people share. Humans have a long tradition of sharing narratives and this is just another example of how this can be leveraged.

When Quinlan and Donaldson started the engagement, there was a general view that sales representatives' knowledge of their product was highly influential on the customer's willingness to buy. The original view was that product knowledge was very important. However, they discovered that product knowledge was secondary to sales representatives' attitude. The implications were that the focus should be moved to developing sales representatives' confidence in their product and its efficacy, not on gaining additional product knowledge. They also realized that sales representatives who had experienced any problems with products, were more positive because they understood what a customer might experience. While newer sales representatives had a more negative attitude, the stories of the more experienced sales representatives allowed them to understand the history and the broader context.

The narrative fragments that came out of the engagement also gave rise to several initiatives that were easy to implement and did not require large change programs. This combination of qualitative and quantitative analysis gives rise to an understanding of what direction you want to move in, and how you can start moving in the desired direction.

"The requirement is more to do with fracturing and deconstructing rather than adapting and nudging." [10]

The use of narratives gives us an understanding of direction and any constraints that need to be observed. [11] It may also identify small changes that would have value, as i,n the Pfizer case study. But what about large changes that are episodic in nature? This is where we need an approach to shared learning so that we know what has value in this context before investing.

We mentioned constraints, but in fact there are both context-free and context-sensitive constraints as Alicia Juarrero talks about in *Dynamics in Action.* [12] When we define the direction to take, we also define the boundary conditions or context-free constraints that we need to observe, so that when moving in a direction we also have guard rails. Context-free constraints may be realized as a set of policy statements. It is important that executives, however, acknowledge the context and if the context changes, policies may need to be reviewed.

What is typically missed are the context-sensitive constraints which are enabling versus constraining constraints. This is the main point that Juarrero makes and it is also reflected in Ackoff's writings.

"From the bottom up, the establishment of context-sensitive constraints is the phase change that self-organizes the global level." [13]

These types of constraints talk about the capabilities of the organization at the ground level that enables higher-level functions. This is so often missed and it is only by looking at an organization's lower level capabilities that we can see the evolutionary potential of the current environment. For example, if we have the capability to automate software system builds then we can look to provision them on demand for testing. If not, then a traditional approach of building a small number of environments and constraining testing is the only viable approach. So if we can automate this task, we remove a testing constraint providing more flexibility and responsiveness, and we enable higher-level functions.

Traditional approaches to systems development lean too often on making assumptions about what we think we know. This leads to problems when these assumptions prove invalid. We try to mitigate this by allowing a margin of contingency, but this is often not sufficient. We need to accept that neither party is privileged to know what they don't know, and that we need an approach to shared learning to understand the evolutionary potential of the current situation, the here and now. [14]

We also need to deal with fine-grained objects, which means that the context is important. By breaking the system down, we can look to combine elements in novel ways that lead to new capabilities. When we have had some exposure to what is possible, we can better understand what works and what doesn't. In this way of working there is an open acceptance that no one party or individual knows the answer(s) and that we need to explore the possibilities. [15] This leads to validated learning and provides a clear understanding of what works and what does not work.

"Knowledge is not determined in advance of our experience; things of strategic and economic relevance are not waiting to be discovered, but are invented as we go." [16]

Once we explore the current environment's evolutionary potential, we are well positioned to support a step-change. For example, in the book *Lead with Respect*, the authors gave an example of executives needing to undertake a system upgrade as their software system had evolved. [17] They were faced with all the issues we commonly see – that lead to a high cost of change, and high risk through loss of knowledge and low skills, as the system has become one that no one wants to change. The question executives needed to answer is what should the system look like? To establish this they looked to changes in the current processes and system. These changes allowed the needs of the new system to be established and for both parties to move forward from an informed position.

Only when there was a clear understanding of the processes and system structure did they look to make an investment. Typically one asks the users what they want, but because there had been no exploration of possibilities or the impact on the existing process, they had no idea. There were too many unknown unknowns that could not be quantified. By experimenting, new knowledge can be created that can allow investment needs to be quantified. [18]

Our focus must be the here-and-now to act accordingly, rather than trying to predict things that may easily lead to analysis-paralysis. We don't need to predict the future if we can move in the right direction. A set of principles for operating in a complex environment includes: work with fine-grained objects, leverage distributed cognition, and ensure dis-intermediation. When we honor these principles, we can engage the workforce via narratives to help establish and understand the direction, and then use shared learning to establish what has agency in the now.

Another example that illustrates these principles is the story about Lotus cars that was reported in 'The Sunday Times.' [19] The new CEO asked for all three existing car models to be broken down into their parts, which were then laid out on tables so that they could be inspected (working with fine-grained objects). All 900 employees of the company were involved in this exercise, and they were asked to tag the components using a traffic light system (using distributed cognition and dis-intermediation). The components were either to be kept, supply renegotiated, redesigned, or discarded. This exercise ensured that everyone was on the same page and understood why these changes were being proposed. The exercise resulted in a weight and savings respectively of around 20 kg and £3,000 along with an improvement in the quality of the cars.

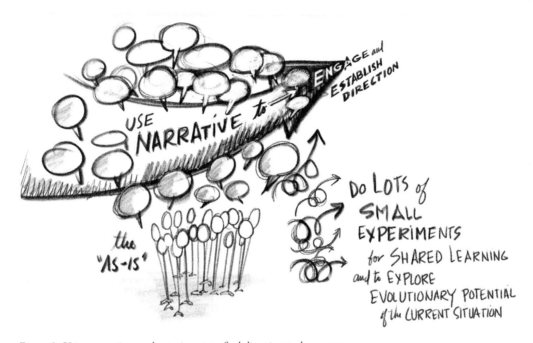

Figure 2. Using narratives and experiments to find direction and next steps

When we have established what has agency we can move to invest. As Peter Palchinsky proposed in the last century: try new things, make them small so that they don't threaten existence, and learn from the experience. [20]

IN CLOSING

We need to change our perspective and acknowledge that today strategy formulation is in the Complex domain of the Cynefin Framework where the system and the agents co-evolve. Consequently, visions have little to no value, as none of us can be sure of the future. As most leaders of organizations are part of an open system, they don't own or control the market, and as such the market and the organization must co-evolve. The Brailsford quote at the beginning of this chapter spotlights that change is the only constant.

The consultant who commands and controls the strategy formation process with idealized futures has outlived his existence. Instead, consultants need to be explorers who are willing to join their clients on a journey of discovery, do experiments, work with narratives, and help executives form, and reform, their strategic direction to solve operational challenges.

In closing I give you Russell Ackoff's thoughts on consultants: "Obviously, breakthrough and creative solutions to problems are more likely to be obtained by the use of educators than consultants." [21]

References

1. Tour de France 2015: Why are Team Sky so successful?, https://www.bbc.co.uk/sport/cycling/33661977

2. Ormerod, Paul, and Rosewell, Bridgett. How much can firms know? 2004, http://repec.org/sce2004/up.28483.1076498136.pdf (accessed September 2015).

3. A power law is where two quantities are related and one quantity varies as the power of the other, for example doubling the length of one side of a square will quadruple it's area.

4. De Geus, Arie P. The Living Company: Growth Learning and Longevity in Business. 1999.

5. Christensen, Clayton M, and Michael E. Raynor. The Innovator's Solution: Creating and Sustaining Successful Growth, Harvard Business Review Press, 2013.

6. Checkland, Peter and Holwell, Sue. Information, Systems and Information Systems: Making Sense of the Field, 1997

7. Niles, John D. Homo Narrans: The Poetics and Anthropology of Oral Literature. Philadelphia: University of Pennsylvania Press, 2010, p.2

8. Mead, Geoff. Telling the Story: The Heart and Soul of Successful Leadership, 2014. Print

9. Edwards, N. Using Stories to increase sales at Pfizer. How "anecdote circles" led to an engaged sales force and improved business results. http://www.engageforsuccess.org/wp-content/uploads/2012/12/Using-stories-to-increase-sales-at-Pfizer.pdf. (accessed 2015).

10. Boulton Jean G., Allen Peter M. and Bowman Cliff. Embracing Complexity: Strategic Perspectives for an Age of Turbulence. 2015, p.25

11. Garvey-Berger and Johnston use the term guard rails in preference to constraints. Berger, Jennifer G, and Keith Johnston. Simple Habits for Complex Times: Powerful Practices for Leaders. 2016.

12. Juarrero, A. (1999). Dynamics in action : intentional behavior as a complex system. Cambridge, Mass.; London: MIT Press.

13. Juarrero, A. (1999). Dynamics in action : intentional behavior as a complex system. Cambridge, Mass.; London: MIT Press. p.6

14. I'm using this in the Darwinian sense that there is a step change in the environment – a metamorphosis

15. This acknowledges what we refer to as messy coherence

16. Chia, Robert C. H, and Robin Holt. Strategy Without Design: The Silent Efficacy of Indirect Action. Cambridge, UK: Cambridge University Press, 2019, p. 99

17. Balle, Michael, and Balle, Freddy. Lead With Respect: A Novel of Lean Practice. 2014. This is well worth reading.

18. Collingridge, J., "Lotus turns it back on the big league," In The Sunday Times, February 8, 2015 accessed via: https://www.thetimes.co.uk/article/lotus-turns-its-back-on-the-big-league-3nhfk2hbqcb

19. Clay Christensen and Michael Raynor speak of moving from emergent to deliberate strategy. Christensen, Clayton M, and Michael E. Raynor. The Innovator's Solution: Creating and Sustaining Successful Growth, Harvard Business Review Press, 2013.

20. Harford, Tim. Adapt: Why Success Always Starts with Failure, Abacus, 2013

21. Ackoff, Russell L. Differences That Make a Difference: An Annotated Glossary of Distinctions Important in Management. Axminster: Triarchy Press, 2010, p.18

What to read next

 Next Full Chapter: Embodied Cynefin: Teaching with the body, Chris Corrigan, p.128

 Next Chronological: It Doesn't Get Happy; it Doesn't Get Sad, Liz Keogh, p.217

 Next Theoretical: With Cynefin we found our own ecology, Anne Caspari and Johann Entz-von Zerssen, p.124

 More on Cynefin Principle 1.3: When Disease Requires a Complexity Framework, Riva Greenberg..., p.153

 More on Cynefin Principle 2.1: Embodied Cynefin: Teaching with the body, Chris Corrigan, p.128

WITH CYNEFIN WE FOUND OUR OWN ECOLOGY

ANNE CASPARI AND JOHANN ENTZ-VON ZERSSEN

ABOUT THE AUTHORS

Anne has an MSc in environmental planning and has worked in many different countries on nature rehabilitation and sustainability projects. In working with ecosystems, she can rely on a solid body of knowledge of how complex adaptive systems work and what tends to get in the way of self-organizing processes. 20 years ago, she started with coaching, adding humans to the equation. In her work with individuals and organizations, she specializes in transformation, change, and leadership. Getting exposed to the Cynefin Framework and Dave's thinking some years ago was a natural fit for her and her practice.

Johann has been a coach for 20 years in different countries, mainly in Germany and Canada. He specializes in training coaches, leadership training, and transformative coaching. Immersing himself for the past several years in the world of sense-making and complexity thinking has added another dimension to his practice. He uses this body of knowledge to help foster change for individuals and on an organizational level. He also runs SenseMaker projects and Cynefin trainings. Johann and Anne are partners in EZC which operates from Germany (www.ezc.partners).

ABOUT THIS CHAPTER

 Vignette

 Theoretical

 Chronology: Piece 26 of 33

WITH CYNEFIN WE FOUND OUR OWN ECOLOGY

ANNE CASPARI AND JOHANN ENTZ-VON ZERSSEN

Our first encounter with Cynefin was through one of Dave's talks. A friend whose critical judgment we trust posted Dave's talk on Facebook. At the time, we were not avid podcast listeners, but we sat down and listened to that one. It was called "How leaders change culture through small actions." After hearing it, we were stunned as it hit home on so many levels. We listened to it again in a way that has since become our habit when listening to Dave's talks: listen, stop, rewind, then listen again to unpack the 'zipped files of meaning' that are woven into Dave's talks. It kept on sinking in, and sinking in, nugget by nugget.

Both of us have been coaches for about 20 years, coming to leadership and Organizational Development (OD) from working with individuals and one-on-one coaching. While we love what we do, there has been this nagging feeling that we are missing something. Specifically, we had a pronounced sense that going about change or growth one person at a time - while it has merit and can be impactful when working with key people, leaders, or so-called multipliers - cannot easily be scaled.

That was not the only thing that hit home listening to Dave's talk. I (Anne) come from 15 years of critical engagement with integral theory, adult development, and all kinds of change theories. When I started working with these theories and frameworks, they helped me immensely. They opened up my thinking and gave me a means to counteract both gross and subtle reductionism in practical work. This was especially helpful to me in my project management work in environmental planning and sustainability contexts. Adult development theory also helped me understand some of the phenomena I encountered in coaching and leadership work.

Over time, however, I experienced a growing scepticism around a new kind of reductionism that crept into most applications of these theories that often went unobserved by the respective communities. Examples include developmental bias ("we need to develop people") in large parts of the integral theory scene and some very formulaic and linear applications of change theories ("step 5: find deeper meaning and purpose"). Since this kind of uneasiness is hard to pinpoint and address, I just noticed that I kept away. I settled at the fringes of these communities and did my own thing.

While listening to that talk by Dave – and many after that – I finally found words to describe my uneasiness; concepts that explained where it came from and frameworks to hold a different kind of approach, backed up by sound theories. I felt such relief!

With Cynefin's complexity thinking, and SenseMaker, its survey and software application, we confirmed that 'data comes before having a framework' – not the other way around. Unlike "a theory of everything" where we look at data through pre-defined quadrants and at people through the biased lenses of predefined levels. No, with the right design principles aka Sensemaker, we can engage with people at the level that they are. No one has to jump through developmental hoops, be at a certain level, or do values/ mindfulness/change training to contribute in meaningful ways.

Basically, in Dave's words, we found a way back to our Cynefin, our place: an ecological, organic approach to the complexity of human growth and change. It allows us to work with developmental theories and leadership development in a complementary way. To work with micro shifts and scaffold their scaling. To engage in complex processes that are not reduced to recipes or "educational trails" pretending to be the real ecology. We don't try to change people nor be like missionaries proud with arrogance about development. We have found our ecology.

In our client engagements we can help most people make sense of the Framework's domains and get out of the "expert" trap. We conducted a workshop a few years ago with about 60 SAP employees where Cynefin made their day. They experienced both relief and excitement when they understood that they could indeed be experts in the Complicated domain, yet didn't have to be (actually they couldn't be!) in the Complex domain. Instead, what they could do was partner with their clients to find solutions together.

Our continuous exposure to Cynefin and complexity thinking, and our ongoing learning journey, has profoundly altered the way we look at change, transformation, and leadership. There is an emerging quality, a different dimension, that has started to define our coaching and leadership development practice from a complexity viewpoint. We now draw on a multitude of perspectives, based on a coherent theory and practice of leadership, for today's disruptive, volatile, and profoundly networked society.

We are committed to working with what is; with probing, sensing, and safe-to-fail experiments for adaptive contexts. We call this, for the time being, "complexity coaching and leadership." We aspire to do work with leaders looking at the whole complex relationship with people's embeddedness in different systems, relational dynamics, and contexts.

From the first time we listened to Dave's talk, stopped, rewound and then listened again, his thoughts and frameworks have opened up and broadened our thinking, coaching and leadership practice. Herzlichen Glückwunsch zum 21. Geburtstag, Cynefin!

What to read next

 Next Vignette: The few Organically Drawn Lines that became Part of my Life, Friso Gosliga, p.149

 Next Chronological: Weaving Well-being into the Fabric of our Organizations..., Marion Kiely..., p.227

 Next Theoretical: When Disease Requires a Complexity Framework, Riva Greenberg..., p.153

EMBODIED CYNEFIN: TEACHING WITH THE BODY

CHRIS CORRIGAN

ABOUT THE AUTHOR

Chris Corrigan lives on Bowen Island, BC, Canada where he is a principal in Harvest Moon Consultants. His work focuses on participatory leadership, facilitation, and evaluation in complex contexts. He publishes a blog and shares resources at www.chriscorrigan.com.

ABOUT THIS CHAPTER

 Full Chapter

 Chronology: Piece 12 of 33

 Narrative

 Cynefin Principles

EMBODIED CYNEFIN: TEACHING WITH THE BODY

CHRIS CORRIGAN

The conventional way to teach Cynefin is by showing a PowerPoint presentation. Common sense tells us to engage people's brains via analytical discourse. However, I believe in, and have experienced, a better way. When we introduce Cynefin through first mobilizing the wisdom of the body and have people reflect on their experience, their understanding of the framework is much deeper and embodied.

I first came across the Cynefin Framework in 2008 through friends in the knowledge management world. As a teacher of facilitation, group process, and leadership, I recognized the power of the Framework to help leaders see a variety of, and decide what approaches to use for, different problems. The Framework helps people understand why complex problems defy orderly solutions. It also helps people make a case for engagement and participation over "command and control" processes for facilitating meetings on complex topics. Consequently, Cynefin found a home in my workshops and courses.

When we try to solve complex problems with the wrong tools and approaches, we often feel stress and confusion, both in our minds and bodies, before we can articulate what is wrong. In my experience, the Cynefin Framework can give people a language that helps them explain their uneasiness. It helps people give words to what they intuitively feel: that working with complexity requires working outside of a traditional linear problem-solving approach. The framework also gives people a way to explain why many efforts to address complex challenges fail. This is why the framework is so powerful once people understand it.

My early experiences teaching the Framework were often met with remarks that it was too heady and abstract to grasp quickly. It was clear to me that I needed to draw on the physical arts to design a good pedagogy for teaching it.

My background is a mix of diverse experiences. I played traditional Irish dance music. I was part of an improvisational theater group, studying and working with Augusto Boal's Theater of the oppressed. I trained in the martial arts. And I learned about the body's ability to grasp ideas, long before the mind makes sense of them. These fields became my source from which I began to draw inspiration and exercises to teach the Cynefin Framework – using the wisdom of the body.

TRAINING DESIGNS

The bulk of this chapter lays out for you different exercises that deliver an experience to a group. My experiments to create these were informed by Dave Snowden's heuristic, "data precedes the framework." After several iterations, I created three challenges that illustrate the Clear, Complicated, and Complex domains. None require any equipment, just a big enough space for a group to stand comfortably in a circle.

When offering these challenges I follow these directions:

1. State the challenge clearly and repeat it once

2. Let the group work itself out

3. Debrief quickly by asking some of the following questions:

    1. What happened?

    2. Who was in charge?

    3. How did decisions get made?

    4. How did you evaluate compliance?

    5. How could you teach others to do this?

ILLUSTRATING CLEAR, COMPLICATED AND COMPLEX

Exercise 1

I invite the group to divide themselves into smaller groups of six or seven people. Then I offer them the following challenge: "Organize yourself by height. You have thirty seconds." I can't think of a time when a group has not been able to accomplish this task. Usually, groups line up by height, tallest to shortest, sometimes forming a circle. Occasionally they get creative and put the tallest person in the middle, with people of descending heights on either side. There is little variation in the solutions to this problem, revealing the effectiveness of a best practice in a tightly constrained system with a clear outcome.

Exercise 2

I mix people up into groups of six to eight and give this instruction, "Organize yourselves by height, birth date, and shoe size. You have five minutes." Over the years, I have watched groups develop dozens of different solutions to this problem. Some of the solutions are static, representing data points on a two or three dimensional set of axes. Some are cumulative, where the group comes up with numbers for each variable, adds them together, and organizes accordingly. Other times, groups create dynamic solutions that involve moving and switching between states. Interestingly, it is rare for groups to learn from or steal other groups' ideas, even when they get stuck.

The debrief is always illuminating and illustrates a knowledge-based, leadership-based approach to problem-solving. There is a requirement to interpret instructions ("Birth date, what does that mean?") and a need to research the hidden data elements of shoe size and birth dates. Sometimes groups find a solution to the challenge that involves only two dimensions because there is an exact correlation between height and shoe size. When we ask if such a solution is repeatable, they realize a weakness: they have merely complied with the criteria of the problem rather than come up with a useful and repeatable solution usable in different contexts.

This exercise also produces "experts." I will often stop the activity before the last group has completed it and ask for someone from one of the other groups to teach the struggling group their solution. When people experience complicated problems and experts are available, their expertise can be captured in documentation that can be taught forward. The teacher has emerged as an expert in this problem in a mere five minutes.

Exercise 3

The first two exercises immerse the group into the world of ordered problems. At this point, I introduce them to another challenge, one I initially learned from Joanna Macy's work, which she calls The Systems Game. This is a common improv game that is played under the title of Assassin or Sun and Moon, and that is the variation I currently use. The set up is as such:

1.   The whole group stands in a circle.

2.   Each person's challenge is to create a solar eclipse, one of the most stunning natural events one can witness.

3.   Each person is the Earth and must secretly choose another person to be their Sun and a different person who is their Moon.

4.   The instruction is: "without touching anyone and in silence, organize yourself so that your Moon is between you and your Sun." I will sometimes give a demonstration. You are asking a person to align themselves with two others, without putting themselves in between the other two people.

5.   "You must always be trying to stay in alignment, no matter what else is happening. If you get into alignment, but something changes, adjust. Your goal is to be in an eclipse for as long as possible."

6.   I then say, "Go."

The room explodes into movement immediately. People are moving all over the place trying to find their Sun and Moon and trying to maintain the alignment of an eclipse. Often, after a minute or so, you begin to hear sounds of frustration. After two minutes, people start giving up or try to game the system. After three minutes, those who have realized that this is an infinite game are playing with joy, and others have checked out. If someone were taking a timelapse picture of the whole exercise, you would see a beautiful complex adaptive system in action.

I begin my debrief asking, "How is THAT like real life?" Then I ask small groups to form and notice the differences between this problem and the two ordered problems. Insights emerge about leadership, constraints, and frustration that there didn't seem to be a solution. People use expressions like "It didn't work!" or "We failed!" revealing the dominance of our linear problem-solving approaches.

In debriefing the exercise, we have the opportunity to explore how emergent strategy works. I often point to moments when a large cluster of people got themselves stuck in a corner or divided into two or three subgroups. Noticing these patterns is fascinating, for there was no deliberate plan to cause the group to do this. Playing back the time-lapse video is delightful.

We can understand emergent learning on the individual level by asking people what strategy they learned in the process that helped them play the game. Heuristics emerge quickly.

The stark difference between this complex exercise and the ordered challenges is a rich way to move into a discussion of the Cynefin Framework and all its implications for leadership, knowledge, decision-making, sense-making, and problem solving.

Exploring these three domains, people usually see that a framework for understanding action in context is helpful. By this time, the group has so much information that you may even be able to ask them to create small groups where they answer questions about constraints, causality, epistemology, leadership, and ontology. Groups can often fill out a blank Cynefin Framework with very little left to teach except to point out applications.

ILLUSTRATING CHAOS AND CONFUSION

While the Clear, Complicated and Complex domains are enough to pursue, if you have more time it's fun to take people into the Chaotic and Confusion domains with their own exercises. These exercises take more time so I typically leave out these two challenges, but it can be useful to illustrate the distinction between them.

I would suggest you start with chaos. I use a milling game from the world of improv theatre in which I give a group a set of paired commands, train them to follow orders, then mix up the orders and finally produce orders at such a rate that the system fails.

It goes like this:

1. Have the group walk around the room, randomly, changing direction, and filling all spaces.

2. Give them an instruction: "When I say 'stop,' you stop and when I say 'go,' you start moving again." Repeat the instruction a few times.

3. Next say: "Now I will add two more instructions. When I say 'clap,' you clap when I say 'bow,' you make a little bow." Ask the group to stop, go, bow and clap for a minute.

4. Now give one more set of instructions: "When I say 'hop' you hop in the air and when I say "woohoo!' you say 'woohoo!'"

5. Now you begin to mix things up. Tell the group, "This time when I say 'stop' you go and when I say 'go' you stop. The other instructions remain the same." Continue giving commands as the group is walking in the space.

6. Then give this instruction: Switch the second and third pair of commands, so that "stop" means "go," "go" means "stop," "bow" means "clap," "clap" means "bow," "hop" means say 'woohoo!'" and "woohoo" means "clap." People will begin to fail because it becomes confusing.

7. Increase the tempo of your commands so that they are coming too fast and furious for people to respond accurately. Some people will find this hilarious. Others will get deeply anxious.

The huge cognitive load in this exercise creates frustration. Some people will stop participating. Notice that this is a form of applying a safety constraint. When people are in deep chaos, a highly structured constraint helps them reset and come back online.

Following this exercise, you can illustrate the difference between chaos and confusion by providing a one-line challenge to the group:

- Ask the group to, "Organize yourselves economically"

This always gives a group pause. They want to know what you mean. In English, the adverb "economically" is ambiguous and also activates biases, assumptions, and broader societal meanings.

Once when I ran this exercise with a group of sustainability activists from mixed economic classes, the group sat in a circle and discussed what "economically" could mean. They came up with:

• Let's just line up by how much money we make.

• How much cash do you have on you right now?

• How about those who come from poor backgrounds, step into the middle…

…and so on. Emotions ran high, biases and privilege got exposed, class warfare broke out, a small trauma was triggered, arguments broke out. They talked about all of it and I never once intervened. It took 45 minutes for the group to come to a solution. One person, who had been watching the whole time, quietly finally spoke up and said, "What if economically means "in the least amount of time and using as little energy as possible?" In that case, I suggest we just line ourselves up by height and be done with it." The group held a collective moment of astonishment and then did just that.

In reflection, people recognized how critical the Confusion domain is and what happens when approaching problems from bias and habit. It was a rich learning moment, and I highly recommend exploring embodied confusion, especially as a contrast to embodied chaos.

COMPLEXITY HEURISTICS USED IN THE DESIGN PROCESS

Over the years, as Dave Snowden continued to develop the Cynefin Framework, he offered more and more heuristics to guide the design of interventions in complex systems. I have found these heuristics useful for designing embodied exercises. Here are the ones I find most instructive:

- **Data precedes the Framework.** Give people data first, it helps them create the Framework later. Each exercise provides participants with experiences that become data as they learn about the nature of a problem. Teaching the Framework after the exercises then becomes a partial sense-making exercise. They reflect on what they learned and use it to explore and understand the Framework.

- **Obliquity.** Complex problems are best addressed indirectly. Teaching Cynefin benefits from this approach as well. Leading with experience invites people to play first and discover the practical reality that different systems require different kinds of interventions. When I teach Cynefin without this indirect grounding, it seems harder for people to understand the value of the Framework.

- **Gamify and challenge.** When you provide a challenge and gamify an experience, people will focus more on the task and less on what is happening. This drives people towards experience and away from sense-making, allowing them to better gather insights about the nature of different problems.

- **Exaptive practice.** Taking lessons from one context and translating them into another context is a key aspect of complexity. Teaching Cynefin through embodied exercises is an example of an exaptive practice.

KEY LESSONS FOR TEACHING

I love facilitating groups with these exercises, and get enthusiastic about the learning that arises. Over the years I have learned a few key lessons that might help teachers use embodied exercises to teach Cynefin.

1. Don't teach anything during the exercises. Separate the experience from the sense-making. It gives a richer set of insights for people.

2. Repeat your instructions twice, and no more. If anyone is confused, let them figure it out or ask others for help. When people struggle with following instructions, the learning experience is richer and can also build capacity in the group as people help each other to understand what is going on.

3. Be sparing with your debrief questions and let people process the experience in small groups before explaining Cynefin. The benefit of using embodied exercises is lost if you spend more time debriefing the exercise than experiencing it.

4. Don't use any specific Cynefin language or explain anything about what is happening during the exercises. As tempting as it is to say "SEE! What you did there is a PROBE!," it is wiser to save all that for later, pointing directly to the moments when people discovered the concepts of anthro-complexity all on their own before they understood how it fits into the Framework.

I sincerely hope my experiences running these exercises can benefit you and the groups you facilitate. There is so much rich learning when people discover rather than are told and when people interact, helping each other, struggling together and building on successes. It is the kind of learning one almost can't forget.

What to read next

 Next Full Chapter: Cultivating Leadership with Cynefin: From Tool to,... Jennifer Garvey-Berger..., p.139

 Next Chronological: Learning with Cynefin, Harold Jarche, p.196

 Next Narrative: Cultivating Leadership with Cynefin: From Tool to,... Jennifer Garvey-Berger..., p.139

 More on Cynefin Principle 1.1: Cultivating Leadership with Cynefin: From,... Jennifer Garvey-Berger..., p.139

 More on Cynefin Principle 2.1: Weaving Well-being into the Fabric of our Organizations..., Marion Kiely..., p.227

CULTIVATING LEADERSHIP WITH CYNEFIN: FROM TOOL TO MINDSET

JENNIFER GARVEY-BERGER, CAROLYN COUGHLIN, KEITH JOHNSTON, AND JIM WICKS

ABOUT THE AUTHORS

The CEO of Cultivating Leadership, Jennifer Garvey-Berger blends deep theoretical knowledge with a driving quest for practical ways to make leaders' lives better. She has written three highly acclaimed books on leadership and complexity and how to grow the capacities we need for the world in which we live. In addition to her writing and research, Jennifer coaches executives and executive teams, designs and teaches leadership programs, and keynotes at leadership and coaching conferences globally. Jennifer has a masters and a doctorate from Harvard University. She loves walking in the mountains with her family, rolling on the floor with her dog, and writing about leading, coaching, and living.

continued/...

ABOUT THIS CHAPTER

 Full Chapter

 Narrative

 Chronology: Piece 3 of 33

 Cynefin Principles

JENNIFER GARVEY-BERGER, CAROLYN COUGHLIN, KEITH JOHNSTON, AND JIM WICKS

ABOUT THE AUTHORS

Carolyn Coughlin has been an executive coach, facilitator, and leadership development specialist for over 20 years. Her journey began in the corporate world, where she was a management consultant first at Price Waterhouse and later at McKinsey and Company. With her fellow Cultivating Leadership partner Jennifer, Carolyn co-designed and runs the Growth Edge Certification series, an endeavor that continues to provide her with endless joy and learning. She also has a keen interest in supporting women to step into leadership positions in greater numbers so that we might finally achieve the power parity toward which we've been (slowly) moving over the last century.

Keith Johnston worked as an activist, writer, and public service leader before completing a Masters and then a PhD focused on leaders' capabilities to work on complex challenges. He grew up and lives in New Zealand and is a founder of the small global leadership consultancy Cultivating Leadership. Keith is a co-author, with Jennifer Garvey-Berger of *Simple Habits for Complex Times: Powerful practices for leaders* (2015).

Jim Wicks loves supporting people and organizations to grow and develop. He draws on 20 years of experience in a variety of senior leadership and technical roles in the finance and health sectors plus over ten years consulting. His lived experience is mixed with a deep knowledge of human development theory and practice, and ideas and approaches from complexity. Jim is a founder and Managing Director of Cultivating Leadership and is a trustee of the Growth Edge Network. He lives in Cork, Ireland with his wife and when he isn't working with clients can be found out in the hills on a bicycle or in the kitchen.

CULTIVATING LEADERSHIP WITH CYNEFIN: FROM TOOL TO MINDSET

JENNIFER GARVEY-BERGER, CAROLYN COUGHLIN, KEITH JOHNSTON, AND JIM WICKS

This chapter describes how over the past decade we have witnessed the concurrent evolution of our firm, Cultivating Leadership, and the ways in which we use Cynefin with our clients and within our company. As we've grown to 50-plus colleagues around the world, we've realized the brilliance of Cynefin in creating new insights and new solutions, and our ability to grow, discard and evolve our tools. Cynefin is a platform upon which we have built much of our work. We used to do Cynefin. Now we live it.

"How do we create the conditions for good things to happen rather than put standards and structures into place to prevent bad things from happening?"

In the beginning, we saw Cynefin as a tool that those in our workshops would find helpful. It was 2010, our little leadership firm was finding a name, a perspective, and our first clients. Looking back, our first slides from this time are absurd – an incomprehensible set of acronyms and arrows. Our participants were confused. And, frankly, so were we.

But we grew and we learned. We began to play with Cynefin in different parts of our programs, moving it from beginning to end and back again to make it more helpful to participants. We used Dave's short video about Cynefin dazzled by his 8,000 views. My goodness, that seemed like a lot of people. (As we write this article, that video has 380,000 views!) We took workshops when Dave would come all the way to New Zealand, and for weeks afterward we would draw Cynefin squiggles in the sand, as we processed what we were learning. We started using the Framework in the book that would become *Simple Habits for Complex Times.* [1]

THE MOVE FROM HEAD TO BODY

We transformed our teaching of Cynefin in 2015 when Keith stopped by a hardware store on the way to a workshop in Adelaide and fashioned a Cynefin Framework out of ropes and other assorted bits. He stepped his way through the ropey framework as he taught it in the room and it came alive for people in a new way. Soon we were getting the participants up on their feet, having them step through the ropes too, feeling into the different domains with their bodies and emotions. One client produced sets of Cynefin ropes in its signature colors, and they became the de rigor Cultivating Leadership accessory. This bodily approach brought Cynefin alive and opened up significant experiences and new possibilities for participants, and us.

At this same time, there was another change sprouting. Our little firm, first the four of us, then six, then 12 people, had blossomed, and we were now 25 people from New Zealand, Australia, the U.S., and the UAE. [2] Suddenly, we found ourselves needing to deal with quality assurance, organizational culture and values, and consistency across program and facilitation teams as we had not done before.

As we grew, we noticed the pulls on us to fall into common traps of other firms before us. Cynefin would classify many of our clients' ways of working as Confused in some way – the mismatch between the situation and the response was so apparent to us looking in from the outside. Yet, even with that cognitive awareness, we found ourselves like our clients, noticing a desire to control things, trying to ensure bad things wouldn't happen, and trying to replicate things that didn't live in the predictable world. To mitigate these pulls, we turned to Cynefin – this time not to shape what we were teaching, but to shape who we were becoming as an organization. Jim, a farm boy from a New Zealand hamlet called Rerewhakaaitu, calls this, "eating our own dog food."

THE MOVE FROM BODY TO ORGANIZATION

Over the last ten years, as Cynefin has moved for us from a tool to a mindset, we have grown. We are now more than 50 people from 14 countries around the world. We have created a deliberately complexity-friendly, developmentally-oriented organization. Cynefin supports us at every turn as we make sense of our system and as we create safe-to-fail experiments to nudge us to the next stage and place. Cynefin helps us notice ourselves and our reactions. And it has led to a new sort of organization with new ways of acting and interacting.

IT BEGINS IN CONFUSION

Cynefin offers us, as leaders in this organization who work with participants in leadership programs, a chance to pull back from our habits and intentionally look at our system and ourselves to create thoughtful approaches. We have long taught that Confusion can be two different states. One is being swamped by the events and paying the consequences for a mismatch between what your habits drive you to do and what the context requires. Another state is being highly aware, like being on a viewing platform with a puzzled curiosity that allows us to see more clearly and discern our way into a new future.

The first time we can remember a move from Confusion to Awareness was in 2014. We had a crisis. Our flagship leadership program for our biggest client, designed by two of us and taught by at least one of the founders through the first cohorts, was now being taught by two associates. As our colleagues taught it, they swapped out some of the original designs for pieces they liked better. Each small change was a minor adjustment, but together, those changes created dissonance in the program's arc that frustrated the participants and led to escalating complaints. The client clamped down on this sort of experimentation – and this sort of associate-led teaching. We four, gripped by fear and anxious to set things right, gathered together in an emergency meeting.

Our anxieties took hold of us. We got caught up in wanting to control, to bring things back to center, to lock things down. We began to discuss ensuring consistency, quality monitoring, and standard operating procedures so that this problem would never happen again. We were hip-deep in the swamp of Confusion, and we were grasping for pre-crafted Complicated solutions to get our Complex challenge back under control.

Then, a cup of tea, a breath, and a climb up the Confusion ladder into the watchtower of Awareness opened our eyes. We saw that we could never actually prevent clients from getting anxious, cohorts from complaining, experimentation from failing. We came back to our compass as leaders in complexity: How do we create the conditions for good things to happen rather than putting standards and structures in place to prevent bad things from happening? We found our feet on solid ground again and began to innovate.

ONCE WE ARE AWARE, WE THRIVE IN COMPLEXITY

After that first crisis, we created a series of experiments to nudge us in the direction of safer experimentation in programs, more support for associates, and transparency about what changes we were making and what we were learning from those changes. The first experiment was an "advice call". [3] The gist of it was this: When you did work that didn't involve one of the firm's leaders, (initially a group cringingly called "homeys" and now called "Cultivators"), you would schedule a small panel of people and ask them for advice. Here was our original formulation for the letter where we announced this experiment:

- You pick (at least) two people, not on the project group to be your advisors. One of those people can be any associate, but one will be what we have taken to affectionately call "homeys."

- One thing Laloux recommends is that as you make your advice panel, you consider who is likely to be most affected by the work you're doing (so if you're doing a (Client A) gig, you might want to include others who have been involved with (Client A) before; if you're doing a mindfulness workshop, you might want to talk with someone who has mindfulness as part of her or his personal expertise or brand.

- You have conversations with those people (at least one upfront and one after) and talk through the program and the issues above. You don't have to take the advice of the others, but you have to consider it. [4]

In the years since the advice call began it became the lifeblood of our organization. These rules have all shifted – some boundaries have dissolved, and others have grown. We were too leader-centric in our original formulation, and now there's no rule that a Cultivator needs to be one of the advice-givers. We were too small in our original aspiration and imagined two or three people meeting. We quickly grew our boundary with the belief that more minds would be better. Now all of us are invited to Zoom in to every advice call, and each of us decides for ourselves which calls we are interested in or to which we can add value. Some calls have six people; others have 26.

Knowing that we were in the Complex domain of the Framework allowed us to iterate and learn about this experiment and have it solve challenges far beyond its original remit. We initially thought of advice calls as a control mechanism, but they quickly became emergent learning events. Now, these advice calls are core knowledge-sharing calls. They connect us to the work across the entire firm. And they connect us deeply to one another because everyone bumps into other people on these calls.

Our new frontier is opening these calls both internally and externally. Externally, we invite the clients we serve and the partners we work with. Internally, we are having conversations about the core ways in which we act as a community and how we can become a more deliberately inclusive firm. We also decide how quickly we should grow and how we handle our changing business model in a Covid-19 world.

We have additional experiments that have become core parts of who we are. And we have experiments that have gone nowhere, or ones that have been helpful and then just drop away over time. For a while we had a monthly Complexity Call where we just talked about the theory and practice of complexity. At first, they were wildly popular, and we geeked out on complexity theory. As these calls became less attended, we decided the time for them had passed. We have tried a variety of ways to encourage peer coaching calls, but none of these ways have been sticky enough to last. We realized that our advice calls encourage asking questions, but we didn't have a place where people could share their deep expertise. Then we started "CLever" calls as a way for colleagues to teach each other about what they know.

More than just the nature of these calls, the way we meet is equally important and was enabled by what we learned probing the complexity space through Cynefin. We start every meeting with a "complexity check-in" – a question posed that everyone answers in turn, and then a second loop to have us make sense of the system that's in the room. For example: What are the patterns we see? What are the outliers? What are the absences or silences – the things that aren't said? We listen to learn to one another, knowing that deep listening is a requirement for taking in multiple perspectives in complexity. These conversations shape our capacity to see our system at that moment and nudge it toward a better future.

OBVIOUSLY, IT'S NOT ALWAYS CLEAR (OR CLEARLY, IT'S NOT ALWAYS OBVIOUS)

From the outset, the design of the processes has been broadly based around Lean, i.e., minimizing the number of, and the steps in, processes and enabling individual discretion. This can be bewildering for new colleagues, who arrive from a big corporation (or even another small consulting firm) to find no expense form or invoicing template. Instead they get the direction, "Just send KB an email." We learned from Cynefin that when too much gets pushed into the Clear domain, it can create the illusion of control, as it decreases redundancy and increases fragility. Because we mostly value flexibility over compliance, it has been tricky to create many systems. Instead, we have relied on flexible people who translate the mess of the individual inputs (on something like an invoice or expense sheet) into a regular and predictable output (like a professional invoice to a client).

As we have grown larger, this trend has strained our Managing Director (Jim) and our Catalyst team – the group most likely to bear the brunt of our desire for flexibility. [5] We have a widespread agreement that we don't want our business model to dip into the Clear domain (to that end we have no automatic sales, we have nothing off-the-shelf, we have no passive income from intellectual property). So we have been working to create support structures in the Clear domain.

One such measure is we have created an internal intranet – we call the "CLoud." Here our growing firm can securely track and share information about clients, about the work we're doing, about our appetite and ability for different sorts of work. It helps us to share resources. It gives us an infrastructure to support us so we can scale without depending as much on individuals.

We want to optimize some of the more Clear parts of our work to increase effectiveness without creating unnecessary bureaucracy. We are aware that our own human behavior, life's unpredictability, and our deep-seated desire for flexibility is located in the Complex domain, and influences how we will do as we attempt to embrace systems and practices more suited to the Clear domain. The implementation of "CLoud" reflected this. The technical bit was easy, but the behavioral change was Complex. Cynefin insights helped the team to focus on the social processes that supported the implementation.

LOVING AND HATING THE COMPLICATED

We find that when we move from Confused into the Complicated domain, we can wrestle with ourselves. Appropriately, we use experts well when we need to; we don't try to solve a challenge that really requires expertise that we don't have. And we value deep expertise in our own colleagues. Those we invite to join us at Cultivating Leadership have some significant knowledge and experience to share with us and the world.

But, we rarely use Complicated processes of analysis. We tell stories for meaning, but we spend less time talking about hard data – numbers of programs, hard measures of client satisfaction, etc. Compared with other businesses, we talk very little about money or collect hard data on where our client leads come from. We are also more likely to want to keep tinkering with a successful leadership program long past the point of adding much value, and we are too often reinventing the wheel. By default we slip back into Confusion and back into Awareness, our familiar dance. But we work hard to collectively remind each other that some things simply are Complicated, and we should treat them as such.

THE MOVE FROM ORGANIZATION TO BEING

Perhaps more than anything else, our use of Cynefin has shown us a way of being in complexity that shapes each moment. As we choose new colleagues, we look for ones who are disposed to lean into their confusion. Cynefin has helped us evolve from trying to be in control, the knowers and the heroes, to being the questioners, the wonderers, the explorers. It has helped us move from over-identifying with our minds and our knowledge to understanding the importance of the body, the spirit, and the intuition. Our clients tell us what most draws them to us is our coherence. How we use the tools and approaches we offer our clients, and how we have grown into being what we advocate in leadership, is what they most want to cultivate in their leaders.

USING CYNEFIN TO CULTIVATE LEADERSHIP

Cynefin has become a platform on which we have built much of our work. Then and now we would rarely talk to a client without drawing the distinctive Cynefin squiggles. Our internal meeting notes are littered with lists and questions across the domains scrawled over notepads and whiteboards. Cynefin's capacity to help us recognize, and respond accordingly, in each domain has profoundly shaped us.

We started with Cynefin being a handy framework to ease leaders into the ideas of complexity. We did Cynefin. Over our company's lifetime, it has grown into a set of tools we employ first on ourselves and then in the world – it has become a set of lenses, a language, a mirror, and a scaffold. We now are Cynefin. And, we continue to grow, as leaders, and evolve with the Framework along with the Cynefin community. We are grateful that this path will continue and that the co-creative Cynefin dance will carry on in this increasingly complex world.

References

1. Berger, Jennifer G, and Keith Johnston. Simple Habits for Complex Times: Powerful Practices for Leaders. Stanford University Press, 2016.

2. Cultivating Leadership, as our name implies, is a firm focused on leadership development. See CultivatingLeadership.com

3. The seed from this idea comes from Laloux, F. (2014). Reinventing organizations: A guide to creating organizations inspired by the next stage in human consciousness. Nelson Parker.

4. This excerpted from the letter to the firm in early 2015.

5. The Catalyst team is the group of staff who creatively support our work.

What to read next

 Next Full Chapter: When Disease Requires a Complexity Framework, Riva Greenberg..., p.153

 Next Chronological: Facilitation Can be Complex..., Vivienne (Viv) Read, p.296

 Next Narrative: The few Organically Drawn Lines that became Part of my Life, Friso Gosliga, p.149

 More on Cynefin Principle 1.1: Facilitation Can be Complex..., Vivienne (Viv) Read, p.296

 More on Cynefin Principle 3.1: The U.S. Navy's Combat Information Center, Trent Hone, p.185

THE FEW ORGANICALLY DRAWN LINES THAT BECAME PART OF MY LIFE

FRISO GOSLIGA

ABOUT THE AUTHOR

Friso Gosliga (1972) is an organizational psychologist born in Friesland (the Netherlands). He has always worked in the field of organizational development, helping people to deal with complex change and uncertainty. Friso is one of the original IBM Cynefin team members, working with Dave Snowden since 2000. He was part of the prototype development team for SenseMaker (in 2004) and has since been running projects all over the world using SenseMaker, Cynefin and insights from complexity theory, in various fields like citizen engagement, monitoring & evaluation and development work. He regularly runs courses for Cognitive Edge about the principles behind Cynefin and SenseMaker and is currently working on a book about complexity and uncertainty.

ABOUT THIS CHAPTER

 Vignette    Narrative

 Chronology: Piece 1 of 33

THE FEW ORGANICALLY DRAWN LINES THAT BECAME PART OF MY LIFE

FRISO GOSLIGA

It must have been somewhere in the autumn of 1999. I was driving from Breda (in the Netherlands) to Frankfurt in the middle of the night with a thermos flask of coffee and a full tank of diesel hoping both the car and I would safely get to our destination without stopping.

As usual, my travels to attend this meeting of the Knowledge Management (KM) Special Interest Group of Lotus Consulting had not been approved by my manager. After all, it didn't add to our bottom line (and his bonus) directly. Moreover, the value of this whole "KM-thing" was unproven. So I took a day off from work to get to the evening session and paid for the hotel out of my own pocket.

There weren't many people in the KM Special Interest Group at Lotus back then and we knew each other mostly through our Lotus Notes discussion groups. Being able to meet face to face was always a bonus. Remember this was when video meetings were something for executive boardrooms and mobile phones were cool if they supported Wireless Application Protocol (WAP).

When I arrived at the meeting venue that evening, I bumped straight into one of the speakers for the night. He was hurriedly getting out of a taxi from the airport. The bearded and bespectacled man was dressed in a bright rugby shirt, and simultaneously collecting his bags, paying the driver and speaking on the phone. It was Dave Snowden, in a scene that anyone who has traveled with him will undoubtedly recognize.

My first encounter with Dave had been a few months earlier, during a KM-course at the infamous IBM La Hulpe Training Centre near Brussels. At that time, Dave was already interested in the use of narrative for mapping knowledge. He demonstrated the power of storytelling by using stories throughout the day's training to deliver his theory, exercises and examples. I was hooked, and equally thrilled when Dave asked me to join the small team of consultants working with him to apply his methods to client projects.

Fast forward to Frankfurt: Similar to our first meeting, Dave spoke about the power of narrative, especially about using narrative for knowledge management. At the time Dave Snowden and Larry Prusak were the KM thought leaders at IBM and he was proposing a more organic, humanistic approach to knowledge management – in a company like IBM.

Dave had the idea to create decision maps by examining the narratives for the building blocks of knowledge: artefacts, skills, heuristics, experience and natural talent – better known by the acronym 'ASHEN'. But how would we gather the stories? Attendees were skeptical about the use of cassette recorders and at the time they were the best option. SenseMaker, the software that we have today, had not yet been created.

Eventually we got onto talking about the well-known Socialization-Externalization-Combination-Internalization (SECI) model of knowledge creation by Nonaka. It was published in 1995 in a book called, The Knowledge-Creating Company. [1] The book describes how knowledge moves between implicit and explicit states through the four socialization processes that give the SECI-model its name. The model didn't sit well with Dave, and our group discussed its strengths and shortcomings at length. I was furiously taking notes as I seemed to be the only one who hadn't read the book yet. (Oops.)

While my recollection of that evening isn't perfect, considering that it happened over twenty years ago, I can still recall an image. It's an image of a small side room off the main lobby, that at the end of the evening contained several very dazed, confused and slightly intoxicated colleagues. We were all looking at a drawing on a whiteboard of something that vaguely resembled a two by two matrix with some weird alterations, a wild collection of arrows drawn all over it, and a bunch of illegible words written in seemingly random places. Again, a familiar scene for anyone who has worked with Dave.

Because the age of the camera-phone hadn't started yet, I don't think there are any pictures. But I do remember the model - it wasn't called a framework yet! It had two dimensions, one dealing with levels of abstraction, the other referring to implicit and explicit states of knowledge. I also vividly remember Dave standing at the whiteboard, coming up with new ideas, growing more and more excited as we asked our questions, and then altering the picture accordingly.

We ended up with something that had four 'spaces' or domains, and those domains were more interesting than the axes themselves. You could tell a little story about each of these domains and how knowledge could move and flow between them. It all seemed to make sense, and even though most of us only caught a fleeting glimpse of this – we were hoping our notes would make sense to us the next day. (Not all of them did, unfortunately.)

At the end of that evening, as I walked back to the hotel across the street, I had the distinct feeling that we in that room had witnessed the birth of something new or at least part of it. Was it a model? A tool, or something else? It was hard to refer to it as it didn't even have a name yet. That wouldn't take long, though.

A few months later, an article by Dave dropped into my Notes mailbox. The vaguely familiar picture in the article immediately triggered the memory of the wild sketches on the whiteboard in the Lotus office in Frankfurt. Little did I know that these organically drawn lines would become an essential part of my professional life for the next twenty one years. The caption read: 'Cynefin.'

Reference:

1. Nonaka, Ikujiro, and Hirotaka Takeuchi. The Knowledge-Creating Company. New York: Oxford university press, 1995.

What to read next

 Next Vignette: How the Cynefin Framework Supports Law Enforcement, Lou Hayes Jr., p.169

 Next Chronological: A Short History of a Long Process..., Mary E. Boone, p.108

 Next Narrative: Welcome to the Cynefinogi (The People of Cynefin), Iwan Jenkins, p.203

WHEN DISEASE REQUIRES A COMPLEXITY FRAMEWORK

RIVA GREENBERG AND BOUDEWIJN BERTSCH

ABOUT THE AUTHORS

Riva Greenberg is a health researcher, health coach, author, advisor and requested inspirational speaker. Having lived with type 1 diabetes for 48 years, her work is dedicated to helping people with diabetes and health professionals work collaboratively in a way that helps both flourish. She is sharing the Flourishing Approach across the world. Riva has written three books and hundreds of articles, spent ten years as a peer-mentor traveling the U.S., has spoken at the UN and is recognized for her humanistic work by professional associations and organizations.

Boudewijn Bertsch helps people bring out the best in themselves and others as a (somatic) coach, thinking partner, and leadership development facilitator worldwide. He originated the 'direct path' to inclusive leadership development; a way of developing people's personal and organizational leadership abilities based on a new emergent worldview. With Riva, he contributes to a relationship- and complexity-based approach to chronic care that encourages the adoption of healthy behaviors.

ABOUT THIS CHAPTER

 Full Chapter

 Theoretical

 Chronology: Piece 10 of 33

 Cynefin Principles

WHEN DISEASE REQUIRES A COMPLEXITY FRAMEWORK

RIVA GREENBERG AND BOUDEWIJN BERTSCH

The Cynefin Framework has been a game-changer in our personal lives. The realization that living with type 1 diabetes (T1D) and managing blood sugar is primarily complex, not complicated, changed our thinking, our actions and lifted our emotional burden. The implications for healthcare professionals is that there are more effective approaches that can expand their repertoire in working with people with T1D.

BOUDEWIJN'S STORY: "I SAW HER BURDEN OF LIVING WITH NEARLY 40 YEARS OF SELF-CRITICISM AND JUDGMENT FALL AWAY."

When I married Riva, she'd been living with type 1 diabetes for twenty-nine years. T1D is among the most intensively self-managed chronic conditions. People with type 1 diabetes must manage their blood glucose (sugar) throughout the day, every day. How well they do this mostly determines how healthy they'll be and helps to reduce their risk of diabetes complications – heart disease, blindness, kidney disease, retinopathy, neuropathy, amputation, hearing loss, adhesive joints and more. Complications are the result of years of higher than normal blood sugars that damage the body's large and small blood vessels. [1]

Riva taught me that her fundamental task to stay healthy is to keep her blood sugar in a targeted range – 70 to 180 mg/dL (3.9 to 10 mmol/L.) She aimed for this every hour of every day. Healthcare professionals trying to help their patients, tell them to "control" their blood sugar to stay in this range. This is believed to be how one best prevents long-term complications, and hypoglycemia (too low blood sugar) that can cause 'real-time' seizures, unconsciousness, and death.

When we married, Riva checked her blood sugar four to six times a day on a simple device called a glucometer (blood sugar meter). Each time she checked and saw the number that indicated her blood sugar, she'd have to make one or more decisions to stay, or get back, in range: Take more insulin? If so, how much? Eat something? If so, what and how much? Take a walk? Or simply do nothing?

Riva 'trained' me early in our marriage to better understand T1D, and believe me it wasn't easy. She would come back from a walk and announce, "If I look pale, what would you do?," "If I'm low, what would you bring me and where do we keep it?" Often she'd show me her blood sugar number and share why she thought she'd got it, the next action she would take, and why. She also shared her confusion when she couldn't explain a number and felt anxious and uncertain about what the right next action was.

Intrigued, and concerned about Riva's welfare, I started to problem-solve with her. At times Riva's numbers seemed a fairly logical result of her efforts. Relying on good habits, experience, and steady determinants, she could get numbers close to what she'd hope for. But frequently, we could only determine what led to a surprising number in hindsight. For instance, struggling over a number she might say:

"Wow, for two days I couldn't figure out why my blood sugar was so high! But I realized my insulin had gone bad and I didn't realize."

She could only have determined this looking backward because so many things were happening simultaneously and affecting the outcome. Yet sometimes even looking back there was no apparent rationale and our search for one was a frustrating and failed exercise.

Ever the researcher, I was keen to crack the puzzle of her blood sugar numbers. I was sure it just needed proper analysis: find the set number of common root causes and she'll be able to manage the variables. In my mind managing blood sugar was simply a matter of analyzing the impact of food, insulin dose, exercise effects, stress levels, and a few other things, and voila, we'd find the golden formula. I assumed that living with T1D was an ordered, mechanical process, one of cause and effect.

But one night while out to dinner I knew different. Riva ordered her meal and started her calculations of how much insulin to take. She guessed at the carbohydrate count in the food she'd eat, the impact of the wine she'd drink, the long walk that morning that could still be lowering her blood sugar level. Since one is taught to take insulin twenty minutes before a meal, as the waiter walked away she plunged the insulin loaded syringe into her leg.

Twenty minutes later the waiter came back and told us an accident in the kitchen would delay our meal another 25 minutes. Riva now had a new situation to contend with: her blood sugar was going to drop too low before the food arrived.

THE INSIGHT

With startling clarity I understood that managing blood sugar is not an ordered cause-effect task, but a complex one and that it relies on constant sense-making. Having been a student of complexity science, I realized:

> *Blood sugar levels are not manufactured or produced by calculations and a treatment decision. Blood sugar levels are an ever emergent property of many (unpredictable and unknown) processes in the body and the interactions Riva has in the world, many of which are also unpredictable.*

Like what just happened at our dinner table in the restaurant.

Many variables known and unknown, seen and unseen, expected and unexpected, separate and together constantly interact to influence blood sugar. I saw that my assumption, and that of Riva and her healthcare professionals – that managing T1D is an ordered task – was on the right side of the Cynefin Framework. But most of the time, it's not. Riva cannot "control" her blood sugar. Mastery for Riva and everyone with T1D is instead – knowing how to influence one's blood sugar and respond to one's number, whatever it is in the moment. People with T1D can only be responsible for their effort, not their result. Despite the prevailing belief, doing one's best is nudging and navigating one's blood sugar in the direction of one's target range; there is no cause-effect control for any specific blood sugar number.

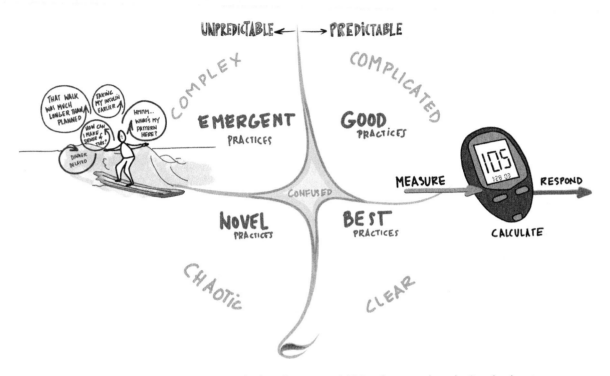

Figure 1. Sense-making Cynefin Framework adapted. Living with T1D is living mostly in the Complex domain.

Among the major influences on blood sugar is the body, which is a socio-biological complex adaptive system. Biological processes including our heartbeat, blood pressure, signaling between gut and brain, digestion, nerve impulses, stress hormones, liver processes and more, interact with each other and influence blood sugar levels. Our body is also subject to life's unpredictability, incalculable factors and interactions within our environment. One time Riva and I were walking to the subway station only to find it was closed and we needed to walk further than planned. That dropped Riva's blood sugar lower than planned. Looking at the Cynefin Framework and Riva as a human being, not a machine, it's clear she lives primarily in the Complex domain.

RELIEF THROUGH INSIGHT

When I shared this reality with Riva, I saw decades of guilt, perfectionism and self-criticism fall from her shoulders. Her negative self-talk now had a mighty combatant: the truth. Using a notebook I drew the Cynefin Framework for her and explained:

"If you were a machine you would always be able to more or less predict your next blood sugar. You'd make a cause-and-effect analysis and calculate your way to a number. You control the outcome by standardizing and manipulating the variables, like food, exercise and the effect of a unit of insulin.

But as a living biological organism, most of the time managing your blood sugar relies on unknown, invisible and constantly changing and interacting variables. Then you take an action and that causes the variables and your blood sugar to fluctuate again. This, in complexity theory, is called a recursive process. You co-create a result to which you respond, which in turn changes the outcome. And this is the very nature of a complex system: the outcome is uncertain and unpredictable, and what you do may have unintended effects. There are too many unknown unknowns.

The good news is that while you can't predict your blood sugar numbers, they are not random, and from the Complex domain you can see patterns, or dispositions. Discovering these, you can influence your numbers in the right direction. Still, there is no certainty, so you cannot be held accountable for the results. Your effort becomes monitoring and knowing what to do when a blood sugar number appears on your meter. That's the criterion for success."

If we look at blood sugar management through the Framework, when blood sugar is extremely high or low, you are in the Clear domain. There are Best Practices to follow to remedy the problem and restore equilibrium.

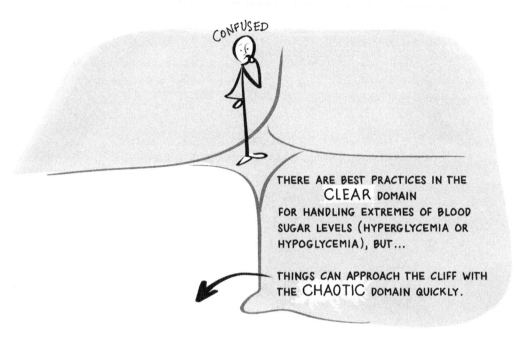

Figure 2, Best practices for T1D exist in the Clear domain

Ironically, it's easy to fall from the Clear domain into the Chaotic. For instance, if a severe low puts you into the hospital, there mistakes can happen – emergency workers may not know about T1D, they may do the wrong thing.

Managing blood sugar is a constant, dynamic movement between the Complicated and Complex domains. In the Complicated domain various good practices may help you recover from a high or low blood sugar event. For example, carrying glucose tablets with you at all times and checking blood sugar at regular intervals.

Predominantly managing blood sugar resides in the Complex domain, however, where one must work with known and unknown unknowns. As such, mistakes will be made, that is normal. For example, because you are distracted you may forget whether or not you already took your insulin before your meal. One heuristic in this domain is safe-to-fail experiments. For example, taking one glucose tablet, not three, to raise blood sugar and injecting small amounts of insulin to lower it, and monitoring the change.

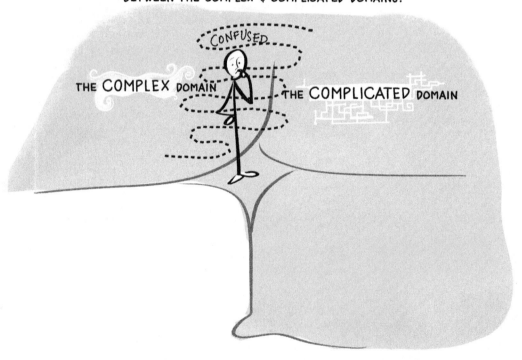

Figure 3. T1D means primarily living in the Complex domain and sometimes the Complicated domain. Stepping into the Confused domain – not understanding why a blood sugar number came up is a normal part of living with T1D.

RIVA'S STORY: A NEW PERSPECTIVE AND RELIEF

Boudewijn's explanation that I live in the Complex domain of the Framework confirmed what I'd always felt but had no language for. We took this photo in 2016 in our subway station; we intuited its truth.

Figure 4. Poster in subway station, Riva on the right.

Further, digesting the Cynefin Framework was liberating. Understanding that I live primarily in complexity, that managing my blood sugar is a constant sense-making activity, knocked the last vestige of guilt, shame and playing the perfectionist game off my shoulders. This buoyed my energy and confidence and helped us both define a path to what we see as 'blood sugar mastery': knowing how to recognize patterns and influence blood sugar, and respond to it to move it in the right direction.

When I was diagnosed in 1972, managing my diabetes would sit squarely in the Clear domain. There were simple rules and they were few: 1) Follow a diabetic diet. 2) Do urine testing to check blood sugar. 3) Inject a prescribed amount of insulin, the same amount every day at 8 AM. There were no glucose meters so I never knew my blood sugar level.

Figure 5. How type 1 diabetes evolved from a Clear recipe-based to a Complex sense-making-based condition.

But today, managing diabetes is constant decision-making. Studies show that people with T1D daily make about 180 decisions. [2] Partly because we have so much more information, new medications and data from devices and, as my fellow T1D advocate, Adam Brown, points out there are innumerable factors to be aware of that influence blood sugar. [3] Cynefin, as a decision-making support framework, is a remarkable tool for health professionals and people with diabetes to improve management, and free people with T1D from self-inflicted blame.

There's also an odd paradox in diabetes. With the release of more diabetes devices, the belief is that blood sugar should be even more "controllable." Yet this is still not true, and it is dangerous. Even with all our devices, only a minority of adults and youth with T1D in the U.S. achieve the American Diabetes Association blood sugar level goals (often indicated by an HbA1c blood test). A two-part study conducted by the T1D Exchange Registry found that while in 2012, only 7% of study participants used a CGM and in 2018, 30% did, participants' blood sugar, across all ages, was higher in 2018 than 2012. [4]

Devices unfortunately allow clinicians to hold tighter to the control myth, and they give people with T1D another reason to see themselves as failing. They can't control their blood sugar even with their devices! Devices can also strengthen health professionals' reliance on technology rather than developing a strong relationship of trust, connection and support with their patients.

Don't get me wrong, devices do have the potential to keep blood sugar in range and individualize treatment, but beyond what I already stated, they come with their own complexities. [5] Using my CGM, I had to learn not to react too quickly. Seeing my blood sugar rise, I tended to inject more insulin, only to drop too low an hour later. As Boudewijn told me, "You need to learn to become comfortable with being uncomfortable in the liminal space between the Complicated and Complex domains."

THE DIABETES CONTROL ILLUSION IS HARMFUL

The idea of "do this and that will happen" is strongly embedded in diabetes self-management. We with diabetes hear it constantly from our doctors. Not because health professionals have any ill intent, but because this is what they learn. Modern medicine stemmed from the scientific revolution when it was thought that the human body was like a machine. This has left practitioners with a deficit treatment paradigm for chronic illness.

Paradoxically, we submit that one reason why people with T1D don't achieve their target values is that they are told that they can. Disappointed by the impossibility of controlling blood sugar, while being told that you can, creates frustration, overwhelm and burnout. The cycle becomes: try, do poorly, blame self, stop managing, and round it goes. In this loop, we operate in the Chaotic and Confused domains; we lose the ability to do sense-making, can freeze, and find decision-making nearly impossible.

Figure 6. When healthcare professionals work from a "control paradigm" they inadvertently may contribute to the patient's disengagement.

REIMAGINING THE DIABETES TREATMENT PARADIGM: HOW THE CYNEFIN FRAMEWORK CAN HELP HEALTHCARE PROFESSIONALS AND PEOPLE WITH T1D

After speaking to many clinicians, a doctor friend who himself has T1D, told us, "Doctors basically learn to apply an engineering frame to a human." [6] That may work for acute care, but translated to chronic conditions it leaves clinicians treating diabetes management as an engineering problem, which resides in the Clear and Complicated domains. We also understand from our friend that clinicians may feel it's risky to give up the idea that people can control their diabetes. "Would patients still look to their health professionals for certainty and clarity, for reassurance and a way through managing their condition?" he wondered aloud. [6]

Medical professionals may also fear a loss of authority as the "expert" and vulnerable beyond comfort to say, 'I'm sorry, you can't control your blood sugar or your diabetes.' If health professionals cannot promise their patients control, they may fear their patients will give up. But this is not true. It is far easier to give up when you measure yourself against an impossible goal than when you acquire skills to succeed with reality.

Health professionals whose repertoire includes working from the Complex domain find it opens up new insights, possibilities, conversations, tools, solutions – and satisfaction for both their patients and themselves. They have found that holding an expanded frame has deepened connection, safety and trust with their patients – powerful agents for improving outcomes.

WORKING FROM THE CYNEFIN FRAMEWORK

We wrote this chapter primarily to support health professionals who work with people with diabetes. We aimed to bring alive the T1D experience of managing blood sugar and have it help you see that it is not a cause and effect equation, but complex.

Meeting your patients in the Complex domain, that by its very nature is energetically dynamic, you are in a place that holds the "evolutionary potential of the present." [7] In other words, it is in this space where you'll find the greatest possibility for emergent solutions to arise. Much to your surprise, it will be less, not more work for you, for these solutions will be the product of thinking together with your patient or at their own suggestion.

Here are some thoughts to help you work with the Cynefin Framework in mind:

- Embrace the notion that those living with type 1 diabetes are generally in the Complex domain of the Cynefin Framework, and that "control as we know it" is not possible.

- Share with patients that while blood sugar and diabetes cannot be "controlled," as we conventionally think of it, there is a way to master both and you will help them to do that. We define mastery, not as never making mistakes, but cultivating the ability to live well and with resilience, knowing how to continually move forward. Success becomes the ability to recognize blood sugar patterns and to know how to influence blood sugar and respond to any blood sugar number to nudge it in the right direction.

- Discover the systems your patient lives in – family, work, community etc. that influence their behavior. Explore context because sense-making is contextual. For instance, it may be appropriate to ask, "Who can help you in your daily life?"

- Please don't use judging words like "non compliant," "non adherent," and "lazy" for instance. Not only do judging words disrespect, and potentially disengage patients, they assume a standardized context while the nature of living with T1D is complex.

The Cynefin Framework is helpful because it can show you how different situations managing T1D require different practices. Here are a few examples of typical events and where they fall on the Cynefin Framework.

Clear domain - Best Practices

- Situations of extremely low and high blood sugars call for best practices. For example, for severe hypoglycemia have an emergency rescue product available and call the national emergency number.

- Teach patients the importance of monitoring blood sugar at regular intervals or wearing a CGM.

Complicated domain - Good Practices

- Have patients understand that because blood sugar levels aren't predictable, there will be times when they will be too high or too low, but still manageable. Help them think through how they can prepare for these situations and what they will do.

- Work with patients to think about how they can make their environment support their health. For instance, they might keep their meter where it's easy to see and use and organize their supplies in one place so they know when to reorder.

Complex domain - Emergent Practices

- Have open dialogues with patients to learn what they do well and help them think through how they can build on that. Listen to their stories.

- Explore with patients their patterns and how to work with them.

- Explore 'safe-to-fail' experiments your patients can undertake to make small improvements.

Confused domain

- If your patient suffers from diabetes burnout and confusion, first and foremost offer your acceptance and understanding. Ask them what they can see is possible now and start from there.

A FINAL NOTE

Working with the Cynefin Framework in mind will likely change the conversation and interaction between health professionals and people with diabetes to be more open, emergent, respectful and constructive. This in kind creates the 'evolutionary potential' we mentioned earlier that influences better outcomes.

The work that Boudewijn and I do in diabetes is informed by the insight that navigating blood sugar and living with type 1 diabetes, is complex. Over the past several years we have designed a health approach for practitioners to use working with their patients. We call it the Flourishing Approach – it primes people to flourish, rather than cope – and it is based, in part, on the Cynefin Framework. The Flourishing Approach is based on complexity science and neurobiology and can help people living with diabetes move toward mastery. [8]

We are indebted to Dave Snowden for giving us the Cynefin Framework. Its profound simplicity explains and enables a more personalized and realistic management approach to type 1 diabetes, and possibly other chronic conditions. Our heartfelt congratulations on 21 years and making such a notable contribution to the world.

References

1. Type 1 diabetes is an autoimmune condition. The pancreas's beta cells no longer produce insulin. In a body that no longer automates insulin production and release, one must 24/7 monitor their blood glucose (sugar) and get an appropriate amount of insulin into one's body to largely coordinate with food intake and exercise. Manually keeping blood sugar in "normal" range is the product of the constantly changing interplay between the impacts on blood sugar and the actions a patient takes, and doesn't take. Type 2 diabetes is a very different disease than Type 1 diabetes and these should not be confused with each other.

2. https://scopeblog.stanford.edu/2014/05/08/new-research-keeps-diabetics-safer-during-sleep/

3. https://diatribe.org/42factors

4. Foster, Nicole C et al. "State of Type 1 Diabetes Management and Outcomes from the T1D Exchange in 2016-2018." Diabetes technology & therapeutics vol. 21,2 (2019): 66-72. doi:10.1089/dia.2018.0384

5. https://asweetlife.org/diabetes-technology-is-better-so-why-are-outcomes-worse/

6. Personal communication with Andreas Stuhr, MD MBA on July 28, 2020

7. We learned this phrase from David Snowden.

8. Greenberg, R., Bertsch, H.B. The Flourishing Treatment Approach: A Strengths-based Model Informed by How People Create Health. On the Cutting Edge Diabetes Care and Education, Vol. 37 Number 6, pp.39-44.

What to read next

 Next Full Chapter: Cynefin and Theory of Constraints: Allies or Adversaries?, Steve Holt, p.173

 Next Chronological: Cynefin and Theory of Constraints: Allies or Adversaries?, Steve Holt, p.173

 Next Theoretical: How the Cynefin Framework Supports Law Enforcement, Lou Hayes Jr., p.169

 More on Cynefin Principle 1.1: Coming of Age: From Framework..., Ann Pendleton-Jullian, p.279

 More on Cynefin Principle 1.3: It Doesn't Get Happy; it Doesn't Get Sad, Liz Keogh, p.217

 More on Cynefin Principle 2: Weaving Well-being into the Fabric of our Organizations..., Marion Kiely..., p.227

 More on Cynefin Principle 3.2: Cynefin and Theory of Constraints: Allies or Adversaries?, Steve Holt, p.173

HOW THE CYNEFIN FRAMEWORK SUPPORTS LAW ENFORCEMENT

LOU HAYES JR.

ABOUT THE AUTHOR

Lou Hayes, Jr. is a career policeman in suburban Chicago. He's held assignments and roles in uniformed Patrol, SWAT/medical, policy, training, investigations, and criminal intelligence. Lou is a co-developer of The Illinois Model™, where theories of adaptability and complexity thinking are applied within policing.

ABOUT THIS CHAPTER

 Vignette　　　　 Theoretical

 Chronology: Piece 28 of 33

HOW THE CYNEFIN FRAMEWORK SUPPORTS LAW ENFORCEMENT

LOU HAYES JR.

I entered U.S. policing at a time when agency accreditation was on the rise. It was a policy-heavy mindset, where standardized procedures and "best practices" were held in high regard. This approach inevitably influenced the way police officers were trained, briefed, acted, supervised, and disciplined.

Such rule-based policing irritated many within the profession. Skeptics like me believed that policy checklists and flowcharts ignored vital aspects such as emotion, judgment, complexity, and other human factors faced in municipal policing.

While assigned to a tactical (SWAT) unit, some colleagues and I took a different approach to operational strategy. As opposed to merely giving the "how" through written directives, pre-programmed responses, and choreographed drills, we gave our learners a strategic thinking framework, by showing the "why" behind decisions. Those nearest the problem would have to be prepared to change a course of action without permission from a command post.

My study inevitably took me to Cynefin. Through the framework, Dave Snowden gave me a new language to better describe phenomena, environments, philosophies, mindsets, and strategies. It was as if he and I were parallel in our work, yet him much farther along in his journey. Cynefin was a missing piece to our project; a project that was widening in scope.

Over the following decade, I found myself immersed in my tactical team's theories while moving through a variety of police assignments, functions, and ranks. Cynefin was among the few foundational frameworks and models that stayed on my mind.

Cynefin became a visualization/template for instructional design, by impacting the (un)structure of training and development programs – from field training recruits, to firearms practice, to tactical drills, to reality-based simulations, to command-level tabletop scenarios. Simply, Cynefin addressed categorical differences in how to efficiently develop skills, understanding, and decision-making from repetitive, technical, closed-loop functions through highly complex, experimental open-loop realms.

Criminal investigations and intelligence also benefited from Cynefin. The framework helped detectives make sense of types of crimes and investigations – and more importantly, the ways they approached these diverse investigations. There is a big difference in the mindset required to investigate a financial cyber-fraud scheme than to disrupt a street gang's emergent crime pattern. Styles of interview and interrogation naturally shifted alongside the broadening of investigative strategies.

Predictably, our intelligence function soon needed a makeover on how it shared information. Analysts had been previously conditioned to rely solely on raw, unadulterated, objective data, looking through a Complicated lens. We'd soon be asking them to develop competing Complex theories that required judgment, discretion, and ultimately bias. In some ways, Cynefin determined which intel approach should be taken based on the types of crimes, the knowledge of offenders, and other clusters of information that could never be seen or crunched by a computer algorithm.

Cynefin has served me well as a police supervisor. I've overseen a variety of teams – tactical units, uniformed Patrol officers, intel and surveillance squads, firearms instructors, and detectives. Some of the teams' roles have been routine and methodical, others extremely dynamic and unpredictable. The style of leadership/management associated with each team, under each circumstance (or system), in each moment is different. Command & Control and Mission Command are two such approaches that can be paired up, at the right time, by more clearly looking at situations via Cynefin.

The U.S. policing community is slowly being exposed to the Cynefin Framework. It holds great value in broadening the approaches, to and design of, policy, training, operational decision-making, supervision, investigations, intelligence, and so much more. I'm so fortunate to have a front-row seat to watching Cynefin grow in my community and shift the mindset towards complexity thinking.

Happy 21st to Cynefin and congrats to Dave Snowden on his impact to so many!

What to read next

 Next Vignette: Learning with Cynefin, Harold Jarche, p.196

 Next Chronological: Shallow Dips into Chaos at the Theatre, Jesko von den Steinen, p.347

 Next Theoretical: Cynefin and Theory of Constraints: Allies or Adversaries?, Steve Holt, p.173

CYNEFIN AND THEORY OF CONSTRAINTS: ALLIES OR ADVERSARIES?

STEVE HOLT

ABOUT THE AUTHOR

Steve Holt is an expert on a variety of improvement methods as a long-time employee of a large aerospace company. In 1997 he discovered the Theory of Constraints and has used it ever since. Steve was certified by the Theory of Constraints International Certification Organization (TOCICO) and later served as a member of the organization's Board. In 2007 he learned about Cynefin and soon began looking for ways to use TOC and Cynefin together. In 2010 he gave the first presentation on Cynefin to the TOCICO annual conference including Dr. Eli Goldratt, the creator of TOC. In 2019 he and Dave Snowden presented a workshop on using Cynefin and TOC together.

ABOUT THIS CHAPTER

 Full Chapter

 Theoretical

 Chronology: Piece 11 of 33

 Cynefin Principles

CYNEFIN AND THEORY OF CONSTRAINTS: ALLIES OR ADVERSARIES?

STEVE HOLT

This chapter compares and contrasts the Cynefin Framework and the Theory of Constraints. While both have their own development paths and differences, there is also alignment and complementarity.

The Cynefin Framework and the Theory of Constraints (TOC) are two philosophies intended to help people make sense of what is going on around them to increase the chances that they make decisions with favorable outcomes. The two were developed independently, and initially, practitioners of each had little or no exposure to the other. Their independent development meant the creation of separate terminology as well. Sometimes the terminology was the same, sometimes it was noticeably different, and sometimes it appeared to be the same, but was different. Over the last decade, as practitioners of each have learned more about the other, these real or imagined differences have sparked debates about whether TOC and Cynefin are aligned allies or adversaries.

Eli Goldratt, an Israeli business management guru, wrote that when two methods come in contact with each other their respective advocates seldom have much knowledge of the other and they tend to look for similarities. [1] But that leads to compromises in which neither has to address their own areas of validity and completeness. It's better, he maintained, to search for areas of disagreement and learn from the differences. In that vein, I will focus primarily on two areas of potential disconnect. One is around the use of the word "constraint" in both Cynefin and TOC and whether or not they are talking about the same thing. The second is whether Goldratt's belief that all systems have an Inherent Simplicity implies that there is no such thing as a Complex System. That would be in direct conflict with the Cynefin Framework.

SNOWDEN AND GOLDRATT: NATURE OR NURTURE?

The creator of the Cynefin Framework, Dave Snowden, and Eli Goldratt, creator of the Theory of Constraints, share several similarities. (Since Dave is still quite with us, while Goldratt is deceased, I will use the past tense, but know that Dave still quite enjoys every behavior I ascribe to him.) Both were physicist-philosophers and ran software companies. Remarkably, both used religion-based teaching stories to emphasize points and they enjoyed argument and debate. Both were natural procrastinators and had the drive to help people make sense of what was going on around them. Goldratt passed away in 2011 and never met Dave Snowden. If they would have met, I have no doubt that the conversation would have lasted for hours and alternated between bouts of total agreement and total disagreement. They would have both delighted in it, and it would have been an event worth buying tickets to.

A BRIEF OVERVIEW OF THE THEORY OF CONSTRAINTS

Eli Goldratt created the Theory of Constraints specifically to help improve the flow in production systems. Goldratt had earned a PhD in Nuclear Physics and was asked by a friend, who was having trouble meeting his production rate, to help a small manufacturing business. Goldratt realized that many of the concepts of flow he had studied academically applied to the flow of a factory, including the impact of features like bottlenecks. He started a production planning software company and wrote a book to market the software, knowing that his approach was counter-intuitive and not taught in business schools. His book, *The Goal*, was Goldratt's way to have potential customers conclude that the method would work for them. It is also how most people first encounter TOC. [2] [3]

Dozens of publishers rejected the book because the genre of "business novel" did not yet exist. Since its first printing in 1984, however, the book has been released in multiple editions and languages and is still very popular and highly ranked on Amazon.

Goldratt proposed that every system with a goal has a bottleneck, or constraint, that determines its output of "goal units." Therefore, improvements in the productivity of the constraint benefits the system. In contrast, "improvements" at non-constraint areas can be harmful for the system if they result in more work than the constraint can handle. Another frequent response to a bottleneck is to hire more people or buy more equipment at the bottleneck, but that can be expensive and time consuming and may not work.

Goldratt recommended a more effective approach to improve systems performance in the Five Focusing Steps. These provide a natural progression of improvements.

As written in the TOCICO Dictionary, V2 the Five Focusing Steps are: [4]

1. IDENTIFY the system's constraint(s).

2. Decide how to EXPLOIT the system's constraint(s).

3. SUBORDINATE everything else to the above decision.

4. ELEVATE the system's constraint(s).

5. WARNING! If in the previous steps a constraint has been broken, go back to step 1, but do not allow INERTIA to cause a system's constraint.

While a common non-TOC first step is to get more of the constraint, in the Five Focusing Steps this is the fourth step. Once you're identified the constraint, steps 2 and 3 typically yield significant improvements at far less cost and effort. The Five Focusing Steps can seem almost simplistic, but can be remarkably insightful.

Many businesses suffer from executives trying to optimize each part of a process, fueled by a fixation on cost-cutting. In traditional cost accounting both Work in Process and Finished Goods Inventory are counted as assets even though they may not be sales. That encourages managers to overproduce to make the numbers look good. Goldratt developed 'Throughput Accounting' to focus on revenue from sales as the key metric, not goods produced. At this point, TOC offers a generic solution for production planning (Drum-Buffer Rope) and finance and measures (Throughput Accounting). Over time, additional generic solutions have been added for analysis and problem solving (the Logical Thinking Process), project management (Critical Chain), supply chain (the Distribution Solution), and strategy (Ever Flourishing Company strategy).

Throughout this development, Goldratt followed an approach that he highlighted in one of his first books, *What is This Thing Called Theory of Constraints?* and in one of his last, *The Choice*. [5] Goldratt's approach was highly dependent on what he saw as the Scientific Method. It depended on using observation and intuition to be the source of hypotheses and then to derive experiments to test for predicted effects. These experiments either confirmed or disconfirmed the predicted effects, which determined whether the assumed cause existed and applied. Over time this creates not a sense of what is true but what is valid within a specific context. Goldratt made the point that truth is something you search for within a religion, while science searches for valid and useful things, even if they are not true.

Looking through a Cynefin lens, we would say that Goldratt used intuition and abductive reasoning to come up with coherent ideas to then test them with safe-to-fail probes. He started with observable negative effects – the UnDesirable Effects (UDEs) – and developed a hypothesis for what might cause them. When he felt confident in predicting what would happen, and why, the Logical Thinking Process logic trees would be used to describe the problem and the solution in terms of inductive and deductive logic. He hypothesized that the cause would also create other effects (inductive reasoning), and that starting with the cause and elements of reality, he could derive the effects (deductive reasoning). This led some to believe that the generic TOC solutions were developed from the logic trees. It's more likely, however, that the logic trees were created after the fact to document the approach and the assumptions behind why they worked.

Nevertheless, this has set up a lingering misperception among people who see the logic trees and assume that TOC is a means of defining the world in terms of linear, deterministic logic. When you read Goldratt's description of how he worked, it is clear that he followed a very Cynefin-like process; he started in the Confusion or Complex domains and ran a series of probes until he had a solid understanding of what was happening. He mostly started in Complex and moved into Complicated, at which point he shared what he had discovered in the form of Complicated domain artifacts.

CONSTRAINTS: HELPFUL OR HARMFUL?

In TOC, constraints are limiting factors that keep you from reaching your goal. The implication is that you want to reduce their impact or remove them. Consider this definition from the Theory of Constraints Dictionary V2:

"Constraint: The factor that ultimately limits the performance of a system or organization. That factor that, if the organization were able to increase it, more fully exploit it, or more effectively subordinate to it, would result in achieving more of the goal." [6]

Figure 1. Don't produce more than the system constraint can handle, it is wasteful

Readers of *The Goal* tend to remember the Boy Scout hike and Herbie, the slowest hiker. On the hike, Herbie was the constraint and the story involves coming up with ways to speed Herbie up. This reinforces the perception that constraints are a problem to be fixed.

Recent versions of the Cynefin Framework seem to present a different view. Consider how the word "constraint" shows up in four of the domains:

- The Clear domain has 'fixed constraints'

- The Complicated domain has 'governing constraints'

- The Complex domain has 'enabling constraints'

- The Chaotic domain has 'no effective constraints'

But are these the same or different principles than those ascribed by TOC? Well, it depends. It's essential to look at the types of constraints in Cynefin to answer the question.

A 'fixed constraint,' as found in the Clear domain, means that there is only one way to do something. You must do Step 1 before you can do Step 2. There is no alternative.

As found in the Complicated domain, a 'governing constraint' means that some specific rules or policies have been imposed on the system to guide what is allowed to be done and how. These frequently vary with context and there are often alternative approaches. For instance, in many countries people drive on the right... except when they pass another vehicle, or swerve to avoid something by driving on the left. There are often no physical barriers to keep them driving on the right, they just do so because that is the policy. That is a governing constraint. Similarly, a traffic signal is a governing constraint. A red light does not physically stop a car from preceding, but drivers are taught to stop and wait for it to turn green by policy.

An 'enabling constraint,' in the Complex domain, is a bit different. It is a limitation, but it enables emergent system behavior that would have otherwise not been possible. Alicia Juarrero in *Dynamics in Action: Intentional Behavior as a Complex System* mentions the way the human knee is constructed makes it unable to bend forward. [7] This is an enabling constraint because it is a limitation, but it also means that we have the necessary movement and control that makes walking and running much easier.

In the Chaotic domain saying that there is 'no effective constraint' means that we cannot perceive any causal relationship between local cause and system effect. We don't know how to influence the system and attempts are essentially random guesses.

Fixed and governing constraints are clearly on the Ordered side of the Cynefin Framework. They are known and defined. Enabling constraints are on the Unordered side of the Cynefin Framework and will result in emergent behavior which is not predictable by analysis, it must be discovered by experimentation.

If we compare TOC and Cynefin versions of constraints, we see that the TOC definition of a constraint is most closely aligned with Cynefin's fixed and governing constraints. Where things get interesting is when we look at enabling constraints. TOC does have the concept of applying a limiting factor to improve system performance but does not call it, or even think of it, as a constraint. In TOC these are referred to as 'Injections' and they are the actions taken to improve system performance. This may include actions to remove constraints seen as limiting.

In his earlier writings, Goldratt also described a 'policy constraint,' a rule or policy that blocked a system from reaching its goal. These rules were likely put in place at a time when they provided real value, but over time they became limitations to system performance, and over constrained a system making things worse.

Examples might include a rule requiring employees to get senior executive approval to spend more than $25 in expenses, or a laborious process to order software. TOC's policy constraints are fully aligned with Cynefin's concept of a governing constraint. I conclude that TOC and Cynefin are in agreement when it comes to constraints, but do not use the same terms in their respective explanations.

POTENTIAL DISAGREEMENT: INHERENT COMPLEXITY OR INHERENT SIMPLICITY?

Perhaps the greatest potential for confusion in comparing TOC and Cynefin is reconciling the existence of Complex Adaptive Systems attached to the Cynefin Complex domain with a concept that Goldratt called 'Inherent Simplicity.' In *The Choice* he said:

"The key for thinking like a true scientist is the acceptance that any real-life situation, no matter how complex it initially looks, is actually, once understood, embarrassingly simple." [8]

That assumption is formalized in the TOCICO Dictionary, V2 as:

Inherent Simplicity: "The concept that nature is simple and harmonious in itself." [9]

This is derived from a line by Isaac Newton frequently quoted by Goldratt which forms the underlying assumption behind Inherent Simplicity:

"Natura valde simplex est et sibi consona." "Nature is exceedingly simple and harmonious in itself." [10]

Goldratt builds on this to conclude that any system, no matter how complex, has an inherent simplicity at its heart. Therefore, improving the system relies on finding that inherent simplicity.

This conclusion is ripe for misinterpretation. I've recently heard this idea used as "proof" that Goldratt denied the existence of Complex Adaptive Systems. Certainly, from a Cynefin standpoint it appears that what he is saying is that what you perceive as a Complex domain situation will be transformed into a Clear domain situation as soon as you find the Inherent Simplicity. That sounds suspiciously like searching for the Philosopher's Stone or a sort of epiphany, or enlightenment.

The reality, however, is actually very much aligned with a Cynefin view of the world. When Goldratt talked about his approach to solving problems in *What is this Thing Called TOC?* [11] and *The Choice*, it's clear that he used abductive reasoning to solve problems, and that's what TOC teaches. [12]

A TOC practitioner starts with observed issues or concerns or symptoms, referred to in TOC as UnDesirable Effects or UDEs. He or she then works backward to identify a causal element or, more recently, a causal conflict, which if present, would cause the UDEs. In the Logical Thinking Process this is referred to as a Current Reality Tree (CRT). Like some of the other Thinking Process methods, the CRT builds on a set of logical tests called the Categories of Legitimate Reservation or CLRs. The CLRs provide the logic tests that the effects exist and that there aren't other causes that would create the same UDEs. Most importantly, it sets the stage to test and see if any other predicted effects are present. If any other effects are predictable from the cause, but are not present, then there must be another cause behind them and not the one hypothesized.

Next the TOC practitioner identifies potential actions, referred to in TOC as injections, that will begin to remove or mitigate the cause identified at the base of the CRT. A similar trail of effect-cause-effect logical relationships is then built and additional injections added, as necessary, to show how the injections can remove the UnDesirable Effects and replace them with Desirable Effects (DEs). That is how the overall system can be improved.

From a Cynefin standpoint, what Goldratt is referring to as Inherent Simplicity, is what happens when you are in a Complex domain situation: you develop a series of coherent safe-to-fail probes, consider the results, possibly run additional, more focused probes and eventually develop sufficient understanding of what's going on to find yourself in the Complicated domain. What had initially appeared to be complex and unpredictable is now controllable. Note that this progression in the TOC approach is consistent with the idea of Cynefin dynamics, in which our perceptions of the domain we are in can change based on our actions.

In terms of creating a practical manifestation of Inherent Simplicity, it's interesting to consider another Newton quote. Newton was the brunt of significant criticism after releasing his Laws of Motion since he did not attempt to explain what gravity was, only how its effects could be calculated. As a response to the criticism, Newton wrote:

"Hypotheses non fingo." [13] Translation: "I feign (or, suggest) no hypotheses."

Newton is saying that his equations explain the observed behavior and, therefore, they are useful, even if no one knows the mechanism by which they work. This is, I believe, very much what Goldratt means by Inherent Simplicity. He's saying that the system may well have a significant amount of Complex domain characteristics, and finding the Inherent Simplicity is finding a heuristic or assumption that enables the overall system to be managed comparatively easily.

That said, we need to remember that Goldratt focused on solving problems primarily in the business world. That is, areas that tend to be either closed form systems or at least have clear bounding conditions. Laws that define how we treat employees and customers, how accounting should work, and even principles of business ethics, mean that those aspects of organizations TOC practitioners look at, are seldom in the domain of so-called, Wicked Problems – problems that cannot be solved by logic or reasoning alone. [14] That said, I believe that TOC could indeed help deal with Wicked Problems.

CONCLUSION

I conclude that Cynefin and TOC are very much aligned, very consistent, and each can help the other. The Cynefin Framework is a sense-making approach that enables you to make sense of what is happening and come up with an idea for an appropriate solution. TOC offers another means of making sense of what is happening by observing and then providing guidance on what might be happening and, most importantly, how to design and assess real or simulated tests to check your assumptions. This provides a means to help the user improve the system and creates a map of the transformation that can be used to explain what happened and why. TOC's Logic Trees provide the means to capture the theory behind the method so that it can be compared to context, and one can check for either applicability or the need for change. This gives Cynefin practitioners a means to not just understand what is happening, but also a tool kit for moving the system forward in more beneficial directions.

Cynefin provides a valuable critical thinking check for TOC practitioners. For example, TOC Generic Solutions for production, project management, distribution, etc. are so well understood, and so widely applicable, that TOC practitioners can frequently conclude that they know what to do after a relatively cursory review of an organization. This 'pattern entrainment' can lead to complacency. Furthermore, when a company leader hears a TOC practitioner claim, after limited research, that they fully understand the company's issues and know what to do, it can appear that the TOC practitioner is a classic aggressive consultant who claims to know what to do, but really doesn't. Insead, the TOC practitioner can use the Cynefin Framework to check their own understanding, and help the client understand what is happening, and why this approach will work.

I see TOC and Cynefin as not just allies, but catalytic allies. Each can benefit the other and I strongly encourage the use of both.

References:

1. Goldratt, Eliyahu. "What is this thing called Theory of Constraints and how should it be implemented?" North River Press, 1990.

2. Goldratt, Eliyahu. "The Goal" North River Press, 1984.

3. For an overview, there is a chapter by chapter summary available at https://www.tocinstitute.org/the-goal-summary.html

4. Cox III, James F., Lynn H. Boyd, Timothy T. Sullivan, Richard A. Reid, and Brad Cartier, 2012, The Theory of Constraints International Certification Organization Dictionary, Second Edition. https://www.tocico.org/resource/resmgr/dictionary/tocico_dictionary_2nd_editio.pdf

5. Goldratt, Eliyahu and Efrat Goldratt-Ashlag, "The Choice: Revised Edition" North River Press, 2010.

6. Cox III, James F., Lynn H. Boyd, Timothy T. Sullivan, Richard A. Reid, and Brad Cartier, 2012, The Theory of Constraints International Certification Organization Dictionary, Second Edition. https://www.tocico.org/resource/resmgr/dictionary/tocico_dictionary_2nd_editio.pdf, p.28

7. Juarrero, A. (1999). "Dynamics in action: intentional behavior as a complex system. Cambridge, Mass," London: MIT Press.

8. Goldratt, Eliyahu and Efrat Goldratt-Ashlag, "The Choice: Revised Edition" North River Press, 2010. p.9

9. Cox III, James F., Lynn H. Boyd, Timothy T. Sullivan, Richard A. Reid, and Brad Cartier, 2012, The Theory of Constraints International Certification Organization Dictionary, Second Edition. https://www.tocico.org/resource/resmgr/dictionary/tocico_dictionary_2nd_editio.pdf, p.66

10. Newton, Isaac "Unpublished Scientific Papers of Isaac Newton: A selection from the Portsmouth Collection in the University Library, Cambridge," 1978, p.35

11. Goldratt, Eliyahu. "What is this thing called Theory of Constraints and how should it be implemented?" North River Press, 1990.

12. Goldratt, Eliyahu and Efrat Goldratt-Ashlag, "The Choice: Revised Edition" North River Press, 2010.

13. Newton, Isaac "General Scholium" appended to 2nd Edition of the Principia https://en.wikipedia.org/wiki/Hypotheses_non_fingo

14. Wicked Problems https://en.wikipedia.org/wiki/Wicked_problem

What to read next

 Next Full Chapter: The U.S. Navy's Combat Information Center: Rapid Success..., Trent Hone, p.185

 Next Chronological: Embodied Cynefin: Teaching with the Body, Chris Corrigan, p.128

 Next Theoretical: The U.S. Navy's Combat Information Center: Rapid Success..., Trent Hone, p.185

 More on Cynefin Principle 1: It Doesn't Get Happy; it Doesn't Get Sad, Liz Keogh, p.217

 More on Cynefin Principle 3.2: The U.S. Navy's Combat Information Center: Rapid Success..., Trent Hone, p.185

THE U.S. NAVY'S COMBAT INFORMATION CENTER: RAPID SUCCESS WITH PARALLEL EXPERIMENTATION

TRENT HONE

ABOUT THE AUTHOR

Trent Hone is a Fellow with Excella in Arlington, VA, and an award-winning naval historian. His work is fueled by an interest in organizational learning and operational effectiveness. He consults with organizations to improve their art of practice, accelerate learning, and innovate more effectively. Trent regularly writes and speaks about organizational learning, strategy, and innovation. Trent's latest book, *Learning War: The Evolution of Fighting Doctrine in the U.S. Navy, 1898–1945*, brings a new and valuable perspective that explains how the Navy harnessed learning mechanisms to accelerate victory. It was the U.S. Naval Institute's Book of the Year for 2018.

ABOUT THIS CHAPTER

 Full Chapter

 Chronology: Piece 24 of 33

 Theoretical

 Cynefin Principles

THE U.S. NAVY'S COMBAT INFORMATION CENTER: RAPID SUCCESS WITH PARALLEL EXPERIMENTATION

TRENT HONE

This chapter briefly reviews the history of the U.S. Navy's Combat Information Center (CIC) and illustrates how Cynefin's recommended approaches can foster new and innovative methods.

INTRODUCTION

For many leaders, Cynefin's recommended approach for dealing with complex challenges is not intuitive. Using parallel, safe-to-fail experiments, and enabling constraints, to foster the emergence of exaptive practices, can be difficult to grasp. Questions immediately come to mind:

- What is safe-to-fail experimentation?
- What is an enabling constraint?
- What does it mean to use exaptive practices?

Example stories illustrating how leaders have successfully used these approaches in the past can help make sense of Cynefin's recommendations with increased clarity.

The introduction of the U.S. Navy's Combat Information Center (CIC) during World War II is an excellent example of an approach that parallels Cynefin's recommended techniques. Although the CIC predates Cynefin by several decades, the story of its origins helps us understand how Cynefin can be applied to overcome a complex challenge. Such challenges require decentralized, non-linear solutions.

The best approach(es) cannot be determined by analysis and investigation. Instead, what's required is engaging with the issue through experimentation and trial. Effective approaches emerge most quickly if experimentation is done in parallel, with multiple hypotheses being tested simultaneously. The results of these experiments will create a better understanding of possibilities and foster the emergence of coherent solutions.

FRAMING THE PROBLEM

The U.S. Navy entered World War II with two new technologies that appeared to offer a crucial advantage. One was radar, which gave the remarkable ability to detect approaching ships and planes. The other, very high frequency (VHF) radio, that allowed ships to communicate with each other in real-time without giving their position away. In theory, these two technologies would permit senior naval officers to rapidly develop situational awareness in combat situations and coordinate the ships under their command with unprecedented clarity. The advantages would be significant in daylight battles; at night, they were expected to be transformational. Unlike trained lookouts, radar could "see" in the dark.

In actual combat, these advantages proved elusive. When Allied forces invaded the island of Guadalcanal in the Solomon Islands in August 1942, they seized its airfield and triggered a lengthy attritional campaign. Possession of the airfield gave the Allies local aerial superiority. To avoid attacks from Allied planes, ships of the Imperial Japanese Navy (IJN) came to the island at night. They regularly landed troops and supplies, shelled the airfield and its defenders, and fought to regain control of the island and its airfield. Five major night battles took place during the campaign. From the start, they illustrated the flaws in the U.S. Navy's prewar expectations.

Rather than unlocking a new, transformational capability, the technologies made things worse. Radar signals reflected off nearby islands made it challenging to separate enemy ships from background echoes. Once a potential target was found, the captain had to choose whether to track it closely, or to continue scanning it to maintain more general situational awareness; early radars could not do both at the same time. Rather than clarifying the situation, VHF radio added to the confusion. Ship captains reported radar contacts to each other; task force commanders asked for clarification and regular updates. Radio circuits became so busy with this traffic that vital orders were lost or delayed, adding to the confusion. This prevented task force commanders from coordinating their forces in real-time.

In hindsight, the results were predictable, and the opposite of expectations. Radio and radar inundated ship captains and task force commanders with unprecedented levels of information. They were expected to absorb it all, assess it, understand its implications, and take decisive action. Instead, they were becoming increasingly confused and disoriented. Command functions broke down. Task forces intended to fight as coherent teams became individual ships struggling to survive in chaotic melees. Friendly fire wrecked several ships; enemy action destroyed many more. Samuel Eliot Morison, who wrote the history of U.S. naval operations in World War II, ably described the confusing nature of the fighting:

"A literally infernal scene presented itself to the participants. The struggle had deteriorated into a wild and desperate melee. The greenish light of suspended star shell dimmed the stars overhead. Elongated red and white trails of shell tracers arched and crisscrossed, magazines exploded in blinding bouquets of white flame, oil-fed conflagrations sent up twisted yellow columns. Dotting the horizon were the dull red glows of smoldering hulls, now obscured by dense masses of smoke, now blazing up when uncontrolled fires reached new combustibles. The sea itself, fouled with oil and flotsam, tortured by underwater upheavals, rose in geysers from shell explosions." [1]

A better approach was needed. From the headquarters at Pearl Harbor, the Pacific Fleet's commander, Admiral Chester W. Nimitz, and his staff assessed action reports to understand why the U.S. Navy's investment in technology was not delivering the expected results. A review of the action reports revealed that ship captains and task force commanders could not make sense of the information available to them fast enough. The information was there; it was available, but officers were unable to use it effectively.

FOSTERING EXPERIMENTATION

Nimitz was an experienced commander who had a reputation for fostering the initiative of his subordinates. That was not a unique skill for U.S. Navy officers of the era, but Nimitz was particularly effective. He had demonstrated this aptitude regularly before the war as the commanding officer of cruiser U.S.S. Augusta (CA-31) and head of the Navy's Bureau of Navigation. While Nimitz served at the Bureau of Navigation, President Franklin D. Roosevelt became familiar with his talents. After the attack on Pearl Harbor, Roosevelt chose Nimitz to lead the Pacific Fleet.

Nimitz suspected the problem in the night battles was "orientation," which John Boyd argued was the "center of gravity for command and control" of military units in combat. Task force commanders and commanding officers failed to make sense of all available information and were unable to use it to their advantage.

To address the problem, Nimitz turned to an approach that the Navy had consistently used in peacetime to successfully foster innovation. Crucially, Nimitz chose this method in the middle of a war when delays might be very costly. The approach used the following steps: [2]

- Frame the problem or challenge

- Establish the constraints

- Encourage parallel experimentation

- Exploit the best-fitting solution that emerges

The challenge had already been identified. Nimitz needed to frame it appropriately and then establish one or more constraints that would encourage a series of parallel experiments. He hypothesized that new structures were needed aboard each ship to process information more effectively. Nimitz was unsure what form these new structures should take or how best to organize them, but he decided not to try to figure that out. Instead, he allowed different solutions to emerge through experimentation.

Nimitz initiated the process of parallel experimentation on November 26, 1942, when he issued a new set of instructions. He ordered each ship of the fleet to create a new shipboard organizational structure. Nimitz framed the problem by stating, "Maximum combat efficiency by individual ships and task organizations can best be attained through full utilization of all available sources of combat intelligence. In this, radar shall be used to the maximum effectiveness." [3] To do that, each ship would establish "a center, in which information from all available sources can be received, assimilated, and evaluated." [4] That center was the CIC. The order to establish one was the enabling constraint.

Figure 1. Combat Information Centers (CiCs) as an enabling constraint.

Nimitz fostered his subordinates' creativity by specifying what the CIC was expected to do while providing virtually no details about how to do it. Each CIC would maintain a master plot of all available information, evaluate it, quickly make sense of it, and share the understanding gained with the ship's captain and its weapons systems. [5] These open-ended instructions left ship and task force commanders free to experiment. The order to establish a CIC was an enabling constraint because it allowed a great deal of contextual sensitivity. Ship captains could organize their CICs however they felt best; feedback rapidly allowed them to see if their experiment was heading in the right direction.

Three distinct feedback loops provided valuable information about the effectiveness of different CIC techniques.

- Combat was arguably the most crucial feedback loop. As the Allied offensive in the Solomon Islands moved past Guadalcanal, the Imperial Japanese Navy continued to fight aggressively. In a series of night battles in and around Kula Gulf in mid-1943, the U.S. Navy learned valuable lessons about the limitations of existing CIC organizations.

- Informal collaborative networks were critical. When ships returned to port, crews shared their experiences and lessons in conferences that had "great value." They learned from each other and spread the most effective techniques through stories they told about their experiences. [6]

- The Pacific Fleet managed the third feedback loop. Nimitz was committed to identifying the most effective techniques and harnessing them for future exploitation. Regular action reports allowed Nimitz and his staff to review the fleet's work and identify the most effective solutions. They periodically brought the officers responsible for them back to Pearl Harbor to codify the most effective techniques. [7]

Early experiments, focused by these feedback loops, led to the emergence of contextually sensitive approaches. One of the most important was a variation based on ship type. Aboard destroyers, the smallest and most nimble ships of the fleet, the executive officer generally assumed responsibility for organizing and running the ship's CIC. [8] Battleships needed a different approach. On battleships, the executive officer already had a specific and well-defined role; he manned the secondary conning station, ready to assume command in case of damage to the primary. A different officer had to be chosen, and because battleships relied on their heavy guns, it was usually someone from within the gunnery department. [9] This flexibility and contextual sensitivity would not have emerged if Nimitz had issued a more prescriptive "solution" to his captains.

Even though this experimentation took place in the middle of a war, and was tested in combat, it is still appropriate to frame it as 'safe-to-fail.' The entire fleet urgently needed improved mechanisms for managing information. The goal was to learn rapidly and develop the best set of techniques. If some ships tried less effective approaches, that would quickly be demonstrated by their performance.

In the months after Nimitz's instructions, many ships suffered from problems like those observed off Guadalcanal. Their ability to manage radar information improved, but was still insufficient because of failure to maintain effective plots, inadequate communication procedures, or interference by commanding officers who felt they knew better. However, other ships showed more promise, and their approaches were the ones that Nimitz and his subordinates began to amplify and exploit. [10] Parallel, 'safe-to-fail' experimentation – as Cynefin recommends – allowed rapid exploration of the available possibilities; failure of some was acceptable if it accelerated the rate of learning, and it did.

The CIC relied on exaptive practice because Nimitz stressed using an existing technique – plotting – in new ways. Plots had been used effectively in the U.S. Navy for decades and were already familiar to ships' officers and crews, but they tended to operate in isolation. In CICs, multiple plots were integrated, allowing the emergence of vastly increased situational awareness. As a 1943 manual stated, the CIC was not "merely a radar plot... under a new name." Instead, it was an "agency for the collection, evaluation, and distribution of combat information." [11]

Plots provided a virtual, top-down view of all contacts' current and past positions, friendly or enemy. CIC Officers could rapidly integrate the visual information displayed on these plots and make sense of it in real-time. Plots became the "brain" of the most effective CICs. Crews used them to develop a clear "picture" of the situation around them and offer it to the captain and other command functions clearly and directly.

A NEW SOLUTION EMERGES

During 1943, as experimentation continued, Nimitz and his staff remained focused on the functions of the CIC and its role as "an information station." However, ship captains and their CIC teams were starting to explore how the CIC could augment naval commanders' cognitive capabilities. [12] Their work moved the CIC beyond an information system and transformed it into a system of distributed cognition.

The most effective argument for broadening the responsibility of the CIC came from combat experience. During a nocturnal aerial attack, a rapid response was essential. In many situations, there was no time to alert the commanding officer to the danger and have him order the antiaircraft guns to fire. Ships that did so often opened fire too late to fight off the attack. Others experimented with an approach where the commanding officer was "on the loop" rather than "in the loop." If an attack was anticipated, the CIC could order the guns to fire as soon as it was detected. This broadened the CIC's responsibilities and allowed it to assume command functions, but it also maximized the opportunity to thwart an attack. Lessons like these made it apparent that the CIC had an essential role in clarifying and simplifying the work of command. [13]

Ultimately, the CIC became a system of distributed cognition fully integrated with the ship's command functions. The work of making sense of available information was divided up among different roles that distributed the cognitive load, and allowed rapid assessment, analysis, and synthesis of incoming information using visual plots as a symbolic information system. Some typical roles were:

- Radar Operator, who observed the radar display.

- Plot Recorder, who made sense of the information provided by the Radar Operator.

- Plotter, who recorded information specified by the Plot Recorder.

- Radio Recorder, who monitored radio traffic and recorded its details.

- Evaluator, who assessed all available information and synthesized it.

- CIC Talker, who communicated the Evaluator's assessment to the captain and other command functions.

Nimitz's instructions provided an enabling constraint that initiated a series of parallel, 'safe-to-fail' experiments using exaptive practice. By framing the problem and specifying desired outcomes – but resisting the urge to impose a solution – Nimitz allowed his subordinates to explore a broad range of possibilities. The result was a transformative capability that exceeded initial expectations. As the CIC helped commanding officers make sense of the world around them, Guadalcanal's confused melees gradually gave way to more coordinated and collaborative operations. When the CIC expanded and became more tightly integrated with command functions, it unlocked its full potential as a system of distributed cognition. Once that occurred, the CIC gave the U.S. Navy an unprecedented ability to manage information, fully capitalize on the potential of new technologies, and maintain situational awareness. The result was a new approach to combat that vastly exceeded earlier capabilities.

CONCLUSION

The U.S. Navy's CIC is an excellent example of how to address a complex challenge using Cynefin's recommended approaches. Nimitz's effective use of parallel, 'safe-to-fail' experimentation, exaptive practice, and enabling constraints unlocked his subordinates' creativity. They quickly arrived at new, unanticipated solutions to managing shipboard information.

Nimitz deliberately avoided imposing a solution and instead concentrated on creating the conditions for a solution to emerge. He provided a direction and then used regular feedback loops to amplify effective approaches and dampen less useful ones. This ensured continued evolution beyond the originally desired outcome so that, as more experience was gained, new opportunities emerged. Ultimately, the CIC merged with ships' command functions, allowing faster sense-making and more rapid responses to threatening situations. This development was unanticipated but welcomed. It would never have occurred if Nimitz and his staff had imposed a preconceived solution.

Leaders who face similar challenges can learn much from Nimitz's example. When confronting complex problems, they must eschew the urge to rapidly identify a solution and impose it upon their subordinates. Instead, they should establish an effective constraint – one that focuses on effort and attention on the desired outcome – and use it to prompt the creativity and initiative of their subordinates. Once coherent approaches begin to emerge, they can use contextually sensitive feedback loops to refine initial ideas and create viable solutions. This will rapidly identify new techniques, allow them to be improved, and ensure that they fit prevailing circumstances. Many will likely exceed initial expectations fostering new ·innovations and sometimes remarkable new systems.

References

1. Samuel Eliot Morison, History of the United States Naval Operations in World War II, (Reprint: Boston: Little, Brown, 1984), V:250.

2. Trent Hone, Learning War: The Evolution of Fighting Doctrine in the U.S. Navy, 1898-1945, (Annapolis, MD: U.S. Naval Institute Press, 2018), pp.337-38.

3. Pacific Fleet Tactical Bulletin No. 4TB-42, Commander in Chief, U.S. Pacific Fleet, 26 November 1942.

4. Pacific Fleet Tactical Bulletin No. 4TB-42, Commander in Chief, U.S. Pacific Fleet, 26 November 1942.

5. Pacific Fleet Tactical Bulletin No. 4TB-42, Commander in Chief, U.S. Pacific Fleet, 26 November 1942.

6. "Action Report for Night of August 6-7, 1943 - Battle of Vella Gulf," Commander Destroyer Squadron Twelve, 16 August 1943; Hone, Learning War, p.248.

7. One of the most notable was Lieutenant Commander Joseph C. Wylie, who had developed one of the first effective CICs while Executive Officer of destroyer Fletcher.

8. "CIC Handbook for Destroyers Pacific Fleet," Commander Destroyers, Pacific Fleet, 24 June 1943.

9. "Tentative Radar Doctrine and CIC Instructions, Battleships, Pacific Fleet," Commander Battleships, U.S. Pacific Fleet, 5 June 1944.

10. One of the most famous experiments occurred on destroyer Fletcher, when the executive officer, Lieutenant Commander Joseph C. Wylie, helped his captain, Commander William R. Cole, navigate their ship through a furious battle unscathed.

11. "CIC Handbook for Destroyers Pacific Fleet," Commander Destroyers, Pacific Fleet, 24 June 1943.

12. Timothy S. Wolters, Information at Sea: Shipboard Command and Control in the U.S. Navy, from Mobile Bay to Okinawa, (Baltimore, MD: Johns Hopkins University Press, 2013), p.208.

13. "CIC Handbook for Destroyers Pacific Fleet," Commander Destroyers, Pacific Fleet, 24 June 1943.

14. Norman Friedman, Network Centric Warfare: How Navies Learned to Fight Smarter Through Three World Wars, (Annapolis, MD: U.S. Naval Institute Press, 2009), p.60.

What to read next

 Next Full Chapter: It Doesn't Get Happy; it Doesn't Get Sad, Liz Keogh, p.196

 Next Chronological: In Pursuit of a Mastery of Risk..., Robert Koch, p.242

 Next Theoretical: Learning with Cynefin, Harold Jarche, p.196

 More on Cynefin Principle 3.1: Coming of Age: From Frameworks..., Ann Pendleton-Jullian, p.279

 More on Cynefin Principle 3.2: Cynefin's Influence on The Flow System, John R. Turner..., p.320

LEARNING WITH CYNEFIN

HAROLD JARCHE

ABOUT THE AUTHOR

A graduate of the Royal Military College, Harold Jarche served over 20 years with the Canadian Armed Forces in leadership and training roles. Harold began his career as an officer with Princess Patricia's Canadian Light Infantry. He completed his service as a Training Development Officer with the Royal Canadian Air Force, where he conducted the analysis and design of training for aircrew and technicians on the newly purchased CH-146 helicopter. Harold works with individuals, organizations, and public policy influencers to develop practical ways to improve collaboration, knowledge sharing, and sense-making. He helps his clients deal with an increasingly complex networked world, and considers social networks and communities of practice, essential components of all our workplaces.

ABOUT THIS CHAPTER

 Vignette   Theoretical

 Chronology: Piece 13 of 33

LEARNING WITH CYNEFIN

HAROLD JARCHE

This is a retrospective on how my work has been influenced by the Cynefin Framework, which I first came across in late 2007, many years after it had been originally published in 1999. It's interesting to note that this was the same year as The Cluetrain Manifesto, which shifted how we think about markets in light of the internet.

"Networked markets are beginning to self-organize faster than the companies that have traditionally served them. Thanks to the web, markets are becoming better informed, smarter, and more demanding of qualities missing from most business organizations." [1]

The Cynefin Framework has had a similar effect as the Cluetrain Manifesto. It has helped us to see that much of our world is not a complicated piece of machinery, but rather an entanglement of complex adaptive systems. From the perspective of Cynefin, I could see that there is no single best way to address our pressing business, societal, or environmental issues, which continue to get more complex, and even chaotic.

The majority of our challenges are not Obvious or Clear, addressed with 'best practice,' as Frederick Winslow Taylor prescribed with his Principles of Scientific Management. [2] Nor are they merely Complicated, addressed by 'good practice.' More of our issues are Complex, addressed through 'emergent practice,' and Chaotic, addressed by 'novel practice.' In 1911 Taylor saw standardization as an improvement on existing ad hoc work methods.

"It is only through enforced standardization of methods, enforced adoption of the best implements and working conditions, and enforced cooperation that this faster work can be assured. And the duty of enforcing the adoption of standards and enforcing this cooperation rests with management alone." - F.W. Taylor

Influenced by Cynefin, I looked for a principle that would reflect work that is more and more focused on dealing with complex challenges. Using Taylor's own format, I developed the principle of network management that – it is only through innovative and contextual methods, the self-selection of the most appropriate tools and work conditions, and willing cooperation, that more creative work can be fostered. The duty of being transparent in our work rests with all workers, especially management.

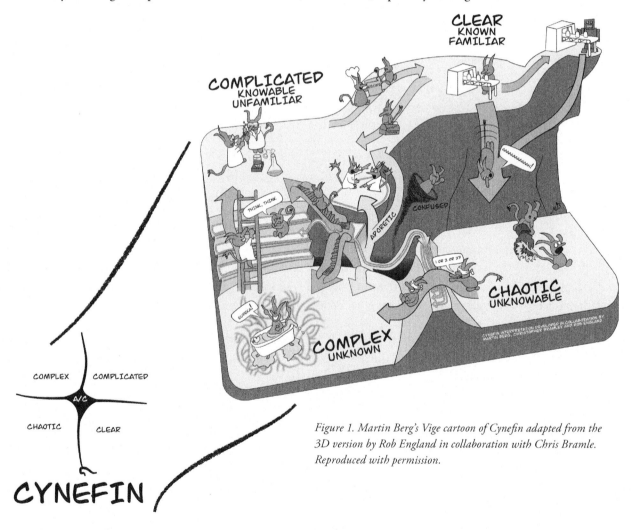

Figure 1. Martin Berg's Vige cartoon of Cynefin adapted from the 3D version by Rob England in collaboration with Chris Bramle. Reproduced with permission.

Cynefin can help us connect work and learning, especially for emergent and novel practices, for which we do not have good or best practices known in advance. When we want to create a conducive learning environment for knowledge workers, the Cynefin Framework helps us to see the inherent weakness of instructional systems design (ISD), which works from the premise of predetermined learning objectives and activities, usually based on good and best practices observed in the workplace.

Instead, we need a learning design model that helps to template 'desirable patterns', recognize 'undesirable patterns,' and provide a variety of 'seeds' for the complexity of the learning environment. Any learning intervention involving several people is arguably in a complex environment, and needs to also allow for emergence. One aspect of complex environments, according to the Cynefin Framework, is that "Cause and effect are only coherent in retrospect and do not repeat." That is also true for most working environments today.

When no one can understand the vagaries of a situation in a changing, complex environment, then the only thing to do is to try out new things based on our best judgment, and then watch, learn, and keep trying new practices. There are few universal 'best practices' or even 'good practices' outside simple or automated processes. There are things that work for some people some of the time. As learning professionals, our job is to understand our organization or client's situation, and look outside to see what others are doing. We have to try things out and see how they work. If we wait for the best practices, we will be too late. This is life in perpetual beta.

A NEW TYPE OF TRAINING DEPARTMENT

Informed by Cynefin, I have made several recommendations for a new type of training department. One of the ways we have addressed simple and complicated problems has been through training. Training works well when we have clear and measurable objectives. However, there are no clear objectives with complex problems. Learning as we probe the problem, we gain insight, and our practices are emergent (emerging from our interaction with the changing environment and the problem). Training looks backwards, at what worked in the past, and creates a controlled environment to develop knowledge and skills.

To deal with increasing Complexity, executives need to support emergent work practices, in addition to allow for training efforts. They must support collaboration, communication, synthesis, pattern recognition, and creative tension, all within a trusting environment to be effective. One method of supporting emergent work is the fostering of communities of practice.

Here are some specific practices for those who lead HR, learning and development, or organizational community efforts.

- Be an active and continuous learner and engage in activities that take you out of your comfort zone so that you know what it's like to be a learner.

- Be a lurker, or a passive participant, in relevant work-related communities (this could be the lunchroom) and listen to what is being said.

- Communicate what you observe to people around you, solicit their feedback, and engage in meaningful conversations.

- Continuously collect feedback from people in the workplace, not just after courses.

- Make it easy to share information by simplifying and synthesizing issues that are important and relevant to fellow workers.

RE-THINKING ACCOUNTABILITY

I also came across articles that Glenda Eoyang wrote as a guest blogger on the Cognitive Edge site, discussing three types of accountability, depending on the stability of the environment. [3]

1. Stable systems > Outcome-based accountability

2. Active, self-organizing systems > Learning-based accountability

3. Random & chaotic systems > Sharing-based accountability

Many of our HR and business practices still work from the assumption that they apply to a stable work environment. But as events from floods and wildfires, to a global pandemic have shown, this is no longer the dominant situation. Some of the project-based work I have done uses learning-based accountability, where we are all responsible for helping the rest of the team learn.

For freelancers and others who live and work on the Web, this becomes a natural way to work. The same can be said for sharing-based accountability, especially among bloggers and others who share online. We have learned that the more you give, the more you get back in the form of feedback and more learning opportunities.

I have wondered out loud, if leaders in an organization are only focused on outcome-based accountability, can they thrive in more active or random environments? Already in 2007, it seemed that most market and socio-economic structures were becoming more random and chaotic. This trend has continued. Reframing the concept of accountability remains an important conversation to start with HR professionals and executives.

CONCLUSIONS

Here are some of my conclusions about complexity, learning, and work developed over the past decade.

- Networks – Our workplaces, economies, and societies are becoming highly networked. That means the transmission of ideas can be instantaneous. There is no time to pause, go into the backroom and develop something to address our challenges. The problem will have changed by then.

- Life in perpetual beta – Not just rapid change, but continual change, requires practices that evolve as they develop. In programming, this has meant a move from waterfall to agile methods. Beta releases are the norm for Web applications, and as we do more on the Web, other practices are sure to follow.

- Complexity – The Cynefin Framework shows that established practices work when the environment or the challenge is simple or complicated. For complex problems, there are no established answers, and we need to engage the problem and learn by probing. This requires an entirely different mindset than training for defined problems and measurable outcomes. The integration of learning and work is not some ideal, it is a necessity in a complex world.

- Networked digital platforms – They give us a better way to engage in collaborative work and help us integrate learning into our daily practice. One such sense-making framework is personal knowledge mastery – a set of processes, individually constructed, to help each of us make sense of our world and work more effectively. PKM keeps us afloat in a sea of information, guided by professional communities and buoyed by social networks.

- Learning – Given our complex and chaotic challenges, the only way to operate as knowledge professionals in an organizational context is where work is learning, and learning is the work. The Cynefin Framework can help us navigate how to approach the nature of our work challenges across the domains that it so neatly describes. It lets us see more clearly so that we can focus our sense-making and knowledge-sharing as we work.

References:

1. https://cluetrain.com/
2. https://en.wikipedia.org/wiki/The_Principles_of_Scientific_Management
3. https://www.cognitive-edge.com/blog/so-what-about-accountability/

What to read next

 Next Vignette: Welcome to the Cynefinogi (The People of Cynefin), Iwan Jenkins, p.203

 Next Chronological: A Cynefin Approach to Leading Safety in Organizations, Gary Wong..., p.357

 Next Theoretical: It Doesn't Get Happy; it Doesn't Get Sad, Liz Keogh, p.217

WELCOME TO THE CYNEFINOGI
(THE PEOPLE OF CYNEFIN)

IWAN JENKINS

ABOUT THE AUTHOR

Dr. Iwan Jenkins is a strategy and leadership consultant focused on the manufacturing and technology sector. His aim is to propel business performance, drive up the capability of employees, and reduce organizational stress. He did this successfully for fifteen years with two global manufacturing companies. In the past twenty years he has helped others be successful through his own consultancy company, The Riot Point Research Corporation. Iwan is a 'sleeve's rolled' consultant. Everything is practical and pragmatic and geared to immediate results, but he's also not frightened of theory and research. Iwan has a PhD in Physical Chemistry, has taught at leading business schools, and published papers in Organizational Psychology publications.

ABOUT THIS CHAPTER

 Vignette   Narrative

 Chronology: Piece 9 of 33

WELCOME TO THE CYNEFINOGI
(THE PEOPLE OF CYNEFIN)

IWAN JENKINS

I am a Welshman, and I come to sing the praises of a Living National Treasure.

Ask the world to list Welsh people of note and their answers will include Tom Jones, Catherine Zeta-Jones, Anthony Hopkins, and/or Michael Sheen. Perhaps, at a push, their responses might extend to Dylan Thomas. The name Dave Snowden, however, is unlikely to appear. Shame! Thus, perhaps, I should refer to Dave as our 'hidden' National Treasure.

But while Dave might fly below the radar in the minds of the general public, the influence of his work has been profound. None more so than the Cynefin Framework. Singing the "Green, green grass of home" by Tom Jones won't get you beyond the rank of Colonel in the U.S. Armed Forces, but familiarity with the Cynefin Framework can.

So, on the twenty-first anniversary of the Cynefin Framework, I'm going to give you an inside edge: the six (tongue-in-cheek) things you need to know if you're a true 'Cynefinite' (or 'y cynefino'). Recite these and you're 'in.'

1. We know Dave Snowden is more important than Anthony Hopkins

Anthony Hopkins may have won an Oscar but I doubt he has shaped the world like our hidden National Treasure.

The Cynefin Framework has aided the definition and resolution of problems in military conflicts, factional disputes, software development, managing food chain risks, and network science. Anthony Hopkins has only silenced some lambs.

And "Cynefin?" Why the name Cynefin? Dave will tell you of his desire for spiritual equivalence to a Japanese term but, in reality, Snowden had no choice. The name was fated. To understand the roots of Cynefin you need to know Dave Snowden. And to understand Dave Snowden, you need to know Wales for the two are linked, intertwined, inseparable – as is Dave and his name for the framework.

2. We are tribal but not obsessed with being a tribe

The Welsh are an anomaly in Northern Europe. We are a tribal community, which is reflected in our language and the name we call ourselves. But we've always been pushed to the margins, literally. And, as a result, we've had to live next to loud neighbors.

We have an unusual language with different roots to the Anglo-Saxons and the Romance languages. The world calls us Wales, the tag derived from Walhaz, an old German expression for 'foreigner' and generally applied to all Celts. We are underdogs who scrap for those who are disadvantaged. We stick together. You'll see it in the words we value.

3. All important words in Wales begin with 'Cy' (kuh)

We call ourselves, Cymry ('kuhm-ree'), people of Cyrmu (Wales). This is a derivative of 'Combrogi,' meaning "fellow countrymen."

We are tellers of tales and defenders of dragons (as you will be now). We have a unique form of poetry (Cynghanedd) for which we give prizes on TV. Imagine that. Words of significance begin with 'Cy' ('kuh)' so if Dave's work was to have consequence, the naming convention was set.

4. We dislike the phrase 'congruent heterogeneity' but accept its accuracy

For all that keeps us together, the Welsh are not homogeneous. We have a fierce regional rivalry. And our landscape and climate are varied too. For one of the smallest countries in Europe, we have substantial topographical diversity.

Ask Dave – he's walked through most of it. Dave's favorite place in the world is on top of Tryfan, a dinosaur-shaped mountain in alpine North Wales. But he's also walked the jagged Western coast, the rolling Eastern border and the billowing southern pastures. Prompt him and he'll tell you that, though brought up in one part of Wales, he feels a sense of home everywhere.

That is Cynefin. Dave took the definition of Nicolas Sinclair in his book on Kyffin Williams, a prominent Welsh painter. Cynefin is… "the place of your birth and upbringing, the environment in which you live and to which you are naturally acclimatised." [1]

5. We accept the best of the Celts but avoid the worst

There's one Welsh trait the Cynefin Framework actively avoids. Thankfully. It is well known amongst the Celts that they, "Don't know what they're fighting for, but they'll fight anyone for it."

In my direct experience, the Cynefin Framework has done the reverse. It has allowed people, with differing backgrounds and perspectives, to come together, to discuss difficult subjects and to agree on a path forward. It has diffused tense urban standoffs, improved conditions at refugee camps, and resolved critical issues in Board Rooms. It has built community and engendered loyalty in places where they have been sorely needed.

6. We know the real gift of the Cynefin Framework is community and loyalty

Perhaps the greatest gift from Dave Snowden of Wales is not just Cynefin, but the outcome of its application – a greater sense of community and loyalty. Remember the Welsh love for supporting the underdog? Remember the essential words meaning community and loyalty? And don't forget the sense of belonging in a range of locations. Not surprising then it's called the 'Cynefin' Framework.

And if through it's application you too have helped others feel involved, together and in more control of their destiny, diolch yn Fawr (thank you very much).

Croeso y Cynefino. (Welcome to the Cynefinites)

References

1.   Kyffin Williams - The Land and The Sea. Published by the Gomer Press, Wales, UK., 2004.

What to read next

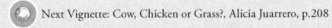 Next Vignette: Cow, Chicken or Grass?, Alicia Juarrero, p.208

Next Chronological: When Disease Requires a Complexity Framework, Riva Greenberg...,, p.153

Next Narrative: Cow, Chicken or Grass?, Alicia Juarrero, p.208

COW, CHICKEN OR GRASS?

ALICIA JUARRERO

ABOUT THE AUTHOR

Alicia Juarrero is the author of *Dynamics in Action, Intentional Behavior as a Complex System* (MIT Press) and co-editor of *Emergence, Self-Organization and Complexity, Precursors and Prototypes* (ISCE). Named 2002 U.S. Professor of the Year by the CASE/Carnegie Foundation for the Advancement of Teaching, Dr. Juarrero has also served on the National Council on the Humanities and the Advisory Board of the National Endowment for the Humanities. She is President and Co-Founder of VectorAnalytica, Inc, developing software platforms to monitor, track, and anticipate outbreaks of infectious diseases.

ABOUT THIS CHAPTER

 Vignette    Narrative

 Chronology: Piece 5 of 33

COW, CHICKEN OR GRASS?

ALICIA JUARRERO

Dave: "Which is the odd one out? Cow, Chicken or Grass?"

Alicia: "Excuse me?"

That was just about the first exchange between Dave and me. I had neither read Richard Nisbett's groundbreaking work on cultural psychology, *The Geography of Thought*, nor did I know Liang-Hwang Chiu's work that Nisbett drew from, so I was duly stumped, as Dave no doubt intended. But it wasn't just intellectual one-upmanship: it was Dave's way of establishing common ground – in our mutual interest in context-dependent relations. He was also communicating his tribal credentials, Welshman, to Cuban.

The exchange took place during a break at a small meeting Dave had organized at the University of Maryland's University College for a few of us interested in how narrative and story-telling elicit nuanced contextual details that other ethnographic techniques do not. Cynefin was a recently established entity within IBM at the time, so this must have been around 2002 or 2003. However, even back then, Dave and Cynthia Kurtz, his colleague, were growing frustrated with a rigid corporate culture that emphasized standard operating procedures and best practices over innovative applications informed by complex systems science. They understood that stakeholders' narratives could provide managers with a far more in-depth understanding of human behavior in business firms and institutions.

I was a faculty member at a community college – a condition far from tribal and closer to the wilderness – and most grateful that the Cynefin website identified my 1999 book as a foundational text. In the book, I wrote a chapter on narrative explanation and the dynamics of action. I think this chapter was the reason I received the invitation to this particular meeting. Dave and I shared the conviction that contextual description is always better than reductionist accounts of complex dynamics, especially complex human dynamics. The very name Cynefin, of course, calls attention to the importance of place as a source of meaning and sense.

As someone trained in studying and understanding the nature of things, I followed the development of the Cynefin Framework – and the practice it informed – with great interest. Cynefin's evolution coincided with transformations in data entry technology that were made possible by the price reduction of mobile devices and the explosive penetration of cell phones worldwide.

Cynefin's development was itself a context-informed process. Dave could now avail himself of easy to use devices that interviewees from most socioeconomic levels and cultures were familiar with. Disintermediation of the interview report's interpretation was now made possible, and that yielded far greater insight and understanding of the dynamics in question. Dave was among the first to recognize this. In the years following 9/11, network and complex science offered new prisms into problems that were proving to be intractable when approached by traditional mechanistic methods.

Unlike many a business consultant, Dave's background in theoretical physics, philosophy, and theology, enriched by street smarts earned as a 1970s radical, allowed him to glimpse connections and implications that others couldn't. It also sculpted his analyses and recommendations into a form that was substantive instead of facile. That Dave's carefully honed demeanor combined that of a mad scientist, priest, and philosopher – all wrapped around the skills of a superb and ruthless debate champion – didn't hurt, especially on this side of the Atlantic, where a British accent is the equivalent of an additional doctorate.

Most significantly, however, was Dave's principled rejection of facile promises of prediction and control. With rhetorical skills that would make Aristotle proud, and informed by a deep understanding of theory, he could communicate in a manner that persuaded top management to accept that context-dependent complex systems cannot be controlled by dictate or decree. He could also encourage them, because science shows that it is possible, to take concrete steps to monitor, probe, and manage conditions that will improve the likelihood that things will proceed in a favored direction. Not being able to control things, therefore, did not mean that top management was without power.

I would have just said, "Managers can only be catalysts. End of story (no pun intended)." Dave's way was much suaver; any recalcitrance on the part of a business executive would be met with, "Let me ask you, have you ever organized a children's birthday party? Okay, so tell me how you went about it." The rest, of course, became the history of Cognitive Edge.

So which of the three, Cow, Chicken, or Grass, is the odd one out? Well, it depends on your cultural framework. Thinking there is one right answer or method is precisely the wrong way of going about managing a complex organization. And that's the point of the test. And that's the point of Cynefin and Cognitive Edge.

Many happy returns, Cynefin!

What to read next

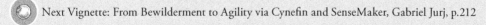

Next Vignette: From Bewilderment to Agility via Cynefin and SenseMaker, Gabriel Jurj, p.212

Next Chronological: Dave and the Cynefin Community..., Peter Stanbridge, p.315

Next Narrative: From Bewilderment to Agility via Cynefin and SenseMaker, Gabriel Jurj, p.212

FROM BEWILDERMENT TO AGILITY VIA CYNEFIN AND SENSEMAKER

GABRIEL JURJ

ABOUT THE AUTHOR

Gabriel Jurj is a dynamic, engaging and commercially aware executive with significant experience in successfully leading Applications Development, Service Delivery and Infrastructure Operations for leading IT, Market Research and Consultancy firms. Acknowledged for possessing strong people management skills, Gabriel excels at leading teams. He employs a distributed approach to management that involves clear objective setting and fostering a culture of shared accountability to successfully execute individual and company objectives. As a natural relationship builder, driven by curiosity, he is continuously exploring new ways and means to advance on the path of science-informed management and leadership practice, guided by complexity thinking and the Cynefin Framework.

ABOUT THIS CHAPTER

 Vignette    Narrative

 Chronology: Piece 33 of 33

FROM BEWILDERMENT TO AGILITY VIA CYNEFIN AND SENSEMAKER

GABRIEL JURJ

In a bit more than a year, our performance improved significantly. We evolved from delivering on time on our commitments less than 17% to a remarkable 100%, Cynefin and SenseMaker being our main contributors. Imagine, as this was largely done with engineers, not one of the easiest groups of professionals to participate in something they aren't familiar with.

From the beginning I considered myself a classic example of a corporate citizen who did not feel comfortable with the static, mechanistic approach to strategy and operations, goals and plans. The business world I lived in missed important aspects, focused too much on profits, and applied one-size-fits-all solutions to any problem too often.

Intuitively, and through my various managerial roles, I knew this was limiting and ignored the day to day challenges in any business. But what was I missing? Why did everybody else seem comfortable with their approach, as if creating a plan and executing it everything would be fine? How could they disregard the end state of the system or the type of problem they faced? It seems like I walked through years of the classical groundhog day playing and replaying embarrassing situations. Where "proper planning" was required, I refused to do it, perplexing and puzzling everyone around me.

On many occasions childhood memories popped up. Those moments of awe in front of a particular toy that I needed to understand how it worked. Similarly, deconstructing today's reality into pieces, I thought, will give me the understanding of how the system works; some connections were visible, others continued to be elusive. The questions rattled in my brain, "What was I missing, what should I do? Climb the wall, go around, or pierce through it?" Over time I realized that it is not as much about 'either-or,' as it is about context and 'and-and.' Unconsciously, I was doing a series of first fit pattern-matching exercises hoping to find the "root cause" of my problems.

As a child, reading was always a big part of my life. The love of books was instilled in me by my mother, a voracious reader. Every day she would grab a book and get lost in it. My habit of reading a book a day had me go through everything I could get my hands on back then to see what the gurus were saying. Not many books were available, but enough to realize that "the solution" didn't exist in those books. From all that I read I found a few recipes and classical case studies that seemed easy to implement but didn't impact much; they attracted early adopters and then faded into oblivion.

Systems theory was often present, mind maps, diagrams, they all looked fine, but didn't match reality. Over years of moving through various roles and organizations, my frustration with the ordered approach to almost everything continued to grow. I knew there must be something else out there, frameworks, tools, and methods more suited to deal with complexity, even if I didn't know what to call them or the situation.

Then I arrived at Waters, the world's leading specialty measurement company focused on improving human health and well-being by applying high-value analytical technologies and industry-leading science. Waters has continually pioneered chromatography, mass spectrometry, and thermal analysis innovations. Whether we are producing new pharmaceuticals, assuring the safety of the world's food and water supplies, or ensuring a chemical entity's integrity in production, we are continually working with our 40,000+ customers to change the world. We are a young organization wanting to "deliver benefit" as our mission statement says. Yes, we have an audacious purpose, but what does that mean in practical terms, I wondered?

I lead the largest software development R & D center in the company, multiple products, all mission-critical. Fast forward, and I'm being tasked to help the organization reach a more mature stage of agility. So three years into the transition from waterfall to agile, we were going through the motions, not knowing how to get from form to substance. Agility, I would brag, is my native state of being. How would I proceed knowing that the beaten path approach wouldn't be of much help?

For me, the essence of agility goes hand in hand with complexity thinking. As Dave says, you can adapt and exapt, deconstruct, recombine, and explore. Through some grace the year before joining Waters I was introduced to Dave Snowden's work and the Cynefin Framework by a good friend and former colleague. Instinctively I sensed the opportunity and I seized it. Having completed the Cynefin foundation course, I engaged with Cognitive Edge and started to draft an intervention. "Theory informed practice" here we come!

"Understanding the present, discovering its evolutionary potential," that's where we started. It meant launching an Agile pulse survey using the SenseMaker tool, the world's first crowdsourcing method for human judgment, meaning, and feeling. One of the most difficult challenges we had was getting people to participate in something they were unfamiliar with. You can imagine journaling, which is a well-known reflection practice, for engineers, is far afield from their affinity for models, recipes, action plans, and Gantt charts. Connecting the "ask" with why it matters, for me did the trick, and we've slowly gotten the stories we needed to make the sense-making endeavor relevant.

As important as the understanding, was the practice. We conducted a series of workshops with several teams to help us get traction. Even though we were moving, a bit slowly for my taste, the travel direction was the right one. We began exploring what's possible, having a scientific "what's possible journey." On one side, managers continued to enhance their theoretical knowledge of the Framework, while on the other side, we were constantly creating opportunities to practice. Resilience was, and still is, one of the most important contributors to our evolution. It is also a constant reminder to meet the system where it is, not where we would like it to be.

Once we were more or less familiar with the basics, I started to press the gas pedal – the alternative to the classic retrospective, Retro Pulse, came out of one of our experiments. The teams involved in this pilot were eager to share their narratives. They were curious to know what new insights would this tool offer for their coding practice and see where all this would take us? For me, it was confirmation how important it is to meet the system where it is.

In Scrum, which was the main approach implemented in our software development process, the whole industry is in a difficult situation. We encounter infantilized roles, people largely follow recipes for success, and they do not possess the tools and heuristics needed to navigate a complex adaptive system or adapt their practice to their teams' particular context. Even for us, although we were getting plenty of qualitative and quantitative insights, we didn't really know how to make sense of it. Again and again, habit had us seeking formulas. "Tell me what to do," was often asked. Faced with this reality, I decided to slow down, be patient, continue the journey, and see what would come next.

One thing I realized was that I needed to continue to invest in our middle management; engineering and project management alongside Scrum masters was critical to our evolution. A parallel experiment was born, the narrative enhanced leadership development program, which is ongoing today.

While all of the above might seem limited in impact, the reality is that in a bit more than a year, we improved our performance significantly. We evolved from delivering on time on our commitments on less than 17% of the cases to an impressive 100%. What the future holds can't be known, but we will keep exploring and experimenting one step at a time.

To conclude, we learned many lessons along the way, and our journey with Cynefin and complexity thinking has just begun. For me, and given my early observations about how work works, the emergent nature of cultural transformation has been the most valuable learning. I hope this is a lesson others can benefit from as well.

What to read next

 Next Vignette: From Cookstown to Cynefin, Anne McMurray, p.272

 First Chronological: The few organically drawn lines that became part of my life, Friso Gosliga, p.149

 Next Narrative: From Cookstown to Cynefin, Anne McMurray, p.272

IT DOESN'T GET HAPPY; IT DOESN'T GET SAD

LIZ KEOGH

ABOUT THE AUTHOR

Liz Keogh is a Lean and Agile consultant based in London. She is a well-known blogger and international speaker, a core member of the Behavior-drive development community and a passionate advocate of the Cynefin Framework and its ability to change mindsets. She has a strong technical background with 20 years' experience in delivering and coaching others to deliver software, from small start-ups to global enterprises. Most of her work now focuses on Lean, Agile and organizational transformations, and the use of transparency, positive language, well-formed outcomes and safe-to-fail experiments in making change innovative, easy and fun.

ABOUT THIS CHAPTER

 Full Chapter

 Theoretical

 Chronology: Piece 21 of 33

 Cynefin Principles

IT DOESN'T GET HAPPY; IT DOESN'T GET SAD

LIZ KEOGH

Most people, myself included, love certainty. We want to develop software to meet our customers' needs. Instead, we're finding out, particularly when our clients say, "I didn't ask for this!" that it's much more complex. The very process we are engaged in is complex and clients can only see what they asked for in hindsight. And still, I'm hopeful partly because of Cynefin.

I learned to program when I was seven years old.

The BBC produced a simple computer for a child to use, as well as a manual for children, replete with beautiful, colorful images and simple programs you could type in. I learned to type, then copy them, and then tweak the program to produce the kind of things I wanted. Sometimes I would experiment, trying to replicate the string art that was so popular in the '70s. My father wrote a program that produced a perfect circle, but its maths were beyond me then.

At that stage, just about everything I tried worked, or if it didn't, I understood quickly why. It was obvious.

I was about nine or so when the computer magazines started coming out. One of them had a game inside: not a tape (we used tapes back then, of course), but an actual line-by-line print-out of the program. I typed it in, saved it, and ran it. It didn't work. I learned later that the magazines weren't produced so that people would type in the games, but that programmers could learn more about how others did code. There were pages and pages of text and I spent several evenings typing after school. I was distressed when it didn't work. I didn't understand the errors it was giving me.

But my father, with more in-depth expertise, was able to see that I had made mistakes in my typing, of course, but there were also mistakes in the print-out. It was my introduction to the complexity of software development. The program was of itself, entirely predictable and complicated, but became complex because of my very human interaction with the computer.

My mother, who'd programmed back in the days of punch cards said, "Back then we always had to write a test along with our code to show that it did what we wanted before we could run it for the calculations we needed. Computing was expensive." And very, very predictable.

At 18, I headed to university. I took a summer job with an engineering group. "Can you program?" they asked me. "A bit," I said.

"Here." They gave me a copy of Kernigan and Ritchie's "C." "Learn this. Here's what we want…"

It took an afternoon to get the program they asked for working, outputting a series of numbers on a port. They were impressed. I began to think that maybe I should code for a living; it was a lot more fun than the soldering iron.

Back in university, I sought out modules with code. I learned about AI: fuzzy logic, expert systems, neural networks whose ability to tell the difference between a cat or a dog emerged retrospectively. It was fascinating, but I was still drawn to the predictability of code. It was clean, undemanding, stress-free.

I took a developer job out of university. My first project was in Visual Basic 6.0; a bit of a mess of procedural, object-oriented, and functional code, different styles, and paradigms mashed together. I hated it. It didn't have the clean lines of the C-programming language. I taught myself Java, which was nicer. I started to pay a bit more attention to the people around me, too. I left Bath, where I'd graduated, and moved to London. It was a shock. So many people, often crammed into tiny spaces. I applied for a job at Thoughtworks, a company that specialized in "Agile" software development. I didn't get the job.

I started working as a contractor. I learned to love desktop User Interfaces (UIs) particularly – they reminded me of the string art – but the way the business side treated my work was annoying. As soon as they saw something, they wanted me to change it. "That isn't what you asked for," I grumbled. But they didn't see what they'd asked for until after they saw it produced.

I was seven years into my career and every project I'd worked on had a clear contract. Every time I started a new contract I wrote what was asked for, including tests that proved it met the request. But not once had the software I developed been used. I figured it was just the way the software world worked. The industry news was rife with project failures. It took luck, I thought, as well as expertise.

Then I realized what was happening. I reapplied to Thoughtworks and this time the UK office had room for me. I joined a project, started pair-programming with the team, and wrote some code the first week. There was no contract. There was just a post-it note and an instruction to talk to someone about what they wanted. It was only changing the font on a receipt – but I saw the impact the first time I had to do a VAT return and could make out the numbers. I had used my own code! Others were using it too. I was excited. Finally, my work was making a difference. This was what I had waited for!

I began learning the methods that the team had used to embrace uncertainty and still move forward, expecting to find a movement that would sweep the world and enable everyone to enjoy the same success I'd just encountered. It seemed inevitable.

It still hasn't happened, and because of Cynefin, I understand why.

SOFTWARE THROUGH THE LENS OF CYNEFIN

Computers are, for the most part, predictable. Programs that start with the same input, rerun, will generally produce the same output. For decades, we thought that it was possible to make predictions about what software should do before developers started coding. Analysts were providing all our requirements up-front, exhaustively checking, and re-checking to ensure that nothing the business needed had been missed. Testers checked the results against test plans. Little emphasis was given to checking with the users that the planned shipments were successful.

As the software ecosystem has grown, it's quicker and quicker to produce powerful code. The Open Source movement has made an astonishing number of code libraries and applications available for free. Modern languages and frameworks provide high-level syntax and shortcuts that make it almost as quick to develop a prototype as it is to provide a sketch. It's no longer necessary, or even helpful, to cement requirements up-front.

Increasingly, organizations that have taken advantage of software's speed and malleability are taking over the marketplace. From nimble start-ups to the FAANG behemoths (Facebook, Apple, Amazon, Netflix, Google), the winners embrace uncertainty and try things out with appropriate safety nets. They are comfortable with uncertainty, and with failing on their way to discover something new and valuable.

In the early 2000s, various leaders of the software world were already beginning to recognize this change. Fourteen of them got together at the Snowbird ski resort in Utah to see if they could distill their thoughts into something useful. The result was the "Agile" movement; still working its way through the software world almost 20 years later.

Anyone who's lived through the last 20 years and watched the rise of the internet will be familiar with new technology's emergent nature. A camera pointed at a coffee pot in Cambridge by an enterprising developer became online video conferencing and applications that let you see who's ringing your doorbell. Maps combined with virtual reality applications became "Pokémon Go." Yet, teams still struggle with a very human quality: the innate dislike all humans have for uncertainty. The Agile movement hasn't taken off the way that we had hoped. Where it has popped up, it's often a token effort, surrounded by all the usual rigor to attempt to force plans to progress as they had been written.

Cynefin offers a lens to help make sense of this world, lending itself readily to software development, through all its different domains.

THE COMPLEX

In 2002 a company called Ludicorp was developing an online multiplayer game "Game Neverending." Part of the tooling of the game allowed players to share images with each other. The game was eventually cancelled, but Ludicorp continued to develop the tools. They eventually repurposed them in 2004, launching Flickr, the photo-sharing site. Another attempt was made to create a similar game, this time under the name "Glitch." Again, the game was abandoned. This time the original tools to allow administrators to talk to each other behind the scenes were repurposed, becoming the messaging service Slack.

Stewart Butterfield, Founder of both projects, said, "The bad news is that they're close to impossible to replicate... if you started with the intent to build a failed massively multiplayer game, you may not end up with a product like this." [1] Their success is correlated in retrospect, but could not possibly have been predicted or designed for – a major aspect of the Cynefin Framework Complex domain.

Even when software doesn't pivot so massively, it often shows some emergent aspects existing in the liminal complex / complicated space. I often hear business people reflect on what they see with terms that signify that emergence. "Ah, that's not quite what I was expecting. That's not going to work, is it?"

Complexity is the domain of innovation, and the desire for something new drives all software efforts. After all, nobody in technology wants to spend money getting something they've already got.

By helping development teams focus on getting feedback quickly – through "spikes," prototypes and proofs of concept – and encouraging them to develop safety nets like good rollback practices and phoenix servers (ready to spring from the ashes of any failure), we can begin to embrace that uncertainty, and the value of Agile practices becomes more apparent.

THE COMPLICATED AND THE CLEAR

There are still aspects of software development that require expertise, rather than experimentation. Responses from the Complicated rather than Complex domain. GPS systems, for instance, remain unchanged. Libraries and code fragments that convert coordinates to distance are similarly stable.

Since developers are stereotypically bored when asked to do the same thing repeatedly, many stable technologies have been open-sourced and many repetitive tasks are automated. Of course, the act of stabilizing something for the first time is complex, and the Open Source and other technological ecosystems can remain dominated by that complexity.

More obvious tools exist for children; graphical languages like Squeak, and code-within-games like the redstone circuitry in Mojang's Minecraft (there's a reason Microsoft bought Mojang).

And, the BBC still hasn't given up its push to get children learning to code. [2]

THE CHAOTIC

I once brought the Guardian newspaper's travel website down for three hours, almost single-handedly. It was a simple error in retrospect; using production-like data in our tests would have caught it. I probably panicked more than the editors did, but it was my first introduction to the urgency of production bugs.

The stories of technological chaos are hard to forget. Microsoft released a chatbot on Twitter, only to find it taught how to be racist and generally offensive. Apple attempted to force everyone to listen to U2, only to find out that customers didn't quite want it. And everyone in the UK knows about the chaos of TSB Bank's meltdown in 2018 when it tried to perform a long-planned upgrade and locked 1.9 million people out of their accounts.

As with any chaotic situation, the trick is to act and act quickly. Of course, the software community has created tools and techniques for helping with that – some of them based on Slack. [3] Great software provides frameworks for more great software, and we're back to complexity again.

THE COMPLACENT

In 2012, a technician at the trading company Knight Capital Group released new software onto seven of its eight servers, forgetting the 8th. A flag that should have been repurposed was turned on, causing the 8th server to release trades into production intended only for test environments. It took the company 45 minutes to find the problem and turn the server off, by which time it had lost $440m, prompting its fire sale. Along the boundary between the Clear and the Chaotic lies complacency – and software development is as prone to it as any other human endeavor.

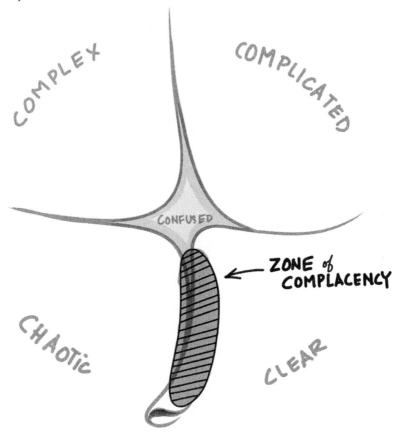

Figure 1. The five Cynefin domains and the zone of complacency

THE CONFUSED

Someone once asked me how I would go about applying Agile techniques to his profession of dismantling nuclear power stations. "I have no idea," I told him. "If we have a nuclear explosion in the code base, we just roll it back to the previous version."

There is inherent safety in software development. At any point before release, the code can be changed, and modern tools and techniques make that change easier than it ever has been before. The companies that can take advantage of that ease of change can move more quickly than others. They can make more profit. All things being equal, every company in the world should have moved to a more Agile way of working by now.

Yet, they haven't.

Across the world, large enterprises are still dominated by big, up-front plans and heavyweight analysis. This confusion feeds my role as an Agile Coach; I am paid to help people negotiate a path to more responsive ways of working.

In risk-averse, long-established firms (and some small start-ups that should know better), the desire to cling to the apparent certainty of plans and budgets is deeply rooted. Trying to persuade executives in organizations to change isn't just a matter of developing software differently. It's about approaching risk in an entirely different way. We have to be transparent about progress, delivering, and getting feedback. Plans are important – they give us coherence; a realistic reason for thinking that what we're about to attempt is a good idea – but assuming that anything will actually follow those plans once we start is a mistake.

It's a technological change for sure: legacy systems, written without the safety net of automated tests and maintainable code, require more careful change. The journey to making something easy to change is loss-leading; it doesn't produce results for some time, and so developers are always under pressure to cut corners. It's an endless battle. Even more than technological, though, asking people to embrace uncertainty is a cultural change, dominated entirely by complexity. That human desire for predictability remains.

So companies go on. They have emerged with products to fill the gaps. They promise success by imposing structures and working methods that fail to address the constraints that are unique to any organization. That is, the back-channels through which work gets done and leadership misbehavior that stops developers from volunteering their creativity. These power structures cause people to own and take control of anything that looks like it might succeed, while abandoning failure. This happens even when failure might be safe for anything except their reputation.

I am hopeful, though.

The introduction of Cynefin to our communities has given change agents a new way of looking at our work. We nudge in directions that are "better" instead of demanding fixed outcomes. We allow change to emerge, trying multiple parallel interventions, instead of pursuing "best practices" that might not be best for the context. We make it safe for ourselves and the companies we work with to fail, allowing for experimentation. And we support the people within the organizations, amplifying the successful experiments they're already trying, and helping them build safety nets for themselves, creating not only a better world but one which will survive and thrive after we're gone.

It's not only our software and technology that's changing, but our understanding of change itself.

References

1.   https://www.youtube.com/watch?v=IS_wpAlkP48
2.   https://www.bbc.co.uk/cbeebies/grownups/coding
3.   https://github.com/monzo/response

What to read next

 Next Full Chapter: Weaving Well-being into the Fabric of our Organizations..., Marion Kiely..., p.227

 Next Chronological: Cynefin Framework in Communications & Media..., Juanita Uribe..., p.336

 Next Theoretical: Weaving Well-being into the Fabric of our Organizations..., Marion Kiely..., p.227

 More on Cynefin Principle 1: Cynefin and Theory of Constraints: Allies or Adversaries?, Steve Holt, p.173

 More on Cynefin Principle 1.3: Cynefin and Strategy, Steve McCrone and Ian Snape, p.257

WEAVING WELL-BEING INTO THE FABRIC OF OUR ORGANIZATIONS WITH THE CYNEFIN FRAMEWORK

MARION KIELY AND ELLIE SNOWDEN

ABOUT THE AUTHORS

Marion Kiely applies anthro-complexity theory and principles to health, safety and wellbeing, with a view to preventing unnecessary suffering, and helping people and the businesses they work for thrive. Based in Ireland, she trains, facilitates, and consults globally via Upstream, the consultancy practice she established in 2016. Marion lectures in University College Cork and brings humor and humanity to her subject matter. Working with stories is a common thread that is interwoven in all aspects of her work.

Ellie Snowden has been involved with Cynefin since it's inception. Not only does Ellie occupy the role of Dave's daughter, but she also works for The Cynefin Center, focusing on topics related to human and environmental health and wellbeing. Ellie's background is in social/medical anthropology and development and she has an ongoing interest in the intersections between embodied and expert knowledge, and how people put them to use to have an affect in the world.

ABOUT THIS CHAPTER

 Full Chapter

 Theoretical

 Chronology: Piece 27 of 33

 Cynefin Principles

WEAVING WELL-BEING INTO THE FABRIC OF OUR ORGANIZATIONS WITH THE CYNEFIN FRAMEWORK

MARION KIELY AND ELLIE SNOWDEN

Executives who want to improve the well-being of their employees, should not assume that well-being is an individual's problem and that the way to solve it is through simple solutions or linear scale surveys. Rather, well-being is a business challenge which goes beyond productivity. It emerges from the sticky web of working conditions and interactions all members of the organization create in their workplace. By gathering employee's stories, you can learn what conditions and interactions matter most to people and, with that information, design policies that truly enhance well-being.

Our journey began in the British Library in April 2018. We had been in contact virtually after being introduced by Dave Snowden, but this was our first meet-up in person. From the get-go we got on great. Ellie was au fait on complexity, anthropology, and Cynefin, and yet despite her familiarity with it (since childhood!) was just beginning to articulate its importance in the area of well-being. Marion was well steeped in occupational health and safety, work-related stress, and mindfulness-based interventions, along with a sprinkling of Cynefin knowledge. We were working on a 'SenseMaker Wellbeing Pulse' and wanted to combine our energies to produce something that would bring value to, and appeal to, those in organizations who have a responsibility, and genuine interest, to influence the area of well-being (Human Resource (HR) executives, Health & Safety (H&S) managers, Occupational Health Advisors). [1]

Alongside our academic interests, we'd both experienced how damaging it can be to work in an unhealthy environment. Marion had gone through burnout, and having survived the ordeal gained many insights into the occupational health process, many of which fell short of 'best practice' advocated by government and industry bodies. Ellie had recently removed herself from a public policy job after experiencing burnout when ironically completing a review of mindfulness interventions in the workplace. She felt restricted by rigid ways of doing research, which minimized stories people shared about their lives, through pre-defined thematic codes and bureaucratic structures.

The fact is that our individual experiences are not an exception. In fact, despite good intentions from line managers, H&S managers and Occupational Health Advisors across industries, well-being is not improving. It seems to have reached a limit as articulated by the following quote from Stavroula Leka, Professor of Work Organization and Well-being at the Business School of University College Cork in Ireland:

> "Even though health, safety and well-being are at the core of workplace and societal functioning and development, the current state of the art indicates that approaches that have been used to promote them have not had the anticipated results. This also applies to mental health in the workplace. A new paradigm is needed to capture the complexity of the modern workplace in relation to mental health." [2]

We invite you to re-imagine where well-being resides as you look at the Cynefin Framework below. While well-being practices are typically on the right side of the Framework, we propose that shifting our view to the left side of the model, primarily to the Complex domain, gives us a new lens from which to see and design practices and policies to improve well-being.

Figure 1. The Cynefin Framework

WELL-BEING: A COMPLEX TOPIC, AND CURRENT METHODS DON'T DO IT JUSTICE

Prior to Marion's introduction to Cynefin, she saw the world through an ordered lens. She was well versed in validated surveys that told you what the problems were by giving you oodles of quantitative data. It was very straight forward: issue the survey designed by the experts, (most comprised of Likert scales and leading questions) and then look at your numbers to see where you were. Its appeal was both its wide use and promotion by many well respected bodies.

We reflected that much of how well-being experts define and measure well-being is as capacities or traits within individuals. The result of focusing on employees, per se, falls short of giving the necessary context as to what conditions in the workplace, and interactions that employees have within it, are truly impacting well-being. Linear surveys do not uncover and discover the rich, complex web of influences responsible for personal and professional well-being, which are very much intertwined. Instead, they analyze things into component parts so that much of well-being work goes on in the Complicated domain and exhibits a linear approach. While surveys do give a high level overview of stress and well-being levels, decision makers end up working with fragmented, and context-poor data. For example, while a survey may reveal we score 3.9 on a 5-point scale of well-being, we still don't know what would move us to a better number, e.g. 4.5.

Context-poor numbers also open us up to data manipulation. What gets measured gets manipulated! This is described as the Cobra effect after a story that originated in India when authorities wanted to reduce the number of venomous cobras. They offered a 2 Rupees bounty for each dead cobra head they were brought. This worked for a while and the amount of cobras reduced. After some time, however, some innovative types opened up cobra breeding farms, whereby they bred cobras and then made a killing in more ways than one. When the authorities found out they stopped the reward scheme, and the cobra breeders let the snakes go free, making the problem bigger than what it was initially!

Figure 2. The Cobra Effect

To do justice to well-being, we must examine the soup that is the biology of our bodies, the evolution and ecology of our species, the social and cultural worlds we inhabit and create (past, present and future), and see how these all tie together in our lives and experiences as persons. [3][4] Ultimately, we must create an environment – physical and psychosocial – that supports individuals to flourish in their interaction with each other. We need to define well-being beyond the Complicated domain, where cause-and-effect thinking, fail-safe formulas and surveys dominate our toolbox.

In business we noticed two dominant reactions to the idea of working with complexity. Either people would nod their heads thoughtfully yet have no clear understanding how to access what that means in practice, or people would bury their heads in the sand and try to ignore the enormity of what was going on. We will provide a grounded and practical way of approaching well-being and how to work with it from a complexity view using the Cynefin Framework as our lens.

LOOKING AT WELL-BEING THROUGH THE LENS OF CYNEFIN

Our definition of well-being in this chapter, is that it is an emergent property of the messy and moveable interactions between people, their relationships, interactions and the organizing practices, procedures and structures in which people find themselves. It is something to be co-created and it emerges over time in a dynamic way. It is not produced or manufactured in a linear (ordered) way.

Well-being is not a problem to be solved, but an opportunity to discover and create an environment where people can flourish. Cultivating well-being is about changing practices in the workplace, not the individuals or wanting/forcing them to change behavior. [5]

Well-intentioned, linear type approaches, as we've mentioned, often manifest in programs that aim to make employees 'more resilient.' But now we know it is not about working on the individual but the ecosystem of your workplace – including structures and hierarchies, policies and people's interactions. Consider interrupting the current approaches you may be using that categorize well-being as simple or merely complicated, by becoming familiar with the Cynefin Framework below. It provides a lens to see well-being from multiple perspectives.

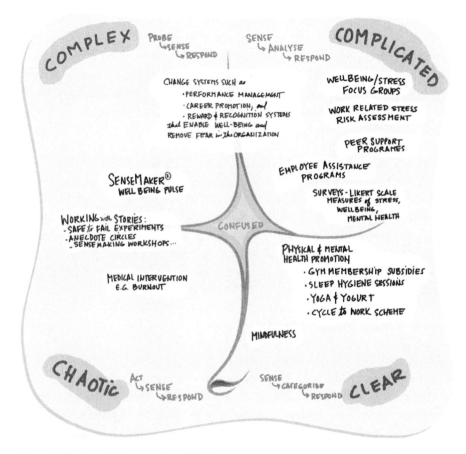

Figure 3. The Cynefin Framework and Wellbeing

Many stressed employees reside in the Framework's Complex, Confused or even at times, Chaotic domain. Well-being 'fixes' tend to come from the Clear and Complicated domain, and by and large they are temporary. Let's say an employee is told to "Practice mindfulness meditation and you'll be stress free." (The Clear domain.) The same employee may be advised to seek the services of an expert, for instance, psychotherapist or yoga teacher. (The Complicated domain). Both these actions may help restore the employee's well-being temporarily, but neither "solution" addresses the workplace practices or environment that is evoking their stress response in the first place (e.g., unachievable workload, bullying). [6]

RE-IMAGINING WORKPLACE WELL-BEING THROUGH YOUR NARRATIVE ECOSYSTEM

LISTEN TO THE STORIES PEOPLE ARE TELLING

In the Complex domain of the Cynefin Framework, people's stories are considered complex adaptive systems. Working with the stories that people tell about their work, gives us insights to relevant (yet often invisible) context to the issues people face. We also get to learn about both what's going well and what isn't. Rather than bringing in the experts and asking hypothesis-informed questions, this is about gathering our internal experts (employees and contractors), and creating a safe space for them to interact, tell their stories, make sense of organizational dynamics and, depending on the method used (software or workshop), get to know each other.

Often stories will tell us what data will not. For example, research into pilot mental health and wellbeing uncovered, through the use of stories, something pilots were concealing. Pilots were creating false names and email addresses to avail themselves of support from psychotherapists. They concealed their identity because if it became known that they were experiencing mental health issues their license could be revoked. This type of information, and level of detail, cannot be gleaned from surveys and big data. Working with stories, particularly when people can share their stories anonymously in a safe environment, without repercussions, you will learn valuable information.

One way to collect stories is to bring people together in a workshop setting and create a small ritual around the sharing of experiences. We can use "anecdote circles" to encourage people to share descriptive anecdotes from their working lives. Ideally we work with a diverse group of people and more than one facilitator in the room to ensure that a range of voices are heard, and this range of experiences can equally be understood from more than one perspective.

Ideally you want to frame the session with a topic, rather than a list of objectives or a too rigid set of questions. Given that asking people to simply "share a story" can be overwhelming for some and prompt too much of an evaluative response, we give some prompts as a catalyst for the session. Here are two prompts we've used that have worked well:

1. Think back to your last week at work, think of one story from your experience when things were made either easier, or more challenging to work here.

2. Which one story from your last week would you share with someone who does not work here? A story which best reflects what it is like to work here?

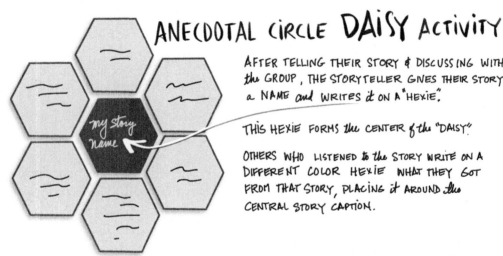

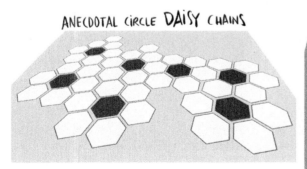

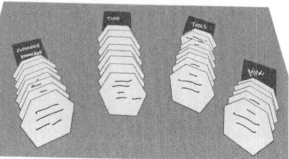

Figure 4. Anecdote Circles

The sharing of stories through this approach enables an open space for the group to then discuss their own feelings and experiences in relation to those of another. We generally hear "This is a luxury we're rarely afforded." By implementing lean processes, some senior executives have gone too close to the bone, cutting off perceived excesses and time-wasting activities. The result is that employees have less opportunities to interact.

Anecdote circles helps to counteract this. They create more opportunities for knowledge sharing, relationship building, and exchanging of stories. We would add that this is also a huge opportunity for collective interpretation of the meaning of events and experiences in the workplace, which has the potential to allow for innovative, contextually relevant practices to emerge.

WORK WITH STORIES TO CO-CREATE SMALL EXPERIMENTS FOR CHANGE

It isn't until we ask, share, and let people reflect and make sense of various perspectives, that we can see what is important to them – and it may be an awakening for them as well. This isn't about 'find and fix,' that is the terrain of the Complicated domain. In the Complex domain, we gain valuable insight into the disposition for any change that might be desired, and the energy available across the network of the organization to make it happen. This allows us to probe, experiment, and monitor what happens as it emerges over time. Having multiple safe-to-fail experiments running in parallel is recommended, as this takes into consideration the Hawthorne Effect. [7] Not focusing on one sole change program allows several small experiments to play out; the system evolves towards a natural disposition rather than one imposed upon it from an idealized standpoint.

Example of one safe-to-fail probe:

One group Marion has worked with was a housing department within a local authority. After much sharing of stories and sense-making, the group looked at what was helping or hindering them getting their work done and looked at developing some actions to nudge the organization in a direction they felt was desirable. Some of the actions weren't big cross-organization change initiatives, they were actions on a small scale. One issue this department had was late rent payments, and all the time-zapping follow-up and chasing that goes with that. Employees had to deal (often face to face) with upset, stressed and sometimes abusive tenants. After a session of anecdote circles and sharing stories and emergent themes, one suggestion explored was to trial giving one or two weeks rent free (possibly at Christmas) to tenants if payments were made on time a previous number of months. If this worked as a pilot in a small scale, it could be considered to amplify across other geographical areas managed by this department. If it didn't, it was to be scrapped. The perception (and hope) was that it would alleviate much time and distress for employees if it worked. Much thought was given to the details and what success or failure would look like, and how the experiment would be amplified or dampened.

When we work with stories and look at creating new pathways forward, we take people on a shallow dive into chaos to spur innovation. This shallow dive gets people side-casting (a complexity-based approach that explores the range of possibilities that experimentally evolve), and seeing what's happening at various spots in the organization. To do this, we give ambiguous instructions and intentionally leave the topic wide open by not promoting or guiding. This can be a bit disconcerting for participants at first. They participate for the day, at times not knowing exactly why they are doing the exercises they are doing, but at the end of the day they have gained many insights as to how the organization operates, and have many ideas for going forward. This process can help to identify the dispositions of the system and, once we climb the gradual ascent to the Complex domain from Chaos, we gain a new perspective from which to base our decisions on regarding direction of travel going forward.

With this probe - sense - respond approach, if something goes well, we amplify. Alternatively, if it takes an undesirable turn, we dampen. What this means is, rather than measure our successes on going from a 4.5 to a 4.9 without necessarily knowing how we got there or whether it's replicable, we propose 'getting more stories like this (that people see to be positive and worthwhile) and less stories like those (that people would like to see less of).' If items that are hindering employees and leading to frustration are allowed to emerge via stories, and if context is explored and understood via developing safe-to-fail experiments, employees will begin to face less hurdles, feel more content and enjoy more flow in their work. Weaving well-being into the fabric of our organizations can deliver for the people in them, daily and in far-reaching ways.

CONCLUSION

Figure 5. Although our eyes may be open to more, we are predisposed to look in the Clear domain, while well-being is mostly in the Complex domain

The monk Buttho spent his life traveling from cloister to cloister. One dark, clouded night he encountered an elderly man, who was obviously in despair, looking for something under the street lantern. "What are you looking for?" Buttho asked. "I am looking for my key, and I desperately need it now," the liman answered, "or my wife will be mad as hell. She is a devil." Buttho was a gentle person and helped him search. After a while Buttho asked: "Are you sure you lost the keys here?", "No", the man answered, "I know for sure I didn't lose them here. But it was the only place where there is any light, so I thought it best to look here because it made no sense to look in the dark." [8]

When we look at well-being through the Cynefin Framework, we recognize that many of the current tools in the well-being toolbox reside in the Complicated domain. We try to improve through analysis and other such tools. While these give us some indication of well-being, they sorely lack the granularity and context-rich information gleaned from working with methods residing in the Complex domain. To only use complicated methods is like standing under the street-lamp, scouring well-trodden territory in the hopes of finding something new. To go beyond this familiar terrain we must dig deeper than what surveys and analysis can tell us. We must provide environments where employees can openly share, to learn what is really helping and hindering them in their work and their well-being.

Sense-making from the complexity perspective enhances policy options for those who want to influence wellbeing in a meaningful way. Well-being is an opportunity to be explored together with the employees who are involved. We advocate to use stories to explore how well-being can be influenced in a positive way.

The use of the Cynefin Framework is our invitation to better identify where aspects of work and well-being reside, and inform us of the most appropriate approach to take. If we can move beyond fear of the unknown, and with our employees light up those dark, hidden corners of the organization, we can weave well-being into the fabric of our everyday lives and move towards a brighter, happier and more productive future.

References:

1. SenseMaker® is software for working with stories and narratives, which gives both quantitative and qualitative data. The SenseMaker® Wellbeing Pulse applies the software to focus on wellbeing. https://sensemaker.cognitive-edge.com/what-is-sensemaker/

2. Leka, S. and Nicholson, P., 2019. Mental health in the workplace. Occupational Medicine, 69(1), pp.5-6.

3. Huppert, F., Baylis, N. (2004) "Well–being: towards an integration of psychology, neurobiology and social science", Philosophical Transactions of the Royal Society of London. Series B: Biological Sciences, 359(1449), pp.1447-1451.

4. Huppert, F., Baylis, N., Keverne, B. (2004) "Introduction: why do we need a science of well–being?", Philosophical Transactions of the Royal Society of London. Series B: Biological Sciences, 359(1449), pp.1331-1332.

5. Crisp, N. (2020) Health is Made at Home: Hospitals are for Repairs, Salus Global Knowledge Exchange

6. We are not in any way undermining the many positive outcomes that can be achieved by practicing mindfulness, but are trying to convey that it isn't something that works for everyone, nor is it something that should be seen as a quick fix solution for stressed employees.

7. Elton Mayo, who undertook research in the Hawthorne Western Electrical plant in 1931, found that the reason people behave in a modified way if they feel their actions are observed is not because of any intervention introduced, but because they feel they are being focused on. This phenomenon is known as the Hawthorne Effect.

8. Zandee, B., Using The Narrative To Understand The Complexity Of Safety Have The Courage To Look In The Dark! [online] Veiligheidskunde.nl. Available at: <https://www.veiligheidskunde.nl/xu/document/cms/streambin.asp?requestid=29675CE1-DE1B-49D2-B3DE-2BEC9073375F>

What to read next

 Next Full Chapter: In Pursuit of a Mastery of Risk: Working with Uncertainty, Change..., Robert Koch, p.242

 Next Chronological: How the Cynefin Framework Supports Law Enforcement, Lou Hayes Jr., p.169

 Next Theoretical: In Pursuit of a Mastery of Risk: Working with Uncertainty, Change..., Robert Koch, p.242

 More on Cynefin Principle 2: Cynefin Framework in Communications & Media..., Juanita Uribe..., p.336

 More on Cynefin Principle 2.2: Facilitation Can be Complex..., Vivienne (Viv) Read, p.296

IN PURSUIT OF A MASTERY OF RISK: WORKING WITH UNCERTAINTY, CHANGE, AND SURPRISE

ROBERT KOCH

ABOUT THE AUTHOR

Robert is an engineer, artist, researcher, risk and resilience practitioner, and a senior manager in the energy sector. His interest lies in complexity-informed approaches to risk and resilience. His team has coordinated national responses to several major power system disaster incidents. Robert has led a variety of international working groups and is the recipient of several national and international awards. He has a Master's degree in Electrical Engineering from the University of Stellenbosch, South Africa. In 2015 he was listed by ESI Magazine as one of the "most influential figures in African power."

ABOUT THIS CHAPTER

 Full Chapter

 Chronology: Piece 25 of 33

 Theoretical

 Cynefin Principles

IN PURSUIT OF A MASTERY OF RISK: WORKING WITH UNCERTAINTY, CHANGE, AND SURPRISE

ROBERT KOCH

The Cynefin Framework is a navigation tool that entices us to think differently about risk – and about our role as risk practitioners and system stewards. We argue that the mastery for the risk practitioner includes all domains of the Cynefin Framework, which offers us exciting new ways to make sense of risks in an organizational context.

EMBRACING THE UNKNOWN

Scattered across history are stories and maps that delineate two kinds of territories; those already explored, and those that lie beyond – demarcated by the words terra incognita and warnings that there might be dragons. As human beings, we journey toward the unknown in search of opportunity, aware that 'dragons' may be lurking. The hope is that we will navigate the uncertainty ahead with the tools and resources at our disposal. Such intentional hope is what activist and writer Rebecca Solnit calls an 'embrace of the unknown.'

"When you recognize uncertainty, you recognize that you may be able to influence the outcomes. Hope is an embrace of the unknown and the unknowable, an alternative to the certainty of both optimists and pessimists." – Rebecca Solnit. [1]

Journeys into the unknown require use of the pioneering tools of our time: the compass, the sextant, the GPS, the Hubble telescope, the Large Hadron Collider. Could the Cynefin Framework be such a tool for risk practitioners? In this chapter we explore the Framework as to how it guides us in working in, and with, uncertainty, change, and surprise. We will probe its use in risk practice and how it helps us to 'make sense of the world, so that we can act in it'. [2]

Figure 1. A map of the journey into the unknown

ON UNCERTAINTY

Risk practitioners understand risk to mean 'the effect of uncertainty on objectives;' a deviation from what is expected that gives rise to opportunity, threat, or both. [3] Risk management practices offer risk professionals an ability to untangle opportunity from threat – and to act by amplifying opportunity and dampening threat. In tracing the history of risk, Peter L Bernstein notes that:

"The boundary between modern times and the past is the mastery of risk: the notion that the future is more than a whim of the gods and that men and women are not passive before nature." [4]

Risk management builds on an extensive body of good practice aimed at 'creating and protecting value.' [3] This body of practice includes processes for identifying sources of risk and assessing the likelihood and consequence of risk events materializing. Controls are established to reduce risk, and risk indicators are identified and tracked to monitor change. Risk maturity assesses the degree to which these processes are embedded in an organization.

The premise is that we have the analytical capabilities to identify and isolate sources of risk and exercise control. While this is undoubtedly true in some contexts, it is less so when we consider the messily-entangled social, technical, ecological, economic, and political worlds we inhabit. Perhaps it is here, in the uncertainty and discomfort this complex world creates, that the journey begins toward an understanding of what a 'mastery of risk' might mean.

ON CHANGE

In his body of work on the resilience of socio-technical systems, David Woods builds on the idea that:

"Resources are finite, surprise is fundamental, and change never stops." [5]

Increasingly, change is accelerating beyond the rate of our (traditional) ability to learn. Often critical change is not visible until it is too late. Even intentional change in organizations is always a step toward terra incognita. Since we often cannot 'control' change, our thinking must move to how we might 'dance' with it.

The Cynefin Framework helps us dance, to navigate both intentional and emergent change. The framework acts as a map of the decision field, orienting us in different territories and helping us to understand the liminal spaces between. It allows us to explore diverse methods for engaging with change and applying them in novel, context-sensitive ways. Examples include methods for increasing agility in project management, [6] decision support, [7] strategy mapping, [8] and narrative-based sense-making. [9]

ON SURPRISE

Surprise can be disorienting, confusing, and overwhelming. It is also where novelty and possibility arise. How we cope with unfolding complexity, in the moment, determines success or failure. [5] Edgar Allen Poe once remarked that:

"It is the unforeseen upon which we must calculate most largely.' [10]

While it is helpful to develop the 'requisite imagination' to identify and prepare for new forms of surprise, our ability to respond must extend to that which we cannot yet imagine. [11] The pursuit of such preparedness seeks to understand how we notice outliers, make sense of events as they unfold, connect those with the agency and resources to respond, and establish a shared sense of purpose in our response. [12]

Perhaps nowhere more than in disaster risk management and response – when moments count – does it become apparent that different decision domains co-exist. For example, a disaster response command center must act rapidly during the initial chaos of a wide-scale power system blackout, relying on clear protocols for generator start-up and on good practice in coordinating a multi-agency response. Such protocols and good practice establish the time and space for real-time decision-making that is messy, despite our best preparation. Experienced disaster responders attest to a kind of 'calmness' that accompanies this messiness. It is grounded in an appreciation of what aspects of our response can be specified upfront (based on good and best practice), and what aspects depend on the patterns of thinking and decision-making that have been nurtured beforehand. [13] It is also cognizant of when our strategies and contingency plans no longer fit a changed context, and is primed to adapt the nature of our response to match the new context – in real-time, and at times under immense stress.

Cynefin helps us to better understand the essence of such preparedness in different contexts, and thereby to respond more intentionally to the unexpected.

ON RESILIENCE

Resilience in the face of chronic or acute adversity is an emergent outcome of the interaction of multiple agents, sensors, barriers, buffers, and enablers in a system. It is an enigmatic word; a noun that feels more like a verb. [14] We do not speak of managing resilience in the same way we speak of managing risk.

Given its trans-disciplinary roots, resilience is defined in various ways – from engineering resilience (the ability to bounce back) to ecological resilience (the ability to shift to a new stable state). [15] A helpful definition from socio-ecological systems thinking is:

"The capacity to sustain development in the face of change, incremental and abrupt, expected and surprising." – Carl Folke [16]

Resilience thinking focuses us on the need for diversity and redundancy, managing connectivity, promoting real-time learning and experimentation, working with slow variables and system feedback, broadening participation, and promoting poly-centric governance systems. [17] It encourages us to work with the world as it is, not as we wish or imagine it to be.

If there is an art to working with uncertainty, change, and surprise, it speaks to 1) how we anticipate and adapt to threats and opportunities, 2) respond to and recover from surprises, and 3) pro-actively transform the systems in which we work.

As a canvas for resilience thinking, Cynefin helps us recognize contextual relevance in working with ideas from various disciplines. It opens us to exploring how ideas such as possibility, ambiguity, metaphor, ritual, connectedness, and identity can be intentionally deployed to enhance resilience.

ON POSSIBILITY

Despite its stated intent – to work with both opportunity and threat – risk management in practice tends to draw our attention to where threats lie. The language of risk itself prompts this; we speak of sources and causes of risk (more than we do of possibilities), and of risk controls (more than we do of enablers). Our navigation of the unknown drifts toward defense over discovery.

As a thinking tool, Cynefin opens us up to novel ways of thinking about risk and developing risk controls. Navigating uncertainty in some contexts takes the shape of 'probing, sensing, and responding' by implementing multiple 'safe-to-fail' experiments. [2] In doing so, we extend our practice from 'engineering a system of controls' to 'nurturing the system' thereby cultivating the conditions from which new possibilities can emerge.

ON METAPHOR

"Reality is mediated by the language we use to describe it, the metaphors we use shape the world, and our interactions to it." – Sonja Foss. [18]

In our attempts to understand organizations better, we have over time, developed particular metaphors. Whether we engage with organizations as well-oiled machines or as eco-systems will profoundly affect how we manage risk and build (or nurture) resilience. Consider these statements:

"The classical mindset is that things go right because systems are well designed and scrupulously maintained, because procedures (and training) are complete and correct, because people behave as they are expected to – in particular that they do what they have been taught to do, and because designers (and analysts) can foresee and prepare for every contingency. If these assumptions are correct, then humans are clearly a liability, and performance variability a threat. The purpose of training and design is to constrain variability so that efficiency can be maintained." – Erik Hollnagel [19]

"Nature and evolution do not favor stability and equilibrium: instead, natural processes select for resilience and adaptability... for characteristics that foster evolvability. Living things learn from the past and anticipate the future and then modify themselves to handle ambiguity, uncertainty, and unwelcome perturbations. Handle and manage, not avoid and eliminate ambiguity and uncertainty." – Alicia Juarrero [20]

Cynefin helps us to not only understand the importance of the metaphors we use to think about organizations, but also to envisage how we might be more mindful in how we apply them in domains that are ordered vs. those that are complex or chaotic.

ON COMPLEXITY

In his writing, the naturalist John Muir ponders how,

"When we try to pick out anything by itself, we find it hitched to everything else in the universe." [21]

In risk management our predisposition is toward analysis and control. In doing so we resort to reductionism in setting objectives, in identifying sources of risk, and in controlling them. In the process, we lose sight of how the system is more than the sum of the parts. Consequently we inadvertently transfer methods helpful in one territory (or metaphor) to another – where they might be less helpful, and at times devastatingly unhelpful.

The pathways to the wrecks of policies and strategies are littered with position papers, roadmaps, plans, counter-plans, and task teams who have focussed on better analyzing "problems" in order to "solve" them. This focus on 'solving problems' loses sight of the dynamic, messy, fragmented, and at times incoherent nature of the real world, where today's 'solutions' often set up the conditions for tomorrow's 'problems.' [22]

Such unintended consequences are everywhere. Some risk controls constrain valuable organizational agility when it matters most. Some amplify the source of risk being controlled (due to unanticipated feedback loops). Indicators that become management targets, can cease to be effective measures of what is really happening in the system. [23]

To the risk practitioner, it can at times feel as if the 'whim of the gods' and the 'forces of nature' prevail.

Perhaps then our pursuit of mastery must lead us elsewhere. Perhaps mastery lies in better understanding the kind of territory we are in and how we should act in it.

There is immense beauty in complexity, if we choose to see it. Complex adaptive systems are open, irreducible, non-linear, sensitive to initial conditions, and carry their history with them. They are constantly changing, display path dependency, and are fundamentally unpredictable. In complexity, the pursuit of mastery leads us to choose to play an 'infinite game' rather than a 'finite game' that has clear solutions and end points. [24] As risk practitioners, our work becomes focused on setting up conditions for beneficial emergence – rather than attempting to 'solve' problems – or to 'control' outcomes.

The Cynefin Framework helps us to appreciate that 'complexity is not simply greater order complicatedness.' [25] Working with complexity is also not reliant on more complicated tools to analyze and control cause and effect. When we develop an appreciation for complexity, and for the limitations of deterministic thinking, we begin to see the world very differently.

"Both the dream of omnipotence and the nightmare of impotence in a fully knowable but deterministic world dissolve with complexity science, which in many ways represents an important cultural awakening." [26]

Perhaps the mastery of risk begins with such an awakening.

ON AMBIGUITY

Ambiguity is characteristic of complexity. It presents us with information that can be imprecise, insufficient, or conflicting, and it allows multiple coherent narratives to coexist. To embrace ambiguity is to be open to nuance, 'the quality of something that is not easy to notice but may be important.' [27]

At the outset of the risk management process, we confront ambiguity when we set out to clarify our objectives. Risk relates to the effect of the uncertainty on objectives, and our objectives are inextricably linked to the objectives of others. Where these are unstated, under-stated, or ignored, risk tends to arise.

The architect, Bjarke Ingels, applies the heuristic 'yes is more' to his work, embracing stakeholders' diverse needs. [28] By intentionally increasing the set of diverse objectives his team works with, novel architectural solutions emerge that meet broad stakeholder acceptance. Examples include a power station in Copenhagen that simultaneously is a ski slope, and 'invisible' flood risk defences in Manhattan that take the shape of human-centric activity spaces. [29]

Such openness to increasing diversity, though counterintuitive, entices us to connect ideas in novel ways. In the process, we open ourselves to possibility, whilst reducing the potential for systemic fault lines that give rise to increased risk.

Objectives should reflect the nature of the world we are working in. They are best explored collectively, and some will only be discovered on the journey.

ON CONNECTEDNESS

Our human connectedness within organizations affects how we respond to uncertainty, change, and surprise. As risk practitioners, we must recognize the different kinds of connectedness that characterize organizations. Formal (day-to-day) organizational structures, (temporary) emergency response structures, and informal networks afford different ways of interacting, making sense and responding.

In working more intentionally with these forms of connectedness, we orient our collective attention to where threat and opportunity might arise.

ON RITUAL

Rituals usher in important transitions in our patterns of thinking as our environment changes. [22]

Activating emergency response structures is a ritualized way of responding to threats in real time. Through pre-agreed protocols, we take on temporary roles, and our collective attention shifts to what is important in the moment. Distributed response structures afford an organization the ability, through this changed attention, to deal rapidly with multiple threats as and where they arise.

Similarly, we can deploy rituals to enhance our ability to notice possibility and respond to opportunity in the moments that matter most. Such rituals can take the shape of day-long strategy games or small intentional moments in the boardroom. Our intent is to create the conditions necessary for beneficial emergence. A transition is necessary when decision makers move from dealing with audit and compliance issues on a meeting agenda, to immersing themselves in strategic risk discussions. [22]

Well-crafted simulation exercises are a form of ritual that help us prepare for the unexpected. These 'as if' interventions disrupt our day-to-day patterns of thinking – allowing us to construct a new reality temporarily. [22] Such exercises can result in new patterns of thinking being carried back to the front line and into the boardroom. An executive might think differently about broader consequences in day-to-day decision-making. A technician might engage differently with a routine, but safety-critical, test in a power station.

The Cynefin Framework helps us consider what rituals to incorporate into our risk practice in order to shift patterns of thinking and decision-making in an organization.

ON IDENTITY

The language of risk is undoubtedly powerful as a tool for 'making the system visible' given its institutional acceptance as a management tool.

An organizational culture that seeks to nurture beneficial emergence is promoted when the practice of 'making the system visible' becomes trans-disciplinary, not relegated to formal corporate roles such as 'risk owner' and 'risk manager.'

We open up possibilities when we promote a shared identity that seeks to transcend our formal roles as atomized corporate agents. An identity such as 'system steward' helps promote such an organization, one that is continually discovering how better to anticipate, adapt, respond, and transform. [17]

ON LEARNING

At the center of the socio-ecological metaphor of organizations lies our human ability to learn. We learn by doing and by being attentive to error feedback. We do so in context, and with others.

Our ability to adapt to our environment and respond to unpredictable conditions is based on:

"The extraordinary ability of our brains to formulate hypotheses and select those that fit with our environment. We systematically generate abstract symbolic thoughts, and update their plausibility in the face of new observations." – Stanislas Dehaene [30]

In working with organizations as complex adaptive systems, we intentionally harness this ability to learn for the future and from the past. In learning for the future, we might undertake multiple safe-to-fail experiments, selecting those that best fit the unfolding context, knowing that these will help us to adapt to the future. In learning from the past we must maintain an awareness that our history is always constructed, 'pieced into meanings aided by our instincts, experiences, and research.' [31] As Maria Popova points out,

"History is not what happened, but what survives the shipwrecks of judgment and chance." [32]

Learning is stifled when we interpret the past through the lens of the present, forgetting that people in the past were living in their present, unaware of future outcomes. [31] We must nurture a curiosity for how it is that surprises emerge. Accountability for what happened is about giving account for our ability to act within the context of the system at the time. The system becomes open to adaptation when we acknowledge human variability and adjust to error. Conversely, as human beings we lose confidence and curiosity when we fear that our errors will be punished rather than corrected. [30]

For this reason we would do well to remain circumspect about the contextual applicability of methodologies we deploy. For example, methods such as root cause analysis can be unhelpful when dealing with complexity. We learn more by considering how, at different levels of the organization, agents act and respond to error feedback, than by tracing path-dependent root causes. [33]

The Cynefin Framework helps us to think about how we learn in the context we are in – whether through novel or emergent practice, or by adopting good or best practices. [34]

Human sensor networks based on narrative-based sense-making help us to identify patterns, small signals, and outliers. [9] They promote an understanding of how the organization actually works, over how we imagine it to work – from day-to-day operations to how we respond in simulation exercises and to incidents and disasters. This form of sense-making translates to organizational learning when we become intentional about shifting the patterns in the stories we tell each other.

ON PRACTICE

Neuroscientist and philosopher Andy Clarke suggests that 'we are all cyborgs.' That is, 'our minds extend out into the world, incorporating tools and other minds in order to think.' [35]

Cynefin is such a tool for connecting minds. It meets Clarke's requirement that 'complexity should reside in the task, not the tool.' [35] Its infusion into risk practice helps us develop a shared vocabulary as we become intentional in our practice in dealing with different decision contexts. It is such intentionality that differentiates a quest for mastery from a drive to embed risk maturity. [36]

LEAVE THE DOOR OPEN

As we return to the question of mastery, we will trace our journey back through the uncertainty, change, and surprise – and consider again the possibilities that arose as we probed the ideas of metaphor, ritual, connectedness, learning, and intentional practice.

Just as complexity is not a higher order of 'complicatedness,' we have seen that mastery is not simply the meticulous codifying of good practices and procedures. The pursuit of mastery is emergent, and the journey toward it ongoing. It is an 'infinite game' in the dynamic, messy, fragmented, and sometimes incoherent world in which we live.

In traversing this world, the Cynefin Framework is a navigation tool that entices us to think differently about risk and about our role as risk practitioners and system stewards. As we continue on our journey toward this particular terra incognita, that is, the mastery of risk, it seems appropriate to embrace the invitation in Rebecca Solnit's *A Field Guide to Being Lost*:

"Leave the door open for the unknown, that's where the important things come from... for, to acknowledge the unknown is part of knowledge." [10]

References

1. Solnit, Rebecca, Hope in the dark, Canongate Books, Ed.3, 2016: xii.

2. Snowden, David J., and Mary E. Boone. "A leader's framework for decision making." Harvard business review 85.11 (2007), p.68.

3. International Standards Organisation 2018. Risk management: Guidelines management systems - requirements, ISO 31000:2018, International Standards Organisation, Switzerland, 2018.

4. Bernstein, Peter L., Against the gods: The remarkable story of risk. New York: Wiley, 1996.

5. Hollnagel, Erik. "Coping with complexity: past, present and future." Cognition, Technology & Work 14.3 (2012), pp.199-205.

6. Snowden, David. "… which way I ought to go from here?", Cognitive Edge blog, 18 March 2018, http://www.cognitive-edge.com/blog/which-way-i-ought-to-go-from-here/

7. Snowden, David. "The OODA loop & Cynefin", Cognitive Edge blog, 10 November 2012, https://www.cognitive-edge.com/blog/the-ooda-loop-cynefin/

8. Wardley, Simon, . "Wardley maps" Medium., 7 March 2018. Retrieved 24 August 2020.

9. Van der Merwe, Susara E., et al. "Making sense of complexity: Using SenseMaker as a research tool." Systems 7.2 (2019), p.25.

10. Solnit, Rebecca. A field guide to getting lost. Canongate Books, 2006.

11. Weick, Karl E., and Kathleen M. Sutcliffe. Managing the unexpected: Resilient performance in an age of uncertainty. Vol. 8. John Wiley & Sons, 2011.

12. A. Antonovsky, "Health promoting factors at work: the sense of coherence," in Psychosocial factors at work and their relation to health, R. Kalimo, M. A. El- Batawi, and C. L. Cooper, Eds. Geneva, Switzerland: World Health Organisation, 1987, pp.153–167.

13. van der Merwe, Liza, Reinette Biggs, and Rika Preiser. "Building social resilience in socio-technical systems through a participatory and formative resilience approach." Systemic Change Journal (2019), pp.1-34.

14. Woods, David D. "Resilience is a verb." Domains of resilience for complex interconnected systems. (2018), p.167.

15. Comfort, Louise K., Arjen Boin, and Chris C. Demchak, eds. Designing resilience: Preparing for extreme events. University of Pittsburgh Pre, 2010.

16. Biggs, Reinette, Maja Schlüter, and Michael L. Schoon, eds. Principles for building resilience: sustaining ecosystem services in social-ecological systems. Cambridge University Press, 2015.

17. Lowe, T., and D. Plimmer. "Exploring the new world: Practical insights for funding, commissioning and managing in complexity." London: Collaborate (2019).

18. Foss, Sonja K. (1988). Rhetorical Criticism: Exploration and Practice (4 ed.). Long Grove, Illinois: Waveland Press (published 2009). p. 249

19. Hollnagel, Erik. "Coping with complexity: past, present and future." Cognition, Technology & Work 14.3 (2012), p.199.

20. Juarrero, Alicia. "Dynamics in action: Intentional behavior as a complex system." Emergence 2.2 (2000), pp.24-57.

21. Muir, John. My first summer in the Sierra. Houghton Mifflin, 1911. pp.185-288.

22. Puett, Michael, and Christine Gross-Loh. The Path: A New Way to Think About Everything. Penguin UK, 2016.

23. Strathern, Marilyn. "'Improving ratings': audit in the British University system." European review 5.3 (1997), pp.305-321.

24. Carse, James. Finite and infinite games. Simon and Schuster, 2011.

25. Blignaut S. 7 Differences between complex and complicated, 7 February 2019. https://www.morebeyond.co.za/7-differences-between-complex-and-complicated-systems/

26. Steve, Maguire, et al. "Introduction." The Sage Handbook of Complexity and Management. Peter AllenSteve Maguire and Bill McKelvey. London: SAGE Publications Ltd, 2011. 1-26. SAGE Knowledge. Web. 28 Aug. 2020, doi: 10.4135/9781446201084.n1.

27. Cambridge dictionary: https://www.google.co.za/amp/s/dictionary.cambridge.org/amp/english/nuance

28. Ingels, B., Floating cities, The Lego house, and other architectural forms of the future, https://www.ted.com/talks/bjarke_ingels_floating_cities_the_lego_house_and_other_architectural_forms_of_the_future?utm_campaign=tedspread&utm_medium=referral&utm_source=tedcomshare

29. Howarth, D., BIG U flood defences for Manhattan move forward, Dazeen, 2018, https://www.dezeen.com/2018/07/20/big-u-storm-flood-defences-east-side-coastal-resiliency-manhattan-move-forward/

30. Dehaene, Stanislas. How We Learn: Why Brains Learn Better Than Any Machine... for Now. Penguin, 2020.

31. Freeman, J. I'm a Historian. I See Reason to Fear - And to Hope. The Atlantic, 2020. https://www.theatlantic.com/ideas/archive/2020/08/historian-historic-times/615208/

32. Popova, Maria. Figuring. Vintage, 2019, p4.

33. Leveson, N.G., 2016. Engineering a safer world: Systems thinking applied to safety (p. 560). The MIT Press.

34. Snowden, D.J. The Ontology Word, Cognitive Edge. Blog, 2010. https://www.cognitive-edge.com/blog/the-ontology-word/

35. Clark, Andy, and Mark Erickson. "Natural-born cyborgs: Minds, technologies, and the future of human intelligence." Canadian Journal of Sociology 29.3 (2004), p.471.

36. Ruspoli T. Being in the World - A Philosophy Documentary, 2010. https://youtu.be/k5QJ8s3qUyA

What to read next

 Next Full Chapter: Cynefin and Strategy, Steve McCrone and Ian Snape, p.257

 Next Chronological: With Cynefin we Found our own Ecology, Anne Caspari and Johann Entz-von Zerssen, p.124

 Next Theoretical: Cynefin and Strategy, Steve McCrone and Ian Snape, p.257

 More on Cynefin Principle 2.1: Cynefin and Strategy, Steve McCrone and Ian Snape, p.257

CYNEFIN AND STRATEGY

STEVE MCCRONE AND IAN SNAPE

ABOUT THE AUTHOR

Steve McCrone's experience in bomb disposal in the New Zealand Army gave him a good understanding of decision making under conditions of uncertainty. Recognizing that traditional management theory is of limited use in fast changing and highly complex environments, Steve has dedicated his career to learning and applying complexity theory principles into his consulting practice – Cornwall Strategic. He has worked with Cognitive Edge since 2010 after attending a Cynefin foundations course. Cynefin forms the framework for Cornwall Strategics's 'Adaptive Strategy' approach. Steve now works with many of New Zealand and Australia's largest corporate and government organizations.

Ian Snape is the Co-CEO of Frontline Mind, a niche digital-backed learning company specializing in resilience, recovery and leadership in complex high-risk environments. In a previous career, Professor Snape balanced a passion for ice climbing, skiing and polar adventures with an academic career at Melbourne University in the defense against the dark arts, as well as leading teams in Antarctic research. As a consultant trainer he facilitates at the interface between innovation, industry and policy where he helps organizations develop strategy and capability. His clients include large corporations, not for profits and front-line agencies such as the U.S. Marine Corps, Police, Ambulance and Prison services. Cynefin underpins his approach to enabling teams and organizations to survive and thrive in a complex, turbulent world.

ABOUT THIS CHAPTER

 Full Chapter

 Theoretical

 Chronology: Piece 18 of 33

 Cynefin Principles

CYNEFIN AND STRATEGY

STEVE MCCRONE AND IAN SNAPE

In today's climate we can no longer reliably consider strategy a noun - a written tome describing a pathway through a prescient future, but must consider it a verb – discovering ways forward and leading employees and the organization with an appropriate heartbeat offering time and resources for experimentation. Strategy is a dynamic movement through the Cynefin domains.

Today's strategies are usually out of date by the time they are printed. They rarely resonate with front-line employees and are typically ignored, sometimes even subverted. We believe strategy is a verb: a continually evolving process that guides attention, decision-making, and action in a way that remains coherent with purpose in a complex, ever-changing world.

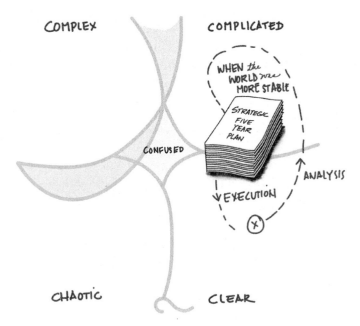

Figure 1. When strategy was a printed document

Developing an organizational strategy is often seen as a higher-order management function where the brains reside in executive and senior suites. But we take a whole-of-system approach, encouraging leaders to involve staff, clients, and stakeholders in a continual process of co-creation and feedforward (feedback coupled to scenario planning or future-shaping using evidence). Strategy and implementation planning, and resultant plans, need to be fit for purpose – just detailed enough to reflect the inherent uncertainty in the system.

Managers who work in complex systems know that plans are susceptible to change and disruption, often in surprising ways. Yet human nature wants to mitigate the effects of change; we use risk management techniques that seek to reduce variation to bring order to opaque or inherently unclear situations.

A strategy often has an inherent dissonance, a struggle between the ordered and the complex. And many managers are initially frustrated by the process of developing and especially implementing strategy. We find that the Cynefin Framework empowers strategic approaches that are appropriate to both ordered and unordered domains. As such we are able to help managers understand their context and how it relates to action, allowing a release of tension between the desire for certainty and the need for exploration.

We have used the Cynefin Framework to guide sense-making and action in models such as:

- Business Model Canvas, [1]
- Boyd's Observe-Orient-Decide-Act (OODA), [2][3]
- Lean Six Sigma and Agile methods, [4]
- Distributed insight collection and analysis through Cynefin's SenseMaker software,
- Facilitation and engagement processes such as Systemic Modeling, [5]
- A portfolio approach to innovation that considers risk and opportunity at different scales and domains of predictability. [6]

We advocate for a thoughtful and dynamic allocation of attention and resources across tactical, strategic, and horizon time-frames. With this we mean a resource distribution that is akin to spread betting, and that is reviewed on a regular basis. For example, just focusing on immediate pain points is often an eternal trap of reactivity, whereas just focusing on the 5-10 year horizon offers little to ensure that we can respond to what is emerging or will emerge in the next few years to survive to reap the benefits of such innovation investments. We invest in activities and culture for high 'probability' (these can be as implicit as explicit) as well as highly asymmetric investments. Taleb refers to this as the barbell approach to innovation, although the best distribution can vary across and within businesses. [7] Of crucial importance, we view Cynefin as a dynamic sense-making framework informing executives when and where to apply some of these approaches to strategy, innovation and culture.

STRATEGIC DIRECTION

An organization's strategic direction can be expressed as a change over time. Some of these changes are the result of deliberate, planned action. Others are a result of a reaction to the emergence of change in the environment. Henry Mintzberg describes strategy as the realized actions resulting from the combination of intended and emergent strategies. [8] Organizations that are led with too much planning and deliberate action can become slow and cumbersome. On the other hand, organizations that are too fluid and rely on emergence can become incoherent and reactionary.

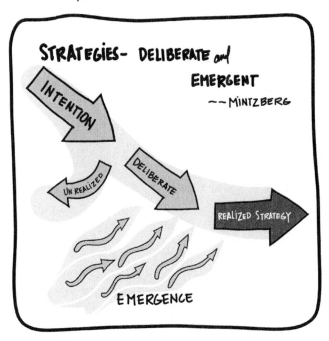

Figure 2. Strategy as a combination of intended and emergent action

Most executives show a preference for an ordered systems approach to strategy, decision making, and resource allocation. So part of our first intervention in most organizations starts with a description of Cynefin and has the client contextualize their strategy opportunities to move forward and their response to those opportunities.

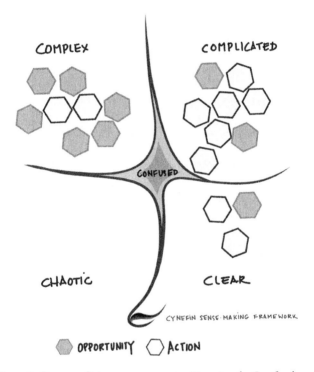

Figure 3. Contextualizing strategy opportunities using the Cynefin domains

STRATEGY IN THE ORDERED DOMAINS

The dominant paradigm for management thinking over the last 50 years has been Systems Dynamics. Systems dynamics (sometimes called systems thinking) uses a mechanical metaphor to treat the organization as a machine. We see this in the language that is used in strategies that are based on systems dynamics. 'Levers for change', 'drivers for growth', 'alignment', 'optimization' etc.

Systems dynamics assume that most of our strategic landscape is known or knowable – through analysis, and that the future will unfold in a predictable or manageable way.

Strategic Planning based on a systems dynamics approach takes the following form:

We assume that the future is known and create the best-imagined future. Then we find a path toward that idealized future. We are certain of our place in the strategic environment and confident in our ability to predict changes. Implementing the plan is a matter of managing resource allocation over time.

The manager's job is to ensure we are on the right path and lead with a command and control mindset. We know this process as Strategy Implementation – the strategy as a separate task from strategy development. Risk management concerns itself with identifying, evaluating, and prioritizing known risks to the strategic direction. Innovation is also a separate process that feeds ideas into the plan.

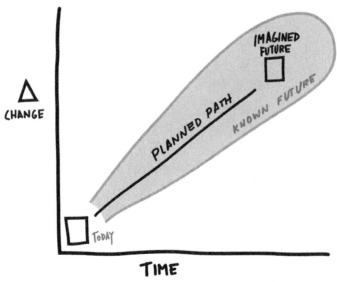

Figure 4. A planned path to a known future

STRATEGY IN THE COMPLEX DOMAIN

"Seeing the world as a ceaselessly complex and adaptive system... involves changing the role we imagine for ourselves... from architects of a system we can control... to gardeners living in a shifting ecosystem that is mostly out of our control." – Joshua Cooper Ramo [9]

When we are certain about our future, we can establish clear goals and priorities. When we are less certain, strategy becomes a series of exploratory steps designed to explore and learn. We conduct small experiments in parallel, gain fast feedback, and enable rapid exploitation of success. Leaders manage the tempo and the direction of the business as a continuous process.

Implementation is immediate because we take direct action now to understand how we can impact the strategic environment. A leader's job is to set the direction and enable their people and teams to test and learn based on their direct understanding of the strategic environment.

• Set the direction to travel

• Create the tempo

• Manage the constraints

In a complex domain we set a new 'mode of operation' for the organization – strategy shifts from planning and implementation toward moving in the right direction at the right tempo. Risk is managed by taking a broad and diverse perspective, detecting the weak signals of change, and responding quickly. Learning from many small failures is like an immune system for the organization. It provides a signal about where to travel and will often offer guidance about what not to do, or what to do less of.

Figure 5. In the Complex domain strategy involves doing multiple small experiments

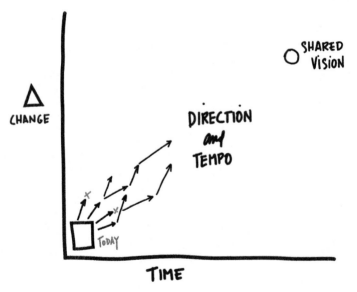

Figure 6. In the complex domain strategy shifts from planning and implementation toward moving in the right direction at the right tempo

COHERENCE WITH PURPOSE (OR MISSION)

The purpose (mission) for the organization should be broad enough to encourage initiative and clear enough to establish intent. We sometimes call this a shared understanding of success. It should provide a sense of direction for all levels of the organization. Senior managers should also clarify the 'main effort' or the broad strategies for movement toward the organizational purpose. The intention here is to create the shortest distance between intention and action by allowing employees to develop micro-strategies coherent with the broad strategic intent. This is 'mission control' and is in stark contrast to the more common 'command and control' exercised by many senior managers who establish their intent and then constrain people through budgetary and planning controls.

Executing the strategy now becomes a matter of allocating resources to move in the right direction at the right tempo. This challenges the concept of alignment because parts of the organization may choose to experiment and explore different opportunities. Coherence comes from our shared understanding of success (purpose) and our shared mental model for movement (Cynefin).

An important role for the leader is to manage the constraints and the resource allocation needed to maintain coherence and tempo.

BOUNDARIES AND DYNAMICS

It may be useful for executives to think of strategy as leading the movement through and between the Cynefin domains. In the core business, we generally have processes, procedures and projects that we can treat as complicated. These are repeatable and we have enough historical information to be reasonably sure of our future. Staff have the skills and experiences needed to guide decision-making and resource allocation. We can reliably forecast and model the system.

The Complicated-Complex transition is like immunity against strategic drift, where a company loses its competitive edge. For instance, the people in the organization become extremely good and efficient at delivering one product or service at the expense of anything else. Hit by a market shock or significant disruption, they are left vulnerable. Enabling some parts of the business to challenge the status quo by conducting multiple safe-to-fail experiments, we can test the assumptions behind a core business. If some of these experiments produce positive results, we should look to amplify them and build an evidence base. We may even take a shallow dive into the liminal complex/chaos domain to stimulate innovation and creativity.

These new emergent ways of doing things, new methods or practices, then replace the old systems once we have confidence in their repeatability. We will then wrap in more defined processes and procedures and provide additional resources. This is the movement from complex to complicated. Be careful not to do this too soon as interventions in the complex will almost certainly have unintended consequences.

We may need to hold and allow sufficient time in the liminal complex/complicated domain to allow for more understanding and refinement. If we push something that's not fit for purpose into the complicated domain too soon, we may drop straight into the Chaotic domain. The advantage of trialing multiple activities at the same time is that we don't expect them to all work, and we only need one or two to do so to be able to keep moving forward. The key to vigilance is using evidence to track success and failure, and continually feed forward into future actions.

Ongoing we continually test the assumptions behind our strategic plan. We establish real-time feedback loops and bring safe-to-fail experiments into 'business as usual.' We notice the temptation to constrain the system in the Clear domain. That may be useful for processes where we need to control for variation but can cause us to tip into chaos if we over constrain things. Be aware too that people who are good at leading and managing in one domain may not be suited in another.

Business issues like culture, engagement, and stakeholder relationships are continuously complex and relationships are almost certainly complex. A good rule of thumb is to assume that almost all human-to-human interactions start in the Complex domain. When we try and standardize these, they seem inauthentic (like call centres) and do not bring out the best in employees. By trying to make these interactions more efficient by standardizing them it destroys meaning and the personal nature of the relationship. We must remain vigilant in such instances, manage in the moment, amplify things we like, and disrupt things we don't.

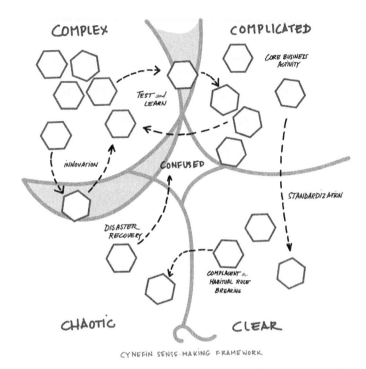

Figure 7. Strategy as leading the movement through and between the Cynefin domains.

PIVOTING

The word 'pivoting' is often used to describe a situation where you need to change quickly in response to a sudden change in the strategic environment. Sometimes this brings the organization into the liminal domain between complexity and chaos. The term implies that you are pivoting or revolving around something. Are you pivoting around your value propositions, your customers or your relationships? We can use Cynefin to contextualize how we pivot, and we link the axis to different aspects of the Business Model Canvas. [1]

A strategic approach to innovating at the boundary of chaos is setting up what we call a rapidly parallel, safe-to-fail portfolio of ideas or projects. We will do them all quickly and relatively cheaply, and test the market to see which land. We then put our attention on what is having early success and quickly kill the other ideas off. The advantage of trialing multiple activities at the same time is that we don't expect them to all work, and we only need one or two to land for us to be able to keep moving forward.

INNOVATION PORTFOLIO DESIGN ACROSS DOMAINS AND TIME-FRAMES

One advantage of using the Cynefin Framework to guide strategic decision-making is it allows people from different parts of an enterprise to share their perspective on the risks and opportunities within their domain. At the enterprise level, risks and opportunities for innovation and strategic change are invariably complex. At lower levels of granularity, there are often parts or functions that are in the Complicated, Clear, or even Chaotic domains. Cynefin can be used very effectively to facilitate diverse stakeholders to consider actions and investments as part of a coherent whole. Such a portfolio, by design, allows for the tension between order and exploration.

Uncertainty and risk/reward. Overall, portfolio design needs to recognize safe-to-fail experimentation that is coherent with the enterprise as a whole. For example, there is little point exploring a fast parallel safe-to-fail pivot, or a significant paradigm shift for a good or service, while simultaneously driving efficiency through continual improvement of lean processes in the same part of the business.

In his book *Antifragile*, Taleb describes a barbell strategy for investing. [7] In that strategy, the bulk of investment is to protect or refine existing assets. When we extend this to enterprise strategy, this implies we gradually protect what is already working in the business. At the other end of the spectrum, he recommends a deliberate high-risk investment in actions that could result in highly asymmetric benefits.

Executives using a portfolio design need to consider uncertainty, risk/reward, and a time-frame.

Timeframe:

- tactical or short-term often months or up to a year or so,

- strategic or medium term perhaps a year to five years, and

- horizon, which could be 5 to 10 year explorations, typically geared towards highly speculative or uncertain aspects of the business.

Let's look at projects and programs in a balanced portfolio for a water utility. They might include:

1. Tactical projects that review approvals and regulations for developers. Often red tape and bureaucratic inefficiency can build up over time as regulations evolve, and utilities struggle with ongoing transformation programs. A review using lean principles of waste reduction might be appropriate in such a context to review the need for multiple touch-points for routine and well-ordered processes. [10]

2. Strategic projects like a short-term partnership with a university to improve cost, time, and precision in water quality testing methods. Lead times might be 4 to 5 years for new methods to meet regulatory approval, and multiple methods might need exploration in the early phases of evaluation.

3. Horizon projects or programs could include investment in a consortium with other utilities and several university groups to look at possible risks, opportunities and synergies from climate change, population growth, hybrid energy systems and emerging trends of how people wish to live in cities. At inception, many of these projects would have poorly defined benefits and pathways at the early stages of investment and design. It might take five years or more before emergent patterns and opportunities become sufficiently visible to warrant deliberate guidance into a complicated program of research and development that have a clear line of sight to operational benefit.

FRACTAL SCALING

A strategy based on movement through the complex domain to establish core capabilities in the ordered domains is fractal - and micro-strategies that are coherent with the mission or purpose can occur at all levels. That means that the relationship between context and movement is the same at any level of the organization. An example of a fractal relationship is the concept of trial and error. The simple process of finding a plausible solution, trialing it, learning from errors and trying again with a modified hypothesis, is self-similar at any scale. 'Trial and error' can be used in assessing shoe size, or in the acquisition of a complementary business.

The organizational strategic plan does not need to be more or less detailed, exact, or defined than the operational plans that flow from the strategy. This self-similar relationship can exist right down to individual resource allocation.

This means that the 'mode of operation' can be established as part of the organizational DNA. There is no need to change or differentiate the strategy development as the organization grows, diversifies, or changes its objectives.

SUMMARY

The role of strategy in the last century was to create a competitive advantage by defining and dominating a market position. The strategy was about creating an idealized future and planning a way to meet that future.

In today's uncertain, volatile and fast-changing world, the strategy is less about position and more about movement. Executives who can quickly detect and respond to opportunity will create a dynamic organization that is resilient to change and capable of exploiting a change in the strategic landscape. The strategy is about designing and constantly adjusting the heartbeat and the direction of the organization.

Recognizing that strategy is a verb, the portfolio acts as a central place of evolving documents to develop and inform relationships across business units and to facilitate conversations about priorities, emerging trends and business intelligence.

We use Cynefin to provide the framework and context for both movement and portfolio design. Sometimes we need to predict, plan and control. At other times we need to explore, experiment and learn. Cynefin allows managers to guide their organization through these transitions with the use of appropriate constraints.

References

1. Osterwalder, A. & Pigneur, Y. (Wiley, 2010). Business Model Generation: A Handbook for Visionaries, Game Changers, and Challengers.

2. Osinga, F. P. B. (Routledge, 2007). Science, Strategy and War: The Strategic Theory of John Boyd.

3. Richards, C. (Xlibris Corporation, 2004). Certain to Win: The Strategy of John Boyd, Applied to Business.

4. Porter, M. E. (Free Press, 1998). Competitive Strategy: Techniques for Analyzing Industries and Competitors.

5. Walker, C. (Clean Publishing, 2014). From Contempt to Curiosity: Creating the Conditions for Groups to Collaborate Using Clean Language and Systemic Modelling.

6. AXELOS. (AXELOS, 2013). Portfolio, Programme and Project Offices P3O®.

7. Taleb, N. N. (Random House, 2012). Antifragile: Things That Gain from Disorder.

8. Mintzberg, H., Lampel, J. & Ahlstrand, B. (Free Press, 2005). Strategy Safari: A Guided Tour Through The Wilds of Strategic Management.

9. Ramo, J. C. (Little, Brown and Company, 2009). The Age of the Unthinkable: Why the New World Disorder Constantly Surprises Us And What We Can Do About It.

10. M. L. (McGraw-Hill, 2002). Lean Six Sigma: Combining Six Sigma Quality with Lean Production Speed.

What to read next

 Next Full Chapter: Coming of Age: From Frameworks and Theories of Change..., Ann Pendleton-Jullian, p.279

 Next Chronological: Coming of Age: From Frameworks and Theories..., Ann Pendleton-Jullian, p.279

 Next Theoretical: Coming of Age: From Frameworks and Theories of Change..., Ann Pendleton-Jullian, p.279

 More on Cynefin Principle 1.3: Cynefin's Influence on The Flow System, John R. Turner and Nigel Thurlow, p.320

 More on Cynefin Principle 2.1: A Cynefin Approach to Leading Safety in Organizations, Gary Wong..., p.357

FROM COOKSTOWN TO CYNEFIN

ANNE MCMURRAY

ABOUT THE AUTHOR

Anne McMurray (BSSc. MSW. MSc. PCC. MBE) is an independent organizational development consultant, specializing in leadership and team development, strategy formulation and change implementation. Anne uses a range of methods to help clients achieve their goals in an increasingly complex environment. She has been a practitioner with Cognitive Edge since 2004. She has supported a wide range of client organizations to use the SenseMaker methodology, to surface the lived experience of key stakeholders, to inform policy and practice in health, education and professional leadership settings. Anne works throughout Ireland and Great Britain, as well as in Europe and Canada, particularly in the areas of health and social services, NGOs, housing, education and local government, as well as with private sector clients.

ABOUT THIS CHAPTER

 Vignette   Theoretical

 Chronology: Piece 7 of 33

FROM COOKSTOWN TO CYNEFIN

ANNE MCMURRAY

Which one is the odd one out: Chicken, Grass, or Cow? The answer is Chicken if you are a Celt. The reason why is because Celts understand the world through relationships. A Germanic answer is likely to be Grass. Germanic languages tend to describe the world through classification. For me, this was an early nugget of Dave Snowden's wisdom that I received when he first introduced me to complexity thinking, and what I call the Cynefin lens of understanding. He is Welsh and I am Irish so we are Celts. Instant rapport. Words create worlds.

Thinking in terms of relationships was instilled in me growing up in Cookstown, Northern Ireland, at the community, town, region, nation, and international levels. In Northern Ireland, most people choose to align with one side against the other: unionist vs. republican. This is reflected in election results and perpetuates division. Few people choose the middle, integrative, connecting ground. For me, that was, and is, the only space.

Systemic problems require systemic solutions. Intractable issues cannot be solved in isolation but only in the context of related problems.

Throughout my career, I have focused on integrating what appears to be in opposition in different types of organizational systems to enable new possibilities to emerge.

During the 1990s, as an organizational development consultant, systems thinkers such as Deming, Senge, and Drucker informed my approach. By 2000 I had run out of road with these approaches. My work was increasingly multi-sectoral, spanning different systems that were tackling what we called then 'wicked issues.' I refer to complex issues such as public health in Ireland, domestic violence, child protection, and social and economic regeneration.

So I began to search for a thought leader who could give me a way of understanding how to work within these complex environments. The search led me to David Gurteen's Knowledge Café meeting in March 2003 in London to hear a guy named Dave Snowden. I had tracked him down through references and articles. I was hopeful for a breakthrough in my thinking and to find someone who could answer my questions.

Just as the session was about to start, David G. explained that Dave S. would not be able to join us due to personal circumstances. My immediate reaction was disappointment and frustration. I had come all this way to go home 'empty brained.' However, in the next sentence, David announced, "…But Dave will give his presentation on the phone through the microphone and I will work the slides for him here in the room."

OK, I thought, so this man is honorable and follows through on his commitments. When Dave Snowden introduced himself and explained that his absence was due to his parents' recent bereavement, my estimation of him soared.

He then delivered his hallmark Cynefin presentation, complete with the gorilla clip and the children's party story to explain entrainment, self-organization, and attractor stimulation. He explained and described the Cynefin domains and it all began to make sense.

He reasoned what I was intuitively beginning to understand through my experiences working with family, community, and organizational systems. He validated different organizational domains and the importance of understanding in which Cynefin domains problems are located to plan the most appropriate interventions. ABIDE, QQE, network incentivization, and 'Future Backwards' are all techniques that are derived from my understanding of the Cynefin Framework. [1][2][3]

I completed the Cynefin practitioner program in 2004. I have since worked with Cognitive Edge using SenseMaker software in a wide range of health and social care related projects. Examples include mental health, end of life care, autism, neurological conditions, school non-attendance, and leadership development. We initiated the 10000 + Voices project in the Northern Ireland health system. The outcomes have led to changes in policy and practice in service provision, and it has been a demonstrator project for other work internationally. Right now we are using the approach to gather nurses' experiences of working through the COVID-19 crisis. We are upscaling this to parts of the UK.

I have introduced the Cynefin Framework to many leaders. It has helped them launch initiatives that have enabled emergence and innovation. I have countless mini examples of application and spread.

I am so grateful that Dave has been my mentor and friend since 2003. And yes I have experienced Olympic-level intellectual gymnastics in conversations with him ranging across physics, philosophy, cybernetics, social anthropology, leadership, organizational psychology, political economics, and rugby. We had a 'sliding doors' beginning. What if I hadn't gone to London? What if the improvised presentation had not worked? What if Dave had ignored a request from an unknown person in Belfast? I believe there are mysterious forces that guide our lives that we can't logic out or explain. In this case, that Dave's and my paths were destined to cross and good work would result.

And I still never understand more than about 50% of what he talks to me about.

References

1. ABIDE is an acronym for five elements that can be used in the complex domain for problem solving. They are:
   - Attractors i.e. the forces that stimulate the patterns of behavior
   - Boundaries that 'hold' the context i.e. time, place, policy, roles
   - Identities i.e. the actors in the situation and the relationships between them
   - Dissonance i.e. diversity and conflict that can unleash creativity and energy
   - Environmental i.e. the context physical or virtual in which the issue is located.
2. QQE is an acronym for Qualitative Quantitative Evaluation. This is a method I use in SenseMaker projects during the results interpretation workshops. It looks at the impact of the various qualitative themes that have emerged.
3. The Future Backwards method was created to aid in widening the range of perspectives a group of people can take on understanding their past and the possibilities of their future.

What to read next

Next Vignette: Not all Those who Wander through Complexity are Lost, Anna Panagiotou, p.277

Next Chronological: The Story of Cynefin 'Coming Home' to Welsh Public Services, Chris Bolton, p.98

Next Theoretical: Coming of Age: From Frameworks and Theories of Change..., Ann Pendleton-Jullian, p.279

NOT ALL THOSE WHO WANDER THROUGH COMPLEXITY ARE LOST

ANNA PANAGIOTOU

ABOUT THE AUTHOR

Anna Panagiotou's roots are in archaeology and research, with a degree in history and archaeology and a PhD in Mediterranean archaeology. In 2019 she made the leap from social complexity to anthro-complexity. She started working at Cognitive Edge, transitioning to a role in the Cynefin Centre in 2020, and deepening her experience with SenseMaker. Anna is involved in several Centre programs, including Climate Change and the response to COVID-19. She is interested in absolutely everything, although material culture holds a special place in her heart.

ABOUT THIS CHAPTER

 Vignette   Narrative

 Chronology: Piece 31 of 33

NOT ALL THOSE WHO WANDER THROUGH COMPLEXITY ARE LOST

ANNA PANAGIOTOU

This is the story of how and why one wayward "academic" (and I cannot add enough quotation marks around that word) met, and eventually got involved with, the Cynefin Framework.

I finished my PhD in 2015, and after much frustration with the lack of funding in my field, I tried to break free. I went looking for employment out in the real world. In late November 2017, I was invited to the Christmas dinner of a company I had applied to, where I was intrigued by a certain bearded Welshman. He was a guest at the same dinner and spent most of the evening gently napping at the table.

In the months following my hiring at the company that held the Christmas dinner, I started hearing people talk about things being "complex" or "complicated," and my ears immediately pricked up. I studied archaeology, and my PhD specifically had to do with what archaeologists call "complex societies." In other words, I have had to do a lot of thinking around what being complex means (in this very human context and based on the material part of people's lives that gets left behind: their stuff, and sometimes themselves too). This also meant I did a lot of thinking about what it means for something not to be complex. What became obvious is that you cannot cleanly split everything into simple or complex categories. And it was also clear that the reasons we have for seeing some things as complex and others not are interesting in themselves.

And so I met the Cynefin Framework, and in the summer of 2018, I also properly met its creator. This time he was awake, keen to talk, and excited about the archaeological perspective. Following that conversation, I was assigned to assist with writing a mini-book on Cynefin. I was given access to the Online Foundations and was encouraged to rummage through Dave's blog to my heart's content to produce a sort of compilation of notes.

The book never came to be, but those months of playing around with the Cynefin Framework, and trying to come to terms with liminal domains, dynamics, and the nature of UnOrder and Disorder (terms that were still in use in 2018) gave me a more intimate understanding of the Framework. By the end of that year, I was a part of Cognitive Edge's training team and eventually moved to the Cynefin Centre.

In the end, what hooked me? What was the connection between the Cynefin Framework and research, and how could anyone curious about the world benefit from it? In a nutshell, Cynefin manages to get to the core of questions that are fundamental to all of science. If you boil it down, we all work on understanding and manipulating subtle, intricate, often hidden webs of connection. These are the literal nature of how our world is: connections and relations are everything. And yet, there are other things too: we can identify (or usually create) areas where we can sever or ignore most of the connections, and control things differently and directly.

Cynefin has also helped me articulate where a sense of ethics fits with research practice. Cynefin acknowledges perspective and perception without saying that everything is relative: material reality exists and the choices we make have material results for ourselves and others. This responsibility to reality, and to others, (unintended consequences and all) is the ethical side of how Cynefin has been my companion in complexity tolerance.

Finally, Cynefin has been a way of understanding this weird life course I'm on. Moving from Greece to London to Berlin, from a PhD to an office job to the Cynefin Centre, could have felt like random bouncing around. But what it is I realize, is navigating complexity – starting from what is available at the time, interacting with the system, trying many different things, and evolving myself, as things around me evolve, and moving not towards a goal, but in a direction of change. In my own life, my personal Cynefin has comforted me and shown me that navigating complexity is not at all the same as being lost.

What to read next

 Next Vignette: Tohu va-Facebook and Dave Snowden, Kendra Rosencrans, p.311

 Next Chronological: Tohu va-Facebook and Dave Snowden, Kendra Rosencrans, p.311

 Next Narrative: Tohu va-Facebook and Dave Snowden, Kendra Rosencrans, p.311

COMING OF AGE: FROM FRAMEWORKS AND THEORIES OF CHANGE TO SCAFFOLDS FOR ECOLOGIES OF CHANGE

ANN PENDLETON-JULLIAN

ABOUT THE AUTHOR

Ann M. Pendleton-Jullian is an architect, writer, and educator. She is a professor and former Director at the Knowlton School of Architecture at Ohio State University, and Distinguished Visiting Professor of Design at the Pardee RAND Graduate School of Public Policy. Previously, she was a Fellow at Stanford University's Center for Advanced Study in the Behavioral Sciences (CASBS) 2018 cohort and an Associate Professor of Architecture at MIT for fifteen years. Her work sits at the intersection of architecture, complexity science, and tools, and ecologies of change.

ABOUT THIS CHAPTER

 Full Chapter

 Chronology: Piece 19 of 33

 Theoretical

 Cynefin Principles

COMING OF AGE: FROM FRAMEWORKS AND THEORIES OF CHANGE TO SCAFFOLDS FOR ECOLOGIES OF CHANGE

ANN PENDLETON-JULLIAN

A framework is a structure designed to support or enclose something, or an abstract setup for solutions to several related problems. It is a complete structure, usually permanent, and gives form to that which it supports, or encloses, or solves. A scaffold, however, is a temporary structure that supports something to emerge on its own terms, it influences as it supports, and is designed to 'scaffold' and steer emergence in today's complex environments.

An anthology of stories and reflections from the Cognitive Edge (CE) community to celebrate Cognitive Edge's 21st birthday is a delicious idea, especially if like me, you can never think about birthday parties without replaying Dave's iconic video on How to Organize a Children's Party in your head. So Happy Birthday Cognitive Edge and congratulations Dave!

Dave Snowden and I met on Nov 7, 2010, at Highlands Forum XVIII in Phoenix Arizona. The topic that brought us together was 'Addressing Complex Problems.' [1] The Highlands Forums were small, closed convenings of the Highlands Forums Group – a cross-disciplinary network of global leaders established in 1995 by the Secretary of Defense. Its aim was to examine questions of emerging interest at the forefront of a range of fields, not just technology. From CEOs to Nobel and Pulitzer Prize winners, to pioneering scientists and journalists, the convenings were small and serious. Most contributors appeared once. I had the inordinate privilege to become one of the seven or so core members of the group, attending the majority of forums for five years until the Department of Defense defunded it. The Phoenix forum was only my second Forum and I was still wall-flowering much of my way in a room of intellectual giants.

Dave stood out. A giant like the others but with uncompromisingly penetrating Welsh wit!! And that was before he even showed his take on intractable problems, the Cynefin Framework, and his micro-narrative sense-making landscapes. I was typically blown away by at least one or two things at each Forum, but this talk was one of the half-dozen, (or so) intellectually-life-changing moments that I most remember from the Forums.

This was the third slide from Dave's 2010 talk:

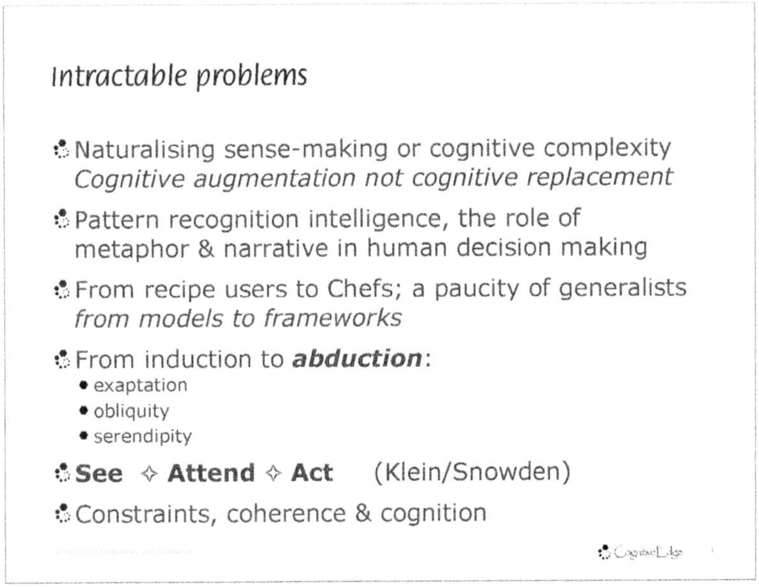

Figure 1. Intractable problems: Third slide from Dave's 2010 talk

If one were to have dropped this slide, it would have made a significant depression in the hard desert caliche, filled with a density of meanings to be unpacked. This is the paradox of Dave, Cognitive Edge, and the community that has emerged around him: human-focused and intellectually uncompromising; intense yet playful; aiming for change but honoring the rhythms that persist; penetrating arrows of insight propelled by rhetorical humor...

And this leads me to the task at hand: to contribute a useful gift to the party.

While all points in Dave's Phoenix Forum slide merit pondering, or re-pondering as they are familiar to most of us, I want to mull on the third point down: "from recipe users to Chefs... from models to frameworks." This notion of moving from models that try to represent reality in various forms (could be mathematically or diagrammatically or physically) so that we can repeat it, to frameworks that loosen the one-to-one hold on what reality is in order to think about ways to work with reality – is a significant shift.

I began my career in astrophysics and then worked for thirty years as a practicing architect, professor and author. Over the past fifteen years, I have developed an expanded "architectural" practice that takes on complex adaptive systems problems – a practice that is motivated to steer change towards better states of what is known as "wicked" problems – those intractable problems that are integrally embedded in complex adaptive systems. I also work with individuals and organizations to steer change and build capacity towards having true agency in the world today. In the summer of 2018 Dave had me speak on my work and new book, *Design Unbound: Designing for Emergence in a White Water World* at the Cynefin Retreat in Whistler BC.

I introduced and sketched a case study of designing for emergence – General Stan McChrystal's transformation of the Joint Special Operations Command (JSOC) – and the generalizable 'framework' for how to make it useful under other conditions and in different contexts. Except it was not a 'framework,' I claimed, but a 'scaffold.' Unexpectedly, this led to an entire discussion of scaffolds vs. frameworks because the difference between them is as important as the analogy is provocative.

So, my party favor for this 21st birthday party is this analogy and how it is part of a virtuous circle that supports the practice of designing for emergence and how it is a class of products that one designs to steer emergent change. This last part will only be a trailer because it has been written about elsewhere. [2]

We all love frameworks, they give our thinking about a problem or project form and structure, while allowing us to remain open to specific content. There are numerous (too many to count) theories of change (ToC) that rely on frameworks upon which to clip their assumptions and methodologies, even supporting the generation of online software. [3] These ToC frameworks are so highly regarded that they have established standards and quality control for the practice of change.

In the mid 1990s, with roots in organizational psychology, sociology, and political science, theories of change promised frameworks of "best practice" for creating social change. But the world has changed exponentially since the 1990s, and we are confronted with increasingly "wicked" problems in which social aspects swamp technical issues, while technology itself is creating disproportionate ripples through all corners of social life and systems, where technological change and its corresponding effects may not level out. Our world is one where everything we do connects to everything else around it in dynamic flows of connectivity and exchange.

'Out of the box thinking' is a different proposition/challenge when the box changes its shape, size, material properties, and even its solidity day-by-day. That makes working on the change complex. There is a certain ironic humor for those in the Cognitive Edge community who work on change in organizations, government, communities, or on behavioral change. And that is the general belief that changing the state of a "wicked" problem can be done through the use of best practices, in strategically planned ways and using standards. To design for today's challenges, we need to design through and for emergence. To do so, we need scaffolds for change, not frameworks. Thus, it is essential to understand the difference.

Scaffolds (they're different than frameworks)

A framework is a skeletal structure designed to support or enclose something, or an abstract setup for solutions to several related problems. It is a complete structure, usually permanent, and gives form to that which it supports, or encloses, or solves. On the other hand, a scaffold is a temporary structure for supporting something until that something can stand on its own.

In architecture, a scaffold usually holds workers and materials during the erection or repair of a building. As a temporary structure for doing work on something, it is not the primary object. It is typically incomplete, it is not left in the system, and it does not give form to the primary object. In fact, its form is usually dictated by the form-to-be of the primary object.

Figure 2. Architectural scaffolds

Biological scaffolds are fascinating, like nano-fiber mats and three-dimensional nano-engineered scaffolding structures that are used in regenerative medicine. These support human tissue, structures and organ growth in the human body compromised by injury or disease. These scaffolds allow cell attachment and migration. They can also deliver vital nutrients or exert specific mechanical or biological influences to modify cells' behavior. In most cases, the scaffold dissolves as the cells grow and the organ or tissue regenerates. Scaffolds support and nurture cell behavior defined by their own needs and "instructions" for growth. They do not determine the final work; they provide for, and in some cases influence, its emergence.

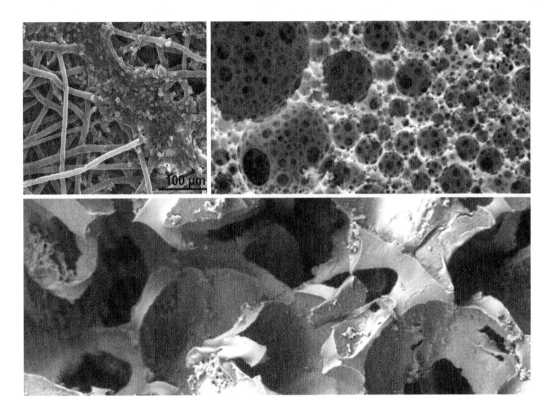

Figure 3. Biological scaffolds

This tiny, tubular, porous scaffold in Figure 3, built by engineers and physicians at the University of Washington, supports and stabilizes fragile cardiac cells and can be injected into a damaged heart. It will foster cell growth and eventually dissolve away. The new scaffold supports cardiac muscle growth and potentially accelerates the body's ability to supply oxygen and nutrients to the transplanted tissue. Ultimately, the idea is that doctors seed the scaffold with stem cells from either the patient or a donor, then implant it when the patient is treated for a heart attack before scar tissue has formed.

Then there is the more 'cyborg' version of the biological scaffolding as in this work coming out of Bioengineering at Harvard University.

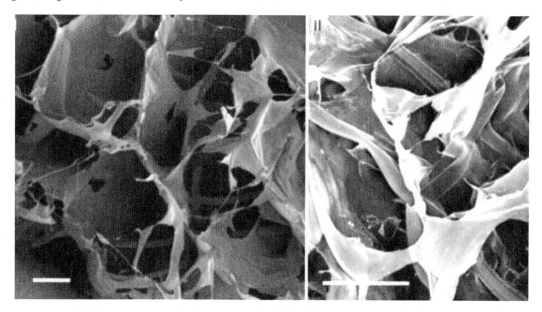

Figure 4. Harvard creates cyborg flesh that's half man, half machine

These 'cyborg' tissues are half living cells, half electronics. As far as the cells are concerned, they're just normal cells that behave normally – but the electronic side actually acts as a sensor network, allowing a computer to interface directly with the cells. In the case of cyborg heart tissue, the researchers have already used the embedded nanowires to measure the contractions and heart rate of the cells.

To create cyborg flesh, as reported by Sebastian Anthony, you "start with a three-dimensional scaffold that encourages cells to grow around them. It is generally made of collagen which makes up the connective tissue in almost every animal. Harvard engineers took normal collagen and wove nanowires and transistors into the matrix to create nano-electric scaffolds (nanoES). Neurons, heart cells, muscle and blood vessels were then grown as normal, creating cyborg tissue with a built-in sensor system." [4]

In biological scaffolding, the scaffold provides the means for the natural emergence of an organ's tissue regeneration. It provides structural support that the organ (such as the 'missing' skin in a severely burned patient) itself cannot, while also creating the necessary conditions and resources (nutrients) for growth. It changes the context for the regeneration of tissue, which follows its own instruction/ruleset. A scaffold, therefore, supports emergence: lower-level rules creating higher-level order.

Scaffolds scaffold (support non-permanently) emergence. And because we can design scaffolds, this metaphor helps us understand how to design for emergence and steering change, whether in an organization or in the state of a "wicked" problem.

DESIGNING FOR EMERGENCE

In his 2007 *Harvard Business Review* article with Mary Boone, Dave defined complex systems this way:

"In a complicated context, at least one right answer exists. In a complex context, however, right answers can't be ferreted out. It's like the difference between, say, a Ferrari and the Brazilian rainforest. Ferraris are complicated machines, but an expert mechanic can take one apart and reassemble it without changing a thing. The car is static, and the whole is the sum of its parts. The rainforest, on the other hand, is in constant flux – a species becomes extinct, weather patterns change, an agricultural project reroutes a water source – and the whole is far more than the sum of its parts. This is the realm of "unknown unknowns."

My colleague and friend John Rendon, who works on these kinds of problems at the scale of governments and nations, has said:

"Complex problems change when you look at them, when you talk with them, and when you engage with them. Interactions are nonlinear and disproportionate; minor changes can have major consequences." [5]

And so:

"The objective is to attain some ability to 'steer' the complex system. But how do we steer a system through a complex, tangled web of interactions?" [6]

Whether applied to self-organized forms of matter-energy or to the unplanned results of human agency, new concepts of (non-linear causality and self-organization) demand a new methodology... a more experimental attitude toward reality and an increased awareness of the potential for self-organization inherent in even the humblest forms of energy. [7]

Designing for emergence is designing for change in a context or system already in motion. How? By introducing an integrated set of components and mechanisms, or even better, ecologies of components and mechanisms with the intention of 'steering' the system in its ongoing self-organization. Designing for emergence is shorthand for designing for emergent behavior in complex systems – those systems that manifest and are driven by emergence. For our purposes, we are interested in complex adaptive systems (CAS) as opposed to complex physical systems, but designing for emergence can apply to both. We are interested in CAS because these are the systems that contain people and it is in these systems that wicked problems form.

Designing for emergence works on the world for the future. The future cannot be designed or engineered; it emerges from actions in the present that are influenced by actions of the past. So, one needs to understand the complex system as it is now, but in relation to its past causality, influences, and entangled events and systems. One needs to also envision what one is aiming for – what would be a desirable, not just default, future state – and then design sets/webs of mechanisms to put into the system to steer it from now to then. The paths imagined are only provisional – all moves are understood to be provisional – things will shift as the context changes. Things will need to be renegotiated as the system gives feedback and adapts.

People who design for emergence understand that contexts are complex and rich as a result of things in motion – flows, exchanges and negotiations – and that inserting new things and actions can direct those flows and exchanges. Small moves can have a tremendous impact on a system already in motion. From new things (policies) to new worlds (a new world engendered by AI), designing for emergence honors the context-in-motion as a complex adapting system. That means one must work at the very operational level of the system, focusing on the dynamics of emergence and exchange within it.

How to do this?

In a keynote talk at the RSD4 Systemic Design conference 2015, Don Norman, Director of the Design Lab at UC San Diego, provided a thorough and clear definition of complex problems. He then referenced the Yale Economist Charles Lindblom's concept of 'muddling through' as the most effective approach for working on complex problems. Seemingly a surrender to complexity, 'muddling through' for Lindblom is not a lack or failure of method, but a system of successive incremental changes – successive small maneuvers that one can do quickly and then assess to move on. The value in Lindblom's process is that doing real work in the system is the means for making progress. But we can do better than tactical heuristic incrementalism. Using the principles of emergence coming from complexity science, we can design for emergence. We can design for change.

In *Design Unbound: Designing for Emergence in a White Water World*, John Seely Brown and I elucidate principles and tools for doing this in the chapter devoted to "Designing for Emergence." We begin by referencing John Holland's framework of four characteristics that belong to the phenomenon of emergence to talk about mechanisms and systems of mechanisms that work with those characteristics – these are ecologies of change. [8]

ECOLOGIES OF CHANGE

Complex problems cannot be solved because any attempt to create a solution changes the nature of the problem. The full landscape of the problem cannot be understood until provisional actions taken to work on the problem are taken. Yet, every one of these provisional actions creates intended and unintended consequences that change the nature of the problem; they change the context itself. Although not solvable in any traditional sense, complex problems can be approached by affecting the way the complex system – the context – around the problem evolves.

Designing for agency and resonance in complex adapting contexts that are continually emerging means that one must work at the operational level of the system itself, and within its functional dynamics. This requires a completely different type of toolbox – one whose tools are not associated with specific tasks at hand but, instead, work on the 'instruction set' that underlies the dynamics of the system – its parts, mechanisms, practices, protocols, the context, and the interdependent relationships among these.

Ecologies of change are specifically useful for steering change, or just having agency, in a whitewater world – one that is rapidly changing, broadly connected, and radically contingent. This is very different than top-down strategic plans, which organize phased management of an operations pathway aimed at a high priority goal, and different than tactical incremental improvement – both of which have value under conditions that are stable, knowable, and hierarchically organized.

Ecologies of change consist of integrated, interacting sets of mechanisms that aim to steer an emerging/unfolding complex adaptive system while it is in motion. Scaffolds can play an important role because they don't impose a deterministic form on the system itself. Scaffolds offer a temporary coherence so that what needs to emerge, can emerge.

NOW WE ARE BACK TO SCAFFOLDS AS THINGS TO BE DESIGNED...

It is the biological scaffolds that we look to as the best metaphor because they allow us to understand the role of the scaffold as non-permanent but offering resources. The cybernetic ones are even more interesting. They enable us to imagine how the scaffold of an ecology of action might leave parts of itself behind – for example, mechanisms and processes for assessment and recalibration, analogous to the heart monitor and pacemaker – to become parts of the system, helping its constituents learn to adapt and evolve.

In chapter 17 of *Design Unbound*, we present the Change Triangle 3.0 as a meta-mechanism for an ecology of change. Two case studies are unpacked: one that was part of a set of case studies that led to the generation of the meta-mechanism and another that was the application of it in another context. The Change Triangle 3.0 is one of two meta-mechanisms in the full book. They are both scaffolds, not frameworks, that operate by designing for emergence.

Returning to this metaphor of a scaffold (as a non-permanent, semi- to fully-surreptitious thing that supports the emergence of a primary thing's emergence), unlike a framework that defines/gives/dictates organizational structure, functional structure, form, or "architecture" of the thing, scaffolds take their cues from the needs of that which they are scaffolding. It is important to understand that they are not crutches or prosthetics. They are not without agency. They have agency in that they support the emergence of the system emerging. They can do this so that the system is sustained as it was meant to be. But they can also catalyze shifts in how the system plays out – from subtle to radical.

PUSHING THE BOUNDARIES OF SCAFFOLD THINKING

In speaking with Dave about scaffolds at the Snowdonia Cynefin Retreat in the fall of 2018, Dave brought up the notion of shadow scaffolds – a very interesting thought! By nature, scaffolds, unlike frameworks, are surreptitious. They not only function in a non-permanent way but also do so quietly and without fanfare – covertly. I assumed that Dave's term 'shadow scaffold' meant scaffolds that do covert, or tacit, work. But, if one takes "shadow" literally to mean a duplicate version of an object, in this case, the scaffold, and one with less dimensionality by one degree, it becomes very interesting. A scaffold that is more surreptitious than the first-order one yet is still related. Without intending to be glibly tautological – a scaffold that scaffolds the scaffold. Interesting indeed!

So what is the work of the shadow scaffold? It could be the work of tacit practices. But if we are after truly novel thinking – novel work that breaks through where other 'solutions' have failed – it could also be the mental muscle work we associate with the imagination. If that is the work the shadow scaffold does, then what is the scaffold itself? How do we scaffold the imagination to make it pragmatically productive, not merely expressive? [9]

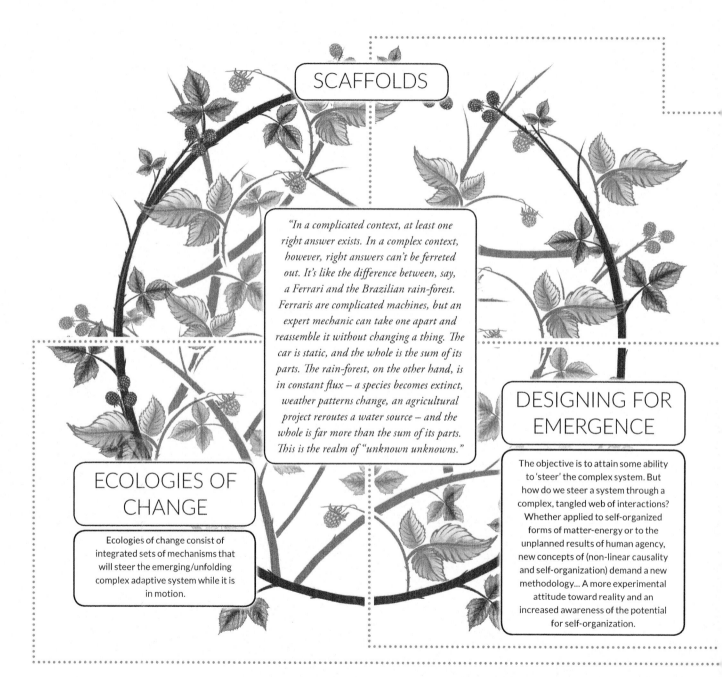

SCAFFOLDS

"In a complicated context, at least one right answer exists. In a complex context, however, right answers can't be ferreted out. It's like the difference between, say, a Ferrari and the Brazilian rain-forest. Ferraris are complicated machines, but an expert mechanic can take one apart and reassemble it without changing a thing. The car is static, and the whole is the sum of its parts. The rain-forest, on the other hand, is in constant flux – a species becomes extinct, weather patterns change, an agricultural project reroutes a water source – and the whole is far more than the sum of its parts. This is the realm of "unknown unknowns."

DESIGNING FOR EMERGENCE

The objective is to attain some ability to 'steer' the complex system. But how do we steer a system through a complex, tangled web of interactions? Whether applied to self-organized forms of matter-energy or to the unplanned results of human agency, new concepts of (non-linear causality and self-organization) demand a new methodology... A more experimental attitude toward reality and an increased awareness of the potential for self-organization.

ECOLOGIES OF CHANGE

Ecologies of change consist of integrated sets of mechanisms that will steer the emerging/unfolding complex adaptive system while it is in motion.

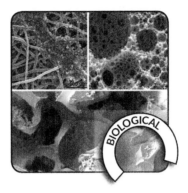

In biological scaffolding, the scaffold provides the means for the natural emergence of the tissue regeneration of an organ. It provides structural support that the organ (such as the 'missing' skin in a severely burned patient) itself cannot, while also creating the necessary conditions and resources (nutrients) for growth. It changes the context for the growth – the regeneration of tissue – which follows its own instructions. A scaffold supports emergence: lower level rules creating higher level order. Scaffolds scaffold (support non-permanently) emergence. And because we can design scaffolds, this metaphor helps us understand how to.

"Complex problems change when you look at them, when you talk with them, and when you engage with them. Interactions are nonlinear and disproportionate; minor changes can have major consequences."

But how to do this? In Design Unbound, Designing for Emergence in a WhiteWater World, Ann Pendleton-Jullian and John Seely Brown elucidate principles and tools for doing this in the chapter devoted to "Designing for Emergence". They begin by referencing John Holland's framework of four characteristics that belong to the phenomenon of emergence to talk about mechanisms and systems of mechanisms that work with those characteristics – these are ecologies of change.

References

1. David Snowden, Welsh management consultant, founder and CSO of Cognitive Edge, a management-consulting firm specializing in complexity and sense-making. Also known for his development of the Cynefin Framework.

2. A. Pendleton-Jullian and John Seely Brown in Design Unbound. Designing for Emergence in a WhiteWater World, Volumes 1 and 2, (Cambridge MA: MIT Press, 2018).

3. "TOCO Software – Theory of Change Community. www.theoryofchange.org. Retrieved July 16, 2020.

4. John Rendon, founder and CEO of the Rendon Group; senior communications consultant to the White House and Department of Defense, in conversation, March 4, 2012.

5. S. Anthony, "Harvard creates cyborg flesh that's half man, half machine" in ExtremeTech, august 29, 2012. https://www.extremetech.com/extreme/135207-harvard-creates-cyborg-flesh-thats-half-man-half-machine

6. John Holland, Emergence: From Chaos to Order, (New York: Basic Books, 1998) p 3.

7. Manuel De Landa, A Thousand Years of Nonlinear History, (New York: Swerve Editions, 2000) pp. 17, 273.

8. In Design Unbound, ApJ and JSB elucidate principles and tools for doing this. Paraphrased from chapter 11, "Designing for Emergence":

    In his groundbreaking book Emergence: From Chaos to Order, John Holland wrote, "the hallmark of emergence is this sense of much coming from little." He then went on to describe four characteristics that belong to the phenomenon of emergence. In emergence:

    1. "Possibilities for emergence are compounded when the elements of the system include some capacity, however elementary, for adaption or learning."(Complex adaptive systems are systems that learn through feedback. They acquire information about the environment and their interaction with that environment. Identifying regularities and irregularities in that information, they form schema or models that allow them to act. Actions then produce new information that feeds back to modify the schema as necessary. In this manner, they adapt. Emergence depends upon systems that learn.)

    2. "Component mechanisms (in an emergent system) interact without central control." (They act in relationship to each other not by directives from a central authority.)

    3. "Possibilities for emergence increase rapidly as the flexibility of the interactions increases."

    4. "Persistent patterns at one level of observation can become building blocks at still more complex levels."

        Holland's characteristics are useful as a framework to talk about designing for emergence as a purposeful approach.

        If we are aiming to design rules that engage with a complex system—one that self-organizes, advances from the inside, and learns because of relationships that depend upon resource and information exchange—then we need to design rules that are about relationships and processes of resource and information exchange between components and their environments/contexts.

And further, following John Holland's parameters for emergence, these rules must scaffold learning in the system. They must stimulate interactions that function without central control. They must encourage flexibility of interactions. And they must inspire the creation of coherent packages of exchanges, communications, and actions that can become building blocks at still more complex levels.

So, designing simple rules that are about interactive relationships and processes of exchange between components within a context, with possibilities for system learning and the ability to aggregate actions for higher order behavior, is a good place to start to think about designing for emergence. Then we need to design the mechanics that set the rules in motion – the mechanisms to drive those rules.

9.   See ApJ and JSB, Pragmatic Imagination, (Blurb, 2016), or Chapter 19, "Pragmatic Imagination" in Design Unbound. Designing for Emergence in a WhiteWater World, Vol. 2: Ecologies of Change, (MIT Press, 2018). Or see "Pragmatic Imagination. A New Muscle for a WhiteWater World" http://www.desunbound.com/assets/papers/a_new_muscle_for_the_white_water_world.pdf

What to read next

 Next Full Chapter: Facilitation Can be Complex (and It Certainly Should Be), Vivienne (Viv) Read, p297

 Next Chronological: Cynefin and Delivery, Greg Brougham, p.113

 Next Theoretical: Facilitation Can be Complex (and It Certainly Should Be), Vivienne (Viv) Read, p297

 More on Cynefin Principle 1.1: Facilitation Can be Complex..., Vivienne (Viv) Read, p297

 More on Cynefin Principle 3.1: Cultivating Leadership with Cynefin...,, Jennifer Garvey-Berger..., p.139

FACILITATION CAN BE COMPLEX (AND IT CERTAINLY SHOULD BE)

VIVIENNE (VIV) READ

ABOUT THE AUTHOR

Based in Australia, Viv Read was one of the first independent practitioners to be trained in Cynefin and associated methods in 2003. An experienced practitioner, facilitator, trainer and mentor, Viv has incorporated the tools and methods into her consulting practice, and has developed a reputation for her skills and expertise in complex facilitation processes. She undertakes collaborative projects with Cognitive Edge and other independent consultants working in Australia and internationally. She is an active member of the practitioner community.

ABOUT THIS CHAPTER

 Full Chapter   Theoretical

 Chronology: Piece 4 of 33   Cynefin Principles

FACILITATION CAN BE COMPLEX (AND IT CERTAINLY SHOULD BE)

VIVIENNE (VIV) READ

This chapter is for those who facilitate groups to make sense of complexity in order to act, and who use complexity-based processes to do so, or are interested in doing so. Our focus is on the Framework's decision support role and its complexity-based tools and methods. Herein, fundamental concepts and principles will help you decide whether this is a path you may wish to pursue.

Every tool and method that we use, or policy that we develop, has assumptions, values, and sometimes the history of the originating culture attached to it. It has been designed to meet a particular purpose and comes from a specific context, and often a particular point in history. Some of these may not be explicit and can get lost or obscured. Some may be sufficiently universal for it not to matter too much. Others have a significant impact. Not knowing what these conditions might be, or taking the time to understand them often makes the tool or method less than adequate.

There is both a skill and an art to revealing a tool's embedded values and assumptions. Similarly, this also applies to how we moderate the tools' impact in the context in which we are using it.

As facilitators, if we work with tools without context, in other words we don't know enough to know the tool doesn't fit the situation, the intervention will suffer, as will the overall outcome.

In my home country of Australia, there had been a revolution in workplaces from the mid to late 1980s. It culminated with the introduction of enterprise bargaining. This move – from a system of standardized terms and conditions of employment for similar job classifications to processes that recognized context, including geography and the specific industry and skills-based career paths – revolutionized industrial relations and workplace practices in all sectors of the economy.

I was privileged to work alongside the late Professor Bill (Gordon William) Ford as he pioneered new approaches to support this new focus. We undertook assignments in some of Australia's leading organizations, including Lend Lease, Carlton United Breweries, Sydney Opera House, ICI, and Westpac. We had developed a language and an integrated and consolidated set of principles and heuristics that helped me make meaning of my own experiences in ways that enabled me to converse effectively with colleagues and clients.

I had already been working in organizational change and workplace reform for some 25 years when I met Dave Snowden and learned about the Cynefin Framework and its complementary tools and methods. Dave's Framework and tools confirmed the importance of understanding context when interacting with systems. I realized later that Dave gave me the theoretical underpinnings of what I intuitively had felt and observed in my work.

Here are a few examples that illustrate what can happen when you don't consider the impact of context.

- The design of imported German equipment for breweries assumed that the workforce consisted of highly skilled operators and technicians. Australian breweries employed operators who were often unskilled immigrants with minimal literacy and numeracy in English. There was a separate technical workforce to deal with more technical issues. Consequently, productivity was always less than 70% on the same equipment compared to German factories.

- Some years ago, Australia purchased submarines that were severely at risk of ever going out to sea. The design assumed sub-mariners were skilled in mechatronics – a combination of skills unheard of in Australia. There wasn't sufficient room on board for the 50% larger crew needed to set sail.

- My attempts to explain Australian terms and conditions of employment to a U.S.-based mining company were somewhat fraught. Australians, who have permanent employment, are entitled to long, paid service leaves – 13 weeks that fall due after ten years of service. Why? Because when Australia was a penal colony, it would take that long to sail home to England to see the family and sail back to resume duties. The reasons are long gone, but the entitlement is embedded. And, no, these terms and conditions are non-negotiable.

These examples repeatedly show that the problems were far more complex, not complicated in terms of the Cynefin Framework, than was initially thought. And workplaces are complex human systems. Because context matters, we also have to rethink how we facilitate in a Complex domain.

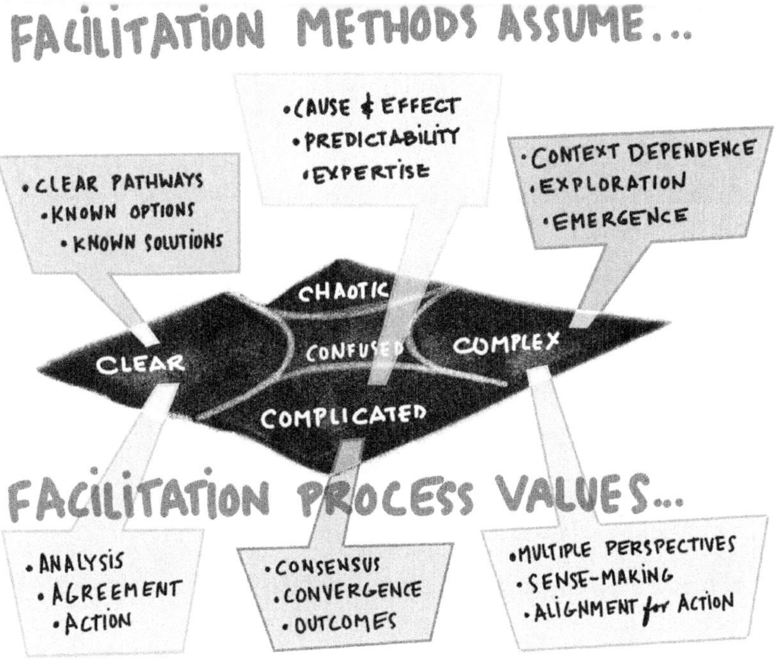

Figure 1. Process and methods... What to use when

THE CYNEFIN FRAMEWORK AND COMPLEX FACILITATION

Over the years, I have become an advocate for the value of complex facilitation. Dave confirmed what I already intuitively knew: when problems are complex, you need to facilitate the people who are entangled in the problem using a complex facilitative approach. Traditional facilitation methods, comparatively, impose an ordered approach on complex issues, often leading to dysfunctional or "same old, same old" solutions.

Let's start with a definition:

Complex facilitation is "the facilitation of complex methods to make sense of complex issues in order to take action..."

Contrast this to the definition of traditional facilitation:

- "Supporting everyone to do their best thinking, a facilitator enables group members to search for inclusive solutions and build sustainable agreements." [1]

- "...contribute structure and process to interactions, so groups are able to function effectively and make high-quality decisions. A helper and enabler whose goal is to support others as they pursue their objectives." [2]

The Cynefin Framework indicates that methods and approaches are valuable yet have limitations - i.e., they work well in one or two domains, but seldom in all domains (bounded applicability). Traditional facilitation methods are useful in ordered systems where outcomes are known. In complex systems, where we deal with messy, tangled problems and messy relationships, they are far less valuable.

The basic principles of complexity we need to understand to facilitate complex processes

According to Cynefin, the way we act in complex systems is by probing, sensing and responding. We shape the interactions with the people in the system, and the system itself, to make space for emergence. Complex facilitation focuses, therefore, on inviting and allowing for opportunities to emerge.

The intent of complex facilitation

To sustain an environment for a group of people that enables a socially constructed shared understanding of complex issues to emerge with sufficient agreement to take action.

This approach is fundamentally different in every way to how traditional facilitation has been taught and practiced. For example, in traditionally facilitated workshops, participants often play a relatively passive role, working towards a particular outcome, and deferring to experts. Or they may be used to being the experts in workshop situations and have others defer to them. Complex facilitation does not allow these patterns to play out but disrupts participants' previous patterns of expectations and expertise. Over the years that I have been practicing complex facilitation, I noticed it could be confronting and uncomfortable for both facilitators and participants at first, however it can also lead to new insights and highly effective workshops.

For participants it means...

They move from known patterns of engagement, where facilitators are responsible for the direction, problem-solving and conflict resolution, to processes with ambiguous instructions, no predetermined outcomes, and minimal to no engagement with the facilitator in the content. The responsibility for producing an outcome shifts from the facilitator to the group.

For facilitators, it means...

A shift from being the expert who is in control of a process and its outcome, to designing and supporting social constructions for participants. That allows for meaning to emerge, with no engagement of the facilitator in content at all. And this means that the facilitator needs to embrace ambiguity and uncertainty as well.

THE PRINCIPLES OF COMPLEX FACILITATION

The various workshop methods and software tools that rely on parts of the Cynefin ecosystem have Cynefin organizing and complexity principles threaded through them. To apply complex facilitation, one needs to understand these principles and how they play out in practice.

Design principles

- Avoid Pattern Entrainment: The initial activity sets the 'pattern' for what will follow. Suppose you start with a traditional activity like setting ground rules (i.e., the facilitator is in charge) or a presentation by the most senior expert in the room. What happens? People fall into old thinking patterns, and nothing new will emerge.

- Design for Distributed Cognition and Multiple Perspectives: As best you can, ensure a variety of perspectives and overall diversity in the group. A facilitator would often be tempted to keep these diverse groups separate to avoid unnecessary conflict, but this also limits the emergence of novelty.

- Enable descriptive self-awareness:

  - Design processes in ways that enable participants to "see the system" and discover insights for themselves i.e., about differences and/or similarities in perspectives, rather than being told or led by the interpretations of external consultants/facilitators.

  - Use different colors, hexagonal post-it notes, and various clustering processes to reveal emergent patterns to participants. These provide insights into different perspectives or aspects of the system. (For those wondering why we use hexagonal post-its: hexagons cluster in ways that squares do not, and help people break out of thinking in categories.)

- Ensure requisite levels of ambiguity and uncertainty:

  - Design processes to be ambiguous so that participants enter into a state of uncertainty. Participants will be uncomfortable, and facilitators need to be prepared for that. This allows for new ideas and meaning to emerge that will enable new actions.

  - Some of the ways we do this include:

    - Ensure multiple processes are run in parallel to increase levels of ambiguity and opportunity to disrupt small group dynamics by moving people between activities.

- Never provide detailed agendas or give all the instructions for an activity up-front. People should not know what is coming next.

- Instructions are slightly ambiguous to allow meaning to emerge from the group.

- It is not the facilitators' role to rescue or give answers.

The facilitation role... 'the heuristics' for a light footprint

- Provide no direct examples or personal experiences, use metaphors instead

- Resist direct comments on behavior, i.e., if someone is dominating a conversation or not participating, the facilitator creates a change in the system to enable a new behavior, they don't comment on the behavior.

- Do not engage with content, only the process, i.e., make changes to the process or the environment that allows different behavior to emerge.

- Apply complex domain principles: make small changes, monitor what happens, dampen or amplify patterns – all at the level of the system.

- There should be more than one facilitator to monitor what is happening to amplify or dampen, and make sure other facilitators are not succumbing to the temptation of engaging with content or providing examples (it is very easy to fall into this trap!).

In sharp contrast, a traditional facilitation role emphasizes [3]

- Leading. A facilitator must be able to keep the training or meeting focused toward achieving the outcome(s) identified beforehand.

- Problem-solving. A facilitator should be skilled at applying group problem-solving techniques.

- Empathizing. A facilitator should be able to "walk a mile in another's shoes" to understand the learners' or team members' feelings.

COMPLEX FACILITATION IN ACTION: A REAL-WORLD EXAMPLE

I offer an example of working with Cynefin and complexity. While it's from an experience I had in 2004, it is particularly noteworthy both because it stands the test of time and is considerable in its scale (and it's a story that also involved Dave).

It was 2004 somewhere in Australia

Some 350 people were gathered in a basketball stadium to discuss the future of the educational system in their state. They were a mixture of teachers, school principals, (government and faith-based) public servants (State and Federal government), parents, and community leaders.

The facilitation space served as a complex human or social system for as long as it was operating. To manage the boundaries of the system, facilitators led and monitored the process as it played out in the whole system. Everyone was always in the same space, so while we had many small groups, there were no separate breakout rooms.

There was enough space to move people around comfortably and sufficient wall space to accommodate a large amount of flip chart material and other data. Only one facilitator (Dave Snowden) had a microphone, Sonja Blignaut and I (Viv) remained on the mezzanine floor with an elevated view of the overall group, i.e., the system.

A step-by-step playbook for complex facilitation

1. **The purpose of this gathering**

We had contracted for a two-day process. We needed to help participants develop enough shared understanding of the current context of the education system, and its challenges, so that two things would happen. 1) there would be agreement on recommendations for action that would move the participants toward the desired new direction and 2) this would emerge throughout these two days.

2.   The participants

The participants were from metropolitan, rural and remote localities and included some 30 indigenous representatives from the State educational system. They were very diverse in terms of status and levels.

The new chief executive (CEO) of the Education Department had been in the role for about six months and was from another state. Nobody knew everybody, everybody knew somebody, and everybody had an opinion on what should happen, as well as who was to blame for what had happened so far. For some of the 30 indigenous representatives, English was a second or third language. Narrative data had been collected from some, but not all, of the participants.

The three facilitators met the CEO the day before the workshop and I briefed the indigenous participants on what to expect from the process. The Minister would speak on day one of the workshop.

3.   The process

There was no presentation to open the session. The Minister, at our request, made his presentation later on day two. There was also no check-in or ground-rule setting. We just dove straight into the first activity.

Several Cognitive Edge complexity methods were used in addition to the pre-collected narrative data. These included Future Backwards and Archetype Extraction. Each method enabled participants to:

- Generate data from their own experience

- Make sense and attribute their personal meaning

- Seek patterns and themes

- Share insights and develop a shared context

- Use the Cynefin Framework as the decision support tool to determine priorities for action

- Develop recommendations based on the principles contained in the Framework

The critical elements of the design of this end-to-end process included:

- Seeking the Minister's permission to move his contribution to day two to reduce the impact and lessen the effect of pattern entrainment.

- Allocating different colored hexagonal-shaped sticky notes (hexies) for different cohorts for all activities. These different colored 'hexies' from the various activities provided visual patterns of the different perspectives in the room, especially once they formed part of mixed clustered outcomes later on in the process.

- Starting with groups of people from similar organizations/professions (i.e., organizing for similarity) and then mixing across different cohorts (organizing for diversity) later.

- Multiple activities happening in parallel.

- There was a regular sharing of information across groups to socialize and share insights, but not to the whole group.

- Introducing the Cynefin Framework as the integrative decision support tool.

- Supporting the process by using artifacts like 'action sheets' based on the domains of the Cynefin Framework. They were used to capture recommendations for the final session. (In Cynefin-speak this is called 'scaffolding.')

4. **Managing the process – complex facilitation principles in action**

As facilitators, we had multiple activities happening simultaneously and we were using deliberate disruption to prevent premature convergence (coming to decisions too quickly). We achieved deliberate disruption by giving instructions like:

- Please select in each group the person who has contributed the most. Ask them to come to the front of the room for an important task. (This is also how we manage dominant voices).

- Move two people at random intervals from each group counterclockwise to another group.

- Form new groups by having one person step out from each group and have them come together in a new group(s).

On average, a group did not have consistent membership longer than 15 to 20 minutes. One or more members were regularly changed to another activity and/or another group. Of course, this contrasted sharply with more traditional approaches and contributed to rising levels of frustration.

With 40 different small groups, the whole system was monitored from the mezzanine level by Viv and Sonja, where one of the additional activities took place. There was constant communication with Dave on the floor of the stadium.

5. **Be prepared for the unexpected**

A common defense for the anxiety created by the ambiguity, is to ask multiple questions and attempt to defer to the facilitator's authority. It can be hard to resist, but the facilitator cannot compromise his or her role by giving in. Some of the questions we encountered included: "Can you give me an example of what you want?" Our answer: "No." "Is this what is expected?" Answer: "Is that what has meaning for you and your colleagues?" "What is the expected outcome?" Answer: "There isn't one".

At one point on the first day, a small group of around 25 school principals looked anxious and somewhat angry. Their concerns were about not knowing what was expected and the anticipated outcomes. When told, "we don't know,' "it will emerge," and "trust the process," they became increasingly angry and decided they would not come back the following day. They were protesting, in their words, "being treated disrespectfully."

They did not come back on the second day. The CEO, who thankfully was a very pragmatic individual, commented, "At least I now know who is not comfortable with ambiguity." In contrast, at the end of that day, representatives from the indigenous community expressed their thanks for creating a process where, "for the first time we have been able to participate equally in a planning process." That was significant because indigenous communities often feel locked out of effective engagement by processes that privilege those who have been trained in complicated methods. The principles of social construction and embracing diversity embedded in complex methods, allow for all perspectives to be included with equity of participation.

THE POWER OF THE CYNEFIN APPROACH

The methods and approaches we used culminated in self-selected workgroups developing action-based recommendations for issues across the Cynefin domains. At 4 p.m. on day two, on mobile stands, 70 recommendations were posted on action sheets representing the Cynefin domains. These had been 'tested' with at least two other workgroups and refined based on feedback.

The CEO and her executive team walked around, read, and had brief (max 3 minutes) conversations with some of the workshop participants for clarity. Each had three different colored dots they could allocate to help them decide when to implement the recommendations:

- Now
- Not now
- Needs further time to consider (one week was the deadline for a response)

Issues that were mapped to the Framework, but not yet considered, were collected and retained in the 'needs further consideration' list. The different colored hexies that created the themes and informed the actions were attached to the recommendations for context – the different colors visibly indicated the different voices for different issues.

The output of these two days was a pleasant surprise. In an elapsed time of two days, 350 people representing multiple perspectives and views, reached a common understanding and enough agreement to agree on 70 specific recommendations for action. All of the ideas were captured in ways that made it easy to address them later. And, people had self-selected and indicated interest on issues they agreed to continue to work on.

HOW DO YOU KNOW IF COMPLEX FACILITATION IS FOR YOU?

This case study illustrates what is possible when you use complex facilitation. To achieve these kinds of results, the actions and behaviors of facilitators need to be congruent with the complexity principles, the processes, the methods, and the tools. That means that the facilitator needs to become comfortable with uncertainty and be willing to accept unexpected developments, disruptions, and a shallow dive into chaos during the intervention. That is what we ask from the participants – and it also applies to the facilitators! When we do this, we enable groups of people to collectively make sense and meaning of complex issues, and we invite the emergence of novelty.

In order to become proficient in complex facilitation methods, you need more than just a step by step playbook. You need to understand the complexity principles embedded in each of these methods i.e., why it works the way it does. You need to let go of the need to design for a particular outcome. Instead, we focus on understanding the purpose and intent of what we are doing, know what kind of participant experience is needed to disrupt old patterns, and enable the emergence of novelty. And throughout, you need to show up in a way that is congruent with the above.

Before you decide if complex facilitation is for you, consider these perspective differences

Traditional facilitation perspective	Complex facilitation perspective
Facilitators are responsible for giving clear and unambiguous instructions so that participants 'get it right and do not fail.'	• There is no right answer. It is about exploration, insights, discovering options and alternatives, not searching for the 'right' answer. We cannot even be sure of what the "right" question is. • Complex issues are not resolved. They are nudged, danced with, managed, and monitored but never resolved.
As a facilitator, I am responsible for the experience that participants have – their level of engagement, comfort, and enjoyment.	• Facilitators are responsible for providing the environment and processes that enable engagement and participation in complexity. • To minimize the realities of disruption, ambiguity, and discomfort would be dishonest. • People may experience the process as frustrating and fail to see the tangible value in the experience for some time – maybe never.
My identity as a 'good and competent' facilitator is directly linked to the visible contribution I have made to the outcomes.	You are not the expert in the room – you don't comment on content, you don't answer questions and you don't ensure a particular outcome. If your identity requires feedback about your role in solving problems and being an expert, then complex facilitation is probably not for you.

Table Traditional and Complex facilitation perspectives

After encountering Cynefin, and its approach to complex facilitation, I have applied its principles and practice extensively in my work. A common experience for me and my colleagues is that using the Cynefin Framework is an approach you "settle into." While it is generally uncomfortable at first, the more you use it, the more you trust the process, and it soon becomes your own 'business as usual.' Above all, working this way provides significantly more effective outcomes for the participants.

I have little desire to go back to any form of traditional 'expert' facilitation. If so inclined, I recommend that any facilitator dip their toe into the adventurous waters of complex facilitation and use the Cynefin Framework as your GPS.

References

1. Kaner, S. Facilitator's Guide to Participatory Decision-Making, 2nd Ed. San Francisco, Calif: Jossey-Bass, 2007. Editorial: Facilitation for development. 2015. Knowledge Management for Development Journal 11(1): 1-10 (no page number was available for the exact quote.)

2. Quoted from web page without exact page number: https://www.cleverism.com/what-facilitation-really-means-and-why-its-key-to-the-future-of-work/ Bens, Ingrid. Facilitating with Ease!: A Step-by-Step Guidebook with Customizable Worksheets on Cd-Rom. San Francisco, Calif: Jossey-Bass, 2000.

3. See International Association of Facilitators (https://www.iaf- world.org)

What to read next

 Next Full Chapter: Cynefin's Influence on The Flow System, John R. Turner..., p.321

 Next Chronological: Cow, Chicken or Grass?, Alicia Juarrero, p.208

 Next Theoretical: Cynefin's Influence on The Flow System, John R. Turner..., p.321

 More on Cynefin Principle 1.1: Embodied Cynefin: Teaching with the Body, Chris Corrigan, p.128

 More on Cynefin Principle 2.2: Cynefin Framework in Communications & Media..., Juanita Uribe..., p.336

TOHU VA-FACEBOOK AND DAVE SNOWDEN

KENDRA ROSENCRANS

ABOUT THE AUTHOR

Having mastered the delicate and complex art of swine showmanship in 1983, Kendra Rosencrans has spent the past 37 years in more relaxing pursuits, like reporting on natural disasters, raising teenagers, and learning Cynefin. A national, award-winning science journalist, Kendra is currently collaborating on Project Numinous, a SenseMaker program to explore stories about the ineffable. She took on a Master's of Divinity and a Doctorate in Organizational Systems in order to have time away from the children, whom she adores. Kendra lives in Kirkland, WA, with her husband, their three teenagers, a cat, and a dog, but no pigs.

ABOUT THIS CHAPTER

 Vignette    Narrative

 Chronology: Piece 32 of 33

TOHU VA-FACEBOOK AND DAVE SNOWDEN

KENDRA ROSENCRANS

I first encountered the Cynefin Framework in 2017. At the time, I was a doctoral student studying narratives and sense-making in relationship to organizational change, but I was not familiar, yet, with Dave's work. Now, as I have studied and applied Cynefin and Dave's concepts of sense-making to my research and work, I have grown to appreciate how Cynefin gives form to the intersections where context, experience, knowledge, and meaning matter.

I work with institutions whose leaders are realizing that the organizational maps and tropes from the past do not make sense for the present or future, but they do not know how to make sense from here. When the way forward is mired in ambiguity or appears unrecognizable, Cynefin provides practical questions and landmarks to reorient decision-makers so that they can make sense of the situation differently and act. In Cynefin, the act of sensing in complexity involves engaging with people's stories from many perspectives and contexts.

Stories matter, and so I will share mine.

My first encounter with Dave, and with Cynefin, was through social media. I was working on my dissertation, and some days, I found scrolling through the 'Book of Face' to be a more productive use of time. I did not know of Dave's work, as strangely, my academic program had not included his theories or work in complexity. However, I started to notice his smart and sharp-witted comments to people in our shared networks that invoked Cynefin, the Bible and references to Hogwarts, among other interesting combinations. In October 2017, Dave had been working through a version of liminal Cynefin, and he posted this sketch, announcing: "More or less the final version of Liminal #Cynefin with disorder resolved."

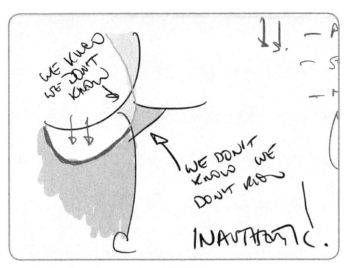

© Dave Snowden, Oct. 26, 2017, Twitter

At the time, not only was I working on a dissertation, but I was the main parent in charge of three kids (one pre-teen and two teen-agers) as my partner worked out-of-state during the week. I was cranky, tired, and stuck. Some days nothing fit together, everything was taking longer than I wanted, and I just wanted to be done. I was uncomfortable and I could not see the end of this creative, but transitional, phase. Dave's sketch placed me in that middle state, oscillating between "I know that I don't know" and "I don't even know what I don't know."

When I looked at that version of Cynefin, I saw the liminal spaces as places of forming and reforming, where not knowing and unknowing collide – like pregnancy. Or, better – like gestation, which is one way of describing that in-between phase where something is becoming, shifting, being created or falling apart, a middle place where there is both a sense of knowing that you don't know, and also not knowing what you don't know. With Dave's Jesuit background and delight in working with layered meaning in mind, I (because of my years in a seminary) also threw in a bit of Old Testament Hebrew and a nod to Genesis 1:2 about the state of the universe at the beginning of Creation as *tohu va-vohu*, formless and void.

I commented, "Seems like there's a pregnancy stage of complex becoming, of moving from tohu va vohu to an organized state that is both known and unknown – before anything "emerges.""

"Yes," Dave posted a few moments later. Then, the intellectual invitation/challenge popped up. "Without form and void? That's cool, expand!"

Gulp. And, awesome!

I offered that I didn't care for the idea of self-organization or autopoiesis, and that I was working on making sense of the difference between liminality, or being on the threshold, and gestation, which is an in-between state for creating something new, and encompasses the tension between resistance and emergence (like birth). Could the liminal in Cynefin be a state of being where there is knowing and not knowing, where something is neither one thing or the other (formless), but is in a space (a void) of becoming?

Dave replied, "Interesting (and rugby awaits) and I can see the birthing metaphor as a type of liminality. But if we look at it in the sense of mask-donning then liminality is not a one way process. I agree that autopoiesis is a poor metaphor for organizations (and possibly in biology as well)."

This short exchange was fun, invigorating, and kindled my curiosity. Dave kindly probed and parried. I survived. It appeared to be a good omen. And, I realized that Dave's posts to social media are a living master class in Cynefin and sense making in real time through his blogs, tweets, posts discussions and sketching. The exchange we had, and others, were good preparation for attending a master class and meeting Dave in person in Vancouver, BC, in December 2017. There, the odd and rich strands of story, philosophy, theology, and complexity started coming together as Dave talked about his idea for Project Numinous, a program for collecting and analyzing stories about encounters that are sacred and powerfully other, *sui generis*, ineffable.

Cynefin means "the place of your multiple belongings." I am happy to have had this serendipitous introduction to you and your tremendous work, Dave, through these digital places of belonging on social media. Congratulations on 21 years!

What to read next

 Next Vignette: Dave and the Cynefin Community: An Intellectual Heaven, Peter Stanbridge, p.315

 Next Chronological: From Bewilderment to Agility via Cynefin and SenseMaker, Gabriel Jurj, p.212

 Next Narrative: Dave and the Cynefin Community: An Intellectual Heaven, Peter Stanbridge, p.315

DAVE AND THE CYNEFIN COMMUNITY: AN INTELLECTUAL HEAVEN

PETER STANBRIDGE

ABOUT THE AUTHOR

Peter Stanbridge is a software engineer who has worked in a number of different roles within Cognitive Edge since its inception, but primarily within software product development. His first degree was in Mathematical Statistics and he has a strong current interest in statistical analytics within SenseMaker, in particular when very large datasets are involved. He has an MSc in Software Engineering from Oxford, but would say that his primary love in life is philosophy and higher critical theology. The principles of naturalizing and democratizing sense making, within organizations and society, is of great interest to Peter, who feels that organizations and countries need to be lead with more empathy, decentralization and a realistic understanding of where people are, not where 'experts' define them to be.

ABOUT THIS CHAPTER

 Vignette    Narrative

 Chronology: Piece 6 of 33

DAVE AND THE CYNEFIN COMMUNITY: AN INTELLECTUAL HEAVEN

PETER STANBRIDGE

It is a great pleasure to be invited to contribute a vignette to Cynefin's 'coming of age' publication. Congratulations on twenty-one years!

My first meeting with Dave in 2003, was by way of a Cynefin-esque methodological challenge. I was part of an IBM project team that had won a European Commission contract to examine the future of Knowledge Management (KM) research. Dave had agreed to contribute.

My immediate task was to explore the different schools of Knowledge Management. I had observed that the literature largely presented lists of two-sided bifurcations of key concepts. I am sure you are familiar with many of these. For example, knowledge as explicit versus implicit, community or individual, innate or acquired, technology or human-based, set of programs or all-embracing, formal or embedded, and so on. Evidently, one had to take sides.

I had figured out that we were going to need to abstract above the idea of individual schools. Still, I hadn't progressed that far in my discussion when Dave interjected with something like, "You consultants are all the same, there you go again, you can't see the world unless it is neatly packaged in lists of choices between two sides..." And so on. I responded that I had studied Hegel's logic of synthesis and even corresponded with John Macquarrie on the subject of Dialectical Theology. Macquarrie had been Lady Margaret's Professor at Christ Church Oxford University and a specialist on dialectical thinking and had shown that the thinking behind these types of lists was a problem. That was my point!

This pleased Dave. He said that he knew John Macquarrie and had published his books when he was part of the editorial team at SCM press. This in turn pleased me. Here was someone who would be able to deal with the nonsense I was reading. (I will add that I was unimpressed with much of the literature, including that from the famous Japanese professor Nonaka.)

But, that aside, this story highlights one of Dave's famous quotes: "You know more than you can say; you can say more than you can write." [1] There is something profound in this that is hidden by the simplicity of its formulation. I experienced it while with Dave.

After he presented a keynote that included this principle at the Stockholm e-challenges conference in 2008, someone speaking to me suggested that Dave's approach was unhelpful for KM because "you can't represent knowledge in writing." Well, of course, Dave hadn't said that at all. Maybe if this chap had seen Dave's library, he would have reached a different judgment: you really can't say everything you would need to every time you say something, even if you could, given infinite time. This may have been my problem during my inaugural phone call with Dave.

Since that auspicious start, I have had the good fortune to spend many hours walking with Dave, often with my wife Julia. These walks, full of discussion, have been wonderful, enjoyable learning experiences. The topics, especially when pragmatic Julia is present, range from peoples, places, histories, philosophies, science, and management theories. (Dave declares that Max Boisot was a polymath, but Dave is a polymath too).

The depth of Dave's thinking is impressive: Quine, 18th century Britain, the meaning of place names, the history of Ireland, chapels in Wales, obscure theologians, places to visit, harmonizing quantum physics with general relativity, and more, were all covered during these walks.

When on a particular walk, deeply engrossed in a conversation about coherence, truth, and method, something dawned on me. I said to Dave, "Are you not promoting 'Scientific Management!!!!?" He looked at me with surprised disbelief and retorted, "What other sort is there? You just have to have the right science." I realized, even though I had been around the Cynefin work for quite some time, how easy it is to miss the context of what someone is saying or writing. Until that moment, I had missed this point.

Related to this point, it appears Dave had been the victim of a critique by Peter Drucker. Dave told me he had been at a conference where he confidently put to rest the use and value of the old fashioned Scientific Management (inaugurated by Frederick Winslow Taylor) when Peter Drucker next took the stage to speak and reprimanded Dave on this.

Drucker spoke of the U.S. at the outbreak of WWII. Essential technologies like lens making (needed for gun and bombsights) were mastered by the Germans (and increasingly the Japanese). In 1941 this was not a good position for the U.S. to be in. But the use of old fashioned Scientific Management enabled the country to rapidly progress in all manner of design and production processes. Thus the basis of Drucker's castigation of Dave. Surely when a country quickly falls into the Chaotic domain, this is not a bad response. I personally think that Drucker had misunderstood what Dave was saying, namely that Scientific Management had its role to play in the right context. That context had gone: you can't say everything.

It is easy to create dichotomies between science or 'respectable philosophy' and fluffy bunny (Dave's term) thinking, or as my philosophy professor put it, Gobbledygook. With this, he meant Heidegger and other postmodernist anti-scientific philosophers. There is a third option. A synthesis might lie in phenomenology, which indicates that our scientific philosophies can never substitute for life itself. That we need to understand "life as lived," is where the Cynefin Framework and SenseMaker excels.

When we capture peoples' experiences as we do in SenseMaker, articulated in their real or imagined stories (or situations given to them), we gain deeper and actionable insights into situations that we have been tasked with managing and controlling. We transcend the limitations imposed by binary and linear thinking and enable a more human-focused way for people to contribute to the decisions that frame their lives.

To end on a personal note, where else in the world could a software engineer, whose primary focus is (obviously) software, work and live in an environment that enjoys this type of discussion? Where else could a non-academic have one's thoughts exposed to such interesting challenges and critiques where thought can progress? Yet this has been my experience working with Dave and the wider Cynefin community. It is intellectual heaven.

Reference:

1.　Dave's quote is adapted from Polanyi's book Polanyi, Michael. The Tacit Dimension. Gloucester, Mass: P. Smith, 1983.

What to read next

 Next Vignette: Shallow Dips into Chaos at the Theatre, Jesko von den Steinen, p.347

 Next Chronological: From Cookstown to Cynefin, Anne McMurray, p.272

 Next Narrative: Shallow Dips into Chaos at the Theatre, Jesko von den Steinen, p.347

CYNEFIN'S INFLUENCE ON THE FLOW SYSTEM

JOHN R. TURNER AND NIGEL THURLOW

ABOUT THE AUTHORS

John R. Turner, PhD, is an assistant professor at the University of North Texas, USA. He currently serves as the Editor-in-Chief for the *Performance Improvement Quarterly* (PIQ) journal. His research interests are in complexity, leadership, performance improvement, team cognition, team science, theory building and testing. He has published multiple refereed book chapters and research articles that can be found under his name at Orcid.org.

Nigel Thurlow is the creator of the award-winning Scrum the Toyota Way training. He has published several peer-reviewed publications on team science, acts as an advisor on several boards at the University of North Texas, has been featured in Forbes, and is a regular contributor for *Chief Executive Magazine*. He is the CEO of The Flow Consortium having previously served as the first ever Chief of Agile at Toyota.

John and Nigel are the co-creators of The Flow System, and co-authors of *The Flow System: The Evolution of Agile and Lean Thinking in an Age of Complexity* and *The Flow System Guide*.

ABOUT THIS CHAPTER

 Full Chapter

 Theoretical

 Chronology: Piece 23 of 33

 Cynefin Principles

CYNEFIN'S INFLUENCE ON THE FLOW SYSTEM

JOHN R. TURNER AND NIGEL THURLOW

This chapter showcases the Cynefin Framework's utility in contrasting open and closed systems and complexity thinking, tame and wild problems, and the Toyota Production System and The Flow System. We highlight Toyota's Flow system as similar to Cynefin, as it enables leaders to better operate in today's ambiguous, complex, disrupted, and unpredictable environment using a unique model of three helixes.

THE BLIND MEN AND THE ELEPHANT

In the fable of 'The Blind Men and the Elephant', most of us recall that several blind men approach an elephant for the first time. [1] After touching parts of the elephant, the blind men discuss their felt experience and try to make sense of it. Each man had a different experience. One associated the elephant's tusk with a spear, another, the trunk with a snake, and yet another the ear with a fan. After discussing each other's experience, the blind men tried to reach consensus as to what this creature was.

The fable ends with the blind men being unable to reach any consensus on what the elephant is. Each man understood one part of the elephant, but no one individual understood the whole. As explained by Mintzberg et al: "Since no one has had the vision to see the entire beast, everyone has grabbed hold of some part or other and 'railed on in utter ignorance' about the rest. We certainly do not get an elephant by adding up its parts." [1] This fable provides us with this insight: failure to understand the whole is due to our inability to expand our thinking beyond our understanding. Thus it is necessary to be open to others' opinions and experiences, and it is essential to know how the individual parts interact with one another, before being able to understand the whole.

THE BLIND MEN AND THE HIPPOPOTAMUS

There is another lesser known fable of the blind men and the hippopotamus. In this version, Xiang contrasted the elephant with the hippopotamus. Elephants are mostly tame, and hippopotami are mostly "aggressive, untamable, and dangerous." [2] When dealing with complexity, the hippopotamus fable is especially relevant. Hippopotami introduce wildness. When dealing with a situation, one of the first things to determine is, are you dealing with an elephant (tame) or a hippopotamus (wild)? Each will require a different approach.

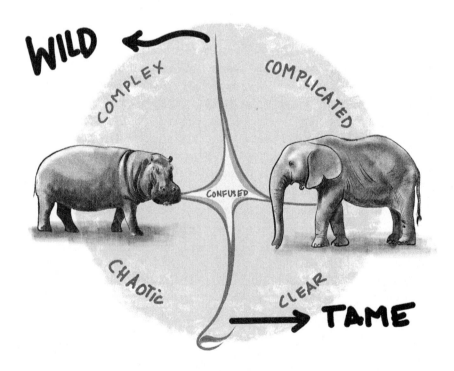

Figure 1. The Cynefin Framework with tame and wild problems

TYPES OF PROBLEMS: TAME (SIMPLE/COMPLICATED) VS. WILD (COMPLEX & WICKED)

Tame problems provide a clear definition of what the problem entails including predefined goals and rules for solving it. Tame problems are Type I problems, simple/complicated problems. Type I problems are those in which there is a consensus on the problem and solution. [3] Examples include calculating waste in a process and solving basic mathematical equations.

In contrast, wild problems can never be truly solved. The problem is ill-defined, there is no clear solution, and many conditions and variables change in real-time. Wild problems cannot be bounded; they consist of complex and wicked problems, identified as Type II and Type III problems. Type II problems, complex problems, have consensus on the problem's definition, but no consensus on how to solve the problem. [3] Examples include cancer research, economic disparity, and terrorism. Type III problems, wicked problems, are problems in which neither the problem nor the solution can be agreed upon. [3] Climate change and pandemics (2003 SARS, 2012 MERS, 2020 COVID-19) are examples.

The traditional approach to problem-solving involves carving a problem into smaller, more manageable sub-problems, a divide and conquer process. While this practice of reductionism has served the scientific community well for some time, it is becoming less effective as the problems we face become increasingly wild or wicked and less traditional or tame. The practice of divide and conquer does not work with wild problems. This approach eliminates complexity, resulting in outcomes that fail when reintroduced back into the wild. These reductionist approaches provide only partial solutions. [2]

> "Such a partial solution, if ever attainable, leaves behind the rest of the wicked problem unanalyzed, but its implementation will also change the dynamics of the socio-ecological system in which the original problem resides."

Attempting to tame wicked problems is most often a faulty undertaking and has also been presented as morally deceptive, "The moral principle is this: whoever attempts to tame a part of a wicked problem, but not the whole, is morally wrong." [4] What is required, however, are more holistic approaches that include the wildness of the problem.

OPEN AND CLOSED SYSTEMS

The contrast between tame and wicked problems can also be applied to open and closed systems. Closed systems operate within prespecified boundaries, open systems do not. "The relatively closed system has rigid, impenetrable boundaries; whereas the open system has permeable boundaries between itself and a broader supra-system." [5] Closed systems have definitive cause-and-effect relationships between their inputs and outcomes; open systems do not and often can obtain similar results using a variety of inputs.

Figure 2. Closed and Open systems

Closed systems are typically bound to protect the system and provide a level of control over the system. In contrast, open systems are not bounded and are influenced by internal and external forces with little control of the system. [6] Using the Cynefin Framework as a guide, we contrasted the differences between system-theoretical approaches and complexity theory. Figure 3 shows this contrast.

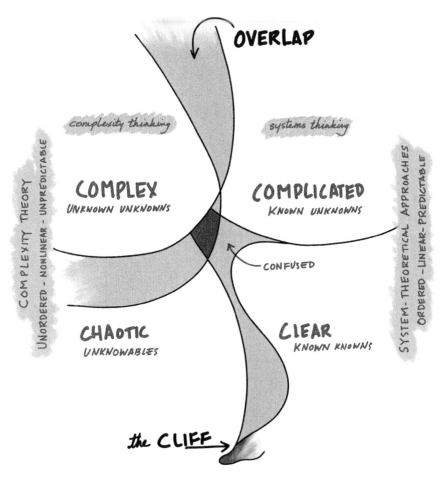

Figure 3. The Cynefin Framework with Systems and Complexity Theory

This contrast, between closed and open systems and system-theoretical approaches and approaches using complexity theory, represents two paradigms that have evolved in parallel over the years, using different perspectives, theories, and methods. The authors acknowledge that there is some overlap between system-theoretical approaches and complexity theory. This overlap, the liminal area in the Cynefin Framework, is identified by the word OVERLAP in Figure 3.

Kast and Rosenzweig recognized that systems could be classified as open or closed, but also acknowledged that a system could be somewhere between, having characteristics of both. [5] This area of overlap is where some system-theoretical approaches are used for addressing problems involving low-levels of complexity. This is also the area where complex adaptive systems reside, sharing similar characteristics between the two domains. However, this overlap is a fuzzy area and represents that there is no clear, definitive separation between these two fields of knowledge.

Equally fuzzy is when a system transitions from being a closed system to an open system and vice versa. The visualization provided in Figure 3 reminds us where this transition may occur and which paradigm to draw from when making the transition.

THE FLOW SYSTEM AND ITS EVOLUTION FROM LEAN

The Toyota Production System

The Toyota Production System (TPS) originated from Eiji Toyoda and Taiichi Ohno from 1948 to 1975 as they developed and refined Toyota's manufacturing processes, which greatly contributed to Toyota's success. The Toyota Production System has evolved into what is now known as lean production, which provides a set of methods or tools (see Figure 4) designed to eliminate waste. The TPS consists of two pillars, Jidoka and Just-in-Time. Jidoka refers to automation with a human touch to represent the interactions required between machines and humans. Just-in-time, underpinned by Kanban, operates on the philosophy of making only "what is needed when it is needed, and in the amount needed." [7] Together, these two pillars make up the TPS house with a foundation in standardized processes with people (customers and employees) at the center (or inside the TPS house). This foundation emphasizes "stability through standardized processes and preventative maintenance." [13] The foundational principles of the Toyota Production System are: Customer 1st, Respect for Humanity, and the total Elimination of Waste (MUDA).

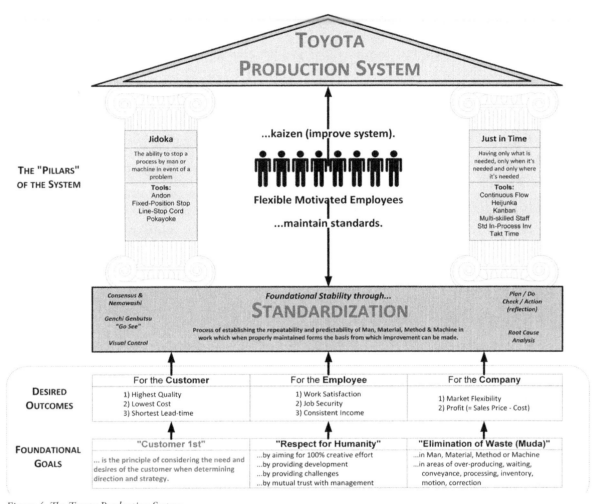

Figure 4. The Toyota Production System

THE TOYOTA WAY

The Toyota Way was first written in 2001 and has been described as the interpretation of TPS for non-manufacturing people. Using a similar house and pillar diagram, the Toyota Way has two pillars, continuous improvement and respect for people. The Toyota Way includes five values in the foundation. [8]

- Challenge. We form a long-term vision, meeting challenges with courage and creativity, to realize our dreams.

- Kaizen. We improve our business operations continuously, always driving for innovation and evolution.

- Genchi Genbutsu. We practice Genchi Genbutsu – believing in going to the source to find facts to make correct decisions, build consensus, and achieve goals at our best speed.

- Respect. We respect others, make every effort to understand each other, take responsibility and do our best to build mutual trust.

- Teamwork. We stimulate personal and professional growth, share the opportunities of development and maximize individual and team performance.

The Toyota Way is a belief system. Others call it organizational culture based on the fundamental principles and values that leverage the Toyota Production System. Where the Toyota Production System provides the methods and tools, the Toyota Way instills a culture for completing organizational goals, "It's the people who bring the system to life: working, communicating, resolving issues, and growing together," while also encouraging and supporting employees to become more engaged. [9]

THE FLOW SYSTEM

The Flow System builds upon the foundations of the Toyota Production System and the Toyota Way by beginning and ending with the customer. All organizational activities are directed toward delivering value to the customer by reducing all non-value-added activities in an organization's process. The Flow System is shown in Figure 5. The principles of The Flow System:

1. Customer First.

2. The FLOW of value.

3. The Triple Helix of Flow.
   - Complexity Thinking
   - Distributed Leadership
   - Team Science

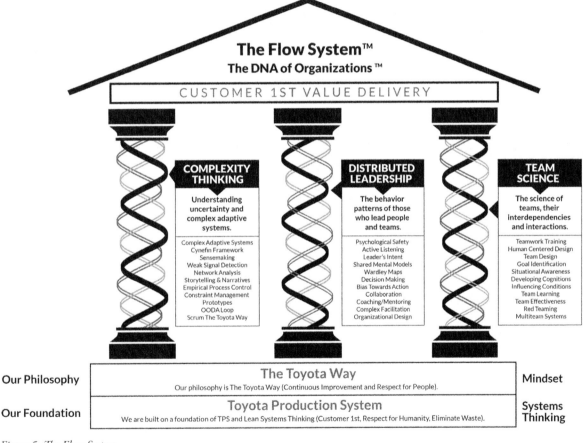

Figure 5. The Flow System

In delivering value to the customer, executives must first achieve a state of flow. Flow is both an individual and a collective (social) construct. At the individual level, flow takes on a psychological meaning as explained by Csikszentmihalyi, "The state in which people are so involved in an activity that nothing seems to matter; the experience itself is so enjoyable that people will do it even at great cost, for the sheer sake of doing it." [10] For executives in organizations to provide a state of flow for their employees, they must facilitate activities that allow their employees to interact freely.

As a social construct, flow is a by-product of interactions in which an organization's structure removes inhibiting constraints, allowing free exchanges of information among agents. Flow is an evolving process that becomes more seamless, natural, and unnoticed over time. [11] Flow is a construct that comes from constructal law that states, "For a finite-size system to persist in time (to live), it must evolve in such a way that it provides easier access to the imposed (global) currents that flow through it." [12]

One way of describing constructal law is in using a free flowing river. The river flows freely, and when interrupted, such as when a boulder falls into the river's path, the river becomes disrupted – at first. Over time, however, the river will organically engineer a new path around the boulder so that the river can flow freely once again. From an organizational perspective, there are countless examples of where flow is disrupted. One example is Conway's Law (13) that introduced the realization that organizations are structured around their lines of communication (hierarchically). The larger the organization, the more lines of communication, the more complexity is introduced into the system and flow becomes disrupted. The key is to reduce the communication channels so that those closest to the work and the customer are able to make necessary decisions to keep developing value, to achieve flow.

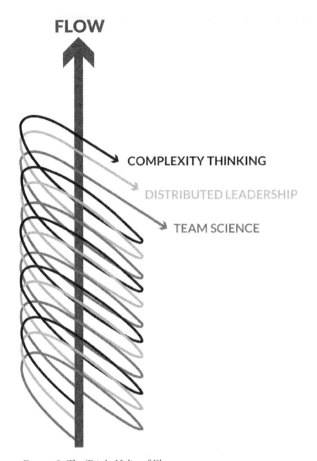

Figure 6. The Triple Helix of Flow

For flow to evolve, The Flow System identified three vital areas of focus in its Triple Helix of Flow, shown in Figure 6. The helixes that make up The Triple Helix of Flow is made up of complexity thinking, distributed leadership, and team science. These must be interconnected before an organization can achieve a state of flow. Complexity thinking incorporates the ability to identify which domain or type of problem executives face before acting. The Cynefin Framework is one of the essential tools leaders can use to aid them in this.

Distributed leadership advances the concept of constructal law by repurposing an organization's structure. Distributed leadership is a hybrid leadership theory that is designed to align organizational goals with today's team-based structures. This hybrid leadership theory incorporates shared leadership as the model of leadership for teams. To manage the interactions between teams, and between teams and organization or executive levels, functional leadership (boundary spanners) roles are implemented. This functional leader would be the new middle management role for organizations structured using multiteam systems (teams of teams).

At the executive levels, the distributed leadership hybrid theory includes instrumental, strategic, and global leadership characteristics. These leadership theories support executives using team-based structures and they face complexity. The composite distributed leadership theory presented in The Flow System is a holistic leadership model that is distributed throughout the organization at all levels (individual, team, organization). Leadership is contextual, each organization will add to, alter, or modify this distributed leadership theory to meet their leadership needs. The distributed leadership theory provides one holistic framework for leaders to implement in complex environments.

Team science offers executives the knowledge to support restructuring team-based structures, such as implementing multiteam systems. The field of team science is also enriched in teamwork training and development to further support leaders in organizations to achieve a state of flow.

Various methods, techniques, and tools are presented for each of these three helixes. The techniques are illustrated in Figure 4 in the rectangular boxes adjacent to each helix. These tools do not offer a prescriptive model; they are only a guide for organizational leaders. Flow is contextual, how each organization achieves a state of flow will be different. The Flow System supports leaders to identify various tools that may work best for them and their contextual setting. It is also necessary to realize that flow is unobtainable without first interconnecting the three helixes into one holistic system. Addressing only one or two of the helixes, while ignoring the other(s), will only result in poor results.

CONTRASTING THE TOYOTA PRODUCTION SYSTEM AND LEAN WITH THE FLOW SYSTEM

The Flow System is a system of understanding to guide leaders when they face complex environments. The Flow System derives its foundation from the principles of the Toyota Production System, Lean thinking, and the Toyota Way. From this foundation, The Flow System builds upon years of knowledge with a primary focus on the customer-first value. While the Toyota Production System, Lean approaches, and the Toyota Way principles and methods have served manufacturing and other industries (e.g., healthcare) well over the years, the problems addressed from these principles are concentrated primarily in the Complicated domain.

As various manufacturing industries become disrupted (e.g., globalization, climate change, terrorism, pandemics), traditional methods no longer adequately assist leaders when exapting or repurposing for today's disruptive environment. For tame and complicated problems (e.g., manufacturing, data entry), the methods provided by the Toyota Production System, Lean thinking, and the Toyota Way provide some of the best practices available today. However, something new was needed for organizations when their leaders encountered more and more wild and complex problems. The Flow System provides organizational leaders with guidelines on how to operate in complexity and when things are wicked and wild.

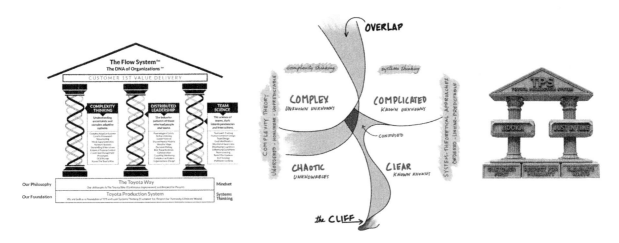

Figure 7. The Cynefin Framework contrasting TPS and The Flow System

In Figure 7, we depict the Toyota Production System and the Toyota Way as belonging to the right-hand side of the Cynefin Framework, as Clear and Complicated and The Flow System as representative of the left-hand side of the Framework, as Complex and Chaotic. This contextualization provides support for organizational leaders to "determine the prevailing operative context so that they can make appropriate choices" when operating in complex environments. [14]

CONCLUSION

We conclude that the Cynefin Framework is essential for leaders because it helps them identify the types of problems or challenges they may face in today's ambiguous, complex, and disrupted environment. Once they know the type of problem, they can decide on their best course of action.

The Toyota Production System provides specific techniques and tools that will help leaders to navigate problems that arise in closed systems. We positioned the Toyota Production System along the right-hand side of the Cynefin Framework (see Figure 7) to highlight its utility in addressing tame problems, like the elephant depicted in Figure 1.

When systems are open and complex, The Flow System supports leaders when they navigate their understanding and reconciliation of wild and wicked problems. We positioned The Flow System along the left-hand side of the Cynefin Framework (see Figure 7), showing its utility when facing wild problems (see Figure 1) – when dealing with the Hippopotamus and not an Elephant! When leaders encounter wild problems, it is necessary to "invest in more meaningful communication and effective relationships between its parts and between itself and its environment." [15] This holistic interconnectivity distributes the interactions between the three helixes that make up the Triple Helix of Flow. The Flow System provides leaders with appropriate tools and techniques for operating in the wild, while identifying organizational areas that require integration (complexity thinking, distributed leadership, team science), resulting in organizations achieving a state of flow.

The examples provided in this chapter highlight our usage of the Cynefin Framework. The Cynefin Framework has also become a necessary component for many other areas of practice and research. These examples, along with the many others found in this book, show how the Cynefin Framework can be contextualized. In the early days of the Cynefin Framework, this very point was emphasized, "Contextualization is also a good example of how the Cynefin Framework concentrates on collective sense-making as a consequence of discourse." [16] The Cynefin Framework is growing more robust now than before. It has reached multiple disciplines, areas of practice, and provides a means of making sense of our environment in many different contextual settings.

References

1. Mintzberg, Henry et al. Strategy Safari: Your Complete Guide through the Wilds of Strategic Management. 2nd edition, Prentice Hall, 2009.

2. Xiang, Wei-Ning. "Working with Wicked Problems in Socio-Ecological Systems: Awareness, Acceptance, and Adaptation." Landscape and Urban Planning, vol. 110, 2013, pp. 1-4, doi:10.1016/j.landurbanplan.2012.11.006.

3. Roberts, Nancy. "Wicked Problems and Network Approaches to Resolution." International Public Management Review, vol. 1, 2000, pp. 1-19, http://www.ipmr.net.

4. Churchman, West C. "Wicked Problems [Editorial]." Management Science, vol. 14, no. 4, 1967, pp. B-141-B-142.

5. Kast, Fremont E. and James E. Rosenzweig. "General System Theory: Applications for Organization and Management." Academy of Management Journal, vol. 15, 1972, pp. 447-465, doi:10.2307/255141.

6. Turner, J. R. and R. Baker. "Complexity Theory: An Overview with Potential Applications for the Social Sciences." systems, vol. 7, no. 4, 2019, p. 23, doi:10.3390/systems7010004.

7. Toyota. "Toyota Production System: Company Information, Vision & Philosophy." Toyota https://global.toyota/en/company/vision-and-philosophy/production-system/#:~:text=Making%20only%20%22what%20is%20needed,muda%2C%20mura%2C%20muri).

8. Liker, Jeffrey K. and Michael Hoseus. Toyota Culture: The Heart and Soul of the Toyota Way. McGraw Hill, 2008.

9. Liker, Jeffrey K. The Toyota Way: 14 Management Principles from the World's Greatest Manufacturer. McGraw Hill, 2004.

10. Csikszentmihalyi, Mihaly. Flow: The Psychology of Optimal Experience. Harper Collins, 1990.

11. Turner, John R. et al. The Flow System: The Evolution of Agile and Lean Thinking in an Age of Complexity. Aquiline Books–UNT, in press.

12. Reis, Heitor A. "Constructal Theory: From Engineering to Physics, and How Flow Systems Develop Shape and Structure." Applied Mechanics Reviews, vol. 59, 2006, pp. 269-282, doi:10.1115/1.2204075.

13. Conway, Melvin E. "How do committees invent?" Datamation, vol. 14, no. 5, pp. 28-31.

14. Snowden, David J. and Mary E. Boone. "A Leader's Framework for Decision Making." Harvard Business Review, vol. 85, no. 11, 2007, pp. 68-76, www.hrb.org.

15. Merry, Uri. Coping with Uncertainty: Insights from the New Sciences of Chaos, Self-Organization, and Complexity. Praeger, 1995.

16. Kurtz, C. F. and D. J. Snowden. "The New Dynamics of Strategy: Sense-Making in a Complex and Complicated World." IBM Systems Journal, vol. 42, 2003, pp. 462-483, http://ieeexplore.ieee.org/servlet/opac?punumber=5288519.

What to read next

 Next Full Chapter: Cynefin Framework in Communications & Media..., Juanita Uribe and Andrés Jiménez, p.336

 Next Chronological: The U.S. Navy's Combat Information Center..., Trent Hone, p.185

 Next Theoretical: Cynefin Framework in Communications & Media..., Juanita Uribe and Andrés Jiménez, p.336

 More on Cynefin Principle 1.3: A Cynefin Approach to Leading Safety in Organizations, Gary Wong..., p.357

 More on Cynefin Principle 3.2: When Disease Requires a Complexity Framework, Riva Greenberg..., p.153

CYNEFIN FRAMEWORK IN COMMUNICATIONS & MEDIA – THE CYNEFIN REVOLUTION

JUANITA URIBE AND ANDRÉS JIMÉNEZ

ABOUT THE AUTHORS

Juanita Uribe has dedicated her professional life to communicating complex things in a way that most people can understand. She started working with children – the wisest people she knows – and then realized that to preserve their innate wisdom she must also work with adults. She has designed and implemented public-private partnerships and programs in citizen, childhood, and youth education and sustainable development for governments, the private sector, and foundations in the U.S. and Latin America. Currently, Juanita represents Cognitive Edge for the Spanish-speaking countries in Latin America.

Andrés Jiménez has a BA from CESA University in Bogota and a Scholar Program Degree in Political Management from George Washington University. He has been National Editor for *Semana Magazine*, Political Counselor for the Colombian Embassy in Washington D.C., former Editor in Chief of *Poder Magazine* and he won the ANIF National Economic Journalist Award in 2006. Andrés worked as Communications Advisor for the President of the Interamerican Development Bank in Washington D.C.

ABOUT THIS CHAPTER

 Full Chapter

 Theoretical

 Chronology: Piece 26 of 33

 Cynefin Principles

CYNEFIN FRAMEWORK IN COMMUNICATIONS & MEDIA – THE CYNEFIN REVOLUTION

JUANITA URIBE AND ANDRÉS JIMÉNEZ

BOHEMIAN RHAPSODY

Before he became the father of modern science, Rene Descartes spent three years as a soldier. He enlisted at age 22 soon after the Thirty Years' War began. At this time representatives of the Catholic king-elect were famously thrown out of a castle window, giving birth to what is known as Prague's Bohemian Revolt. Though Descartes was a Catholic, he enlisted with a Protestant Prince, Maurice of Nassau, and was trained – and trained others as well – in calculating cannonball trajectories, mining, and military construction for ballistic defense and attack.

Descartes soon switched allegiances to the Catholic Duke Maximilian of Bavaria. While stationed somewhere near Neuburg on the Danube – in what today is Southern Germany – he had his famous "night of visions," a series of three dreams on November 10th and 11th, 1619, which changed history. They may be apocryphal since Descartes' notes about these dreams did not survive. Still, Adrien Billet, a 17th Century biographer of Descartes, preserved an account of them in his book La vie de M. Descartes. [1] [2]

According to Billet, in the last of Descartes' three dreams, "the Spirit of Truth" appeared in the middle of the night and told him that the conquest of nature was to be achieved through measure and number. Therefore, the then 23 year-old "was bold enough to conclude that the Spirit of Truth had chosen him to use this dream to reveal the treasures of all the disciplines of learning (…)." [3]

MEASURE AND NUMBER WOULD CONQUER NATURE

Descartes woke-up, and history would never be the same – the Cartesian view of the world had seen the light of day. [4] Newtonian science and the Enlightenment would soon take this idea and run with it: believing the universe to be a machine, claiming that predictability and order define all of reality, and that merely mapping the rules of this complicated, but ultimately linear cosmos is enough to conquer nature. [5] [6] Anything and everything can be understood and predicted if you break it down into its constituent parts and figure out its governing laws. [4] Undoubtedly these assumptions, grounded in Cartesian/Newtonian reductionist, materialistic models are beneficial in highly ordered domains. But they fail miserably when circumstances become more complex.

Dave Snowden's work on complexity and leadership through the Cynefin (Decision Support) Framework is among the top-ten citations globally. Cynefin is a Welsh word that famously signifies something akin to the multiple factors in our experience that influence us in ways we can never understand. Dave's work in anthro-complexity and complexity science provides robust evidence that ordered systems – although highly valuable for civilization – tend to impose rules unnecessarily, snuffing out creativity, and constricting freedom. That's when "The Spirit of Truth" comes back to haunt civilization with a vengeance, ominously whispering... "Please, enough," but Chaotic systems inevitably take over. Sound familiar?

The Cynefin Framework allows decision-makers to move away from the ancient dichotomy of order vs. chaos into something more sophisticated: complex adaptive systems, a.k.a ecosystems. Ecosystems exist in nature; they are not defined by their structure but by their connectivity. In ecosystems, as in organisms, everything is connected to everything else. Cynefin states many of these connections cannot be known. Restrictions and boundary conditions remain mostly undefined. [7]

Regardless of Descartes' dreamy epiphanies, humanity – like the human brain and nervous system – has always been a complex adaptive system. The ubiquitous connectivity provided by the internet, social media, and digital messaging services, such as WhatsApp and Telegram, is fast becoming infinitely more complex.

As British organizational theorist Max Boisot pointed out, "data itself can be thought of as an energetic phenomenon that links us in our capacity as knowing subjects to an external physical world." [8] The most obvious signs of this in media, communications, and political consulting emerged in 2016 – the annus horribilis for pollsters everywhere – when public opinion surveys began to fail catastrophically. This clearly happened with Brexit in the UK, the U.S. presidential election that chose Donald Trump as leader of the free world, and the Peace Plebiscite (October 2, 2016) that was supposed to mark the end of Colombia's 52-year armed conflict, to name just a few examples. How was it that a tried-and-tested tool for measuring public opinion, which had been used extensively and somewhat accurately since World War II, suddenly stopped working?

The answer provided by Cynefin is quite simple. Increased connectivity has, in turn, increased civilization's complexity by orders of magnitude – perhaps exponentially, turning it into a highly complex adaptive system. This system cannot be measured or managed with tools designed for highly structured ones. Explaining this to now President of Colombia Ivan Duque's campaign strategists and pollsters, in 2018, was quite a challenge to put it mildly. Yet they eventually became complexity thinking converts. This was thanks in part to the fact that the Chief Campaign Strategist, Gloriza Ramírez, currently Ambassador in Rome, was a pertinacious "out-of-the-box" thinker.

The conversion happened during a flight between Washington D.C. and Bogota, while Gloriza happened to be sitting next to me for several hours and couldn't get away! The result was the campaign applied SenseMaker (a tool designed by Cognitive Edge based on the Cynefin Framework) to gaze beyond the prevailing propaganda. In contrast to polls and surveys, SenseMaker allows for the collection of micro-narratives from respondents whose own interpretations are then aggregated. Clusters of stories are made apparent in the process, allowing for a better understanding of the system.

The Duque campaign realized, through applying SenseMaker, that one of his much-media-hyped opponents had very little true popular support. However, trusting this result was in itself a leap of faith, since linear thinkers roam the planet and seem to be particularly fond of congregating around political campaigns. And they were armed – of course – with traditional polls and surveys, conveniently published by all major media outlets in Colombia at the time, showing how formidable this particular straw challenger was.

Again, insight prevailed, the campaign placed its trust in SenseMaker and Cynefin, which allowed it to concentrate scarce resources towards facing the real challenger. Like Brexit, the Trump election, and the Peace Plebiscite, many inside the campaign itself could not believe their eyes when the tallies for the 2018 first electoral round were finally revealed (Duque 39.4%, Petro 25.08%, Fajardo 23.78%, and Vargas an eye-popping 7.3%). The rest is history.

So we humans have found tools to measure high complexity domains, but the Cynefin Framework provides much more than mere measuring tools. Whereas in the ordered domains, measurements and statistics can provide enough knowledge, in the complex domain people make sense through experiences (personal, or third person) and stories. The media deals with narratives. That is exactly what vectors are (the micro-narrative methodology, instead of numbers, uses vectors: the direction in the speed of travel through the intensity of effort). These are meta-narratives, designed with the potential to nudge humans towards positive outcomes. Cynefin was conceived to help influence social behavior for genuine, sustainable change through a complexity, not engineering approach. Its remarkable advantage I can attest to.

THE OBJECTIVITY BIAS

When I was 15 years old and was about to graduate from high school, I worked as a journalism apprentice at *El Espectador*. This was the most respected and oldest-running newspaper in Colombia. Founded in 1887 as a Liberal outlet in defiance of our previous 1886 Constitution, it was instituted by one of the most Conservative regimes that emerged in Latin America during the second half of the 19th century. *El Espectador* bravely soldiered on for 134 years, surviving being shut down by a military dictatorship (1956), the murder of its Editor In Chief, Guillermo Cano, (1986) by Pablo Escobar, and the leveling of its headquarters by a Medellín Cartel bombing (1989). It recently announced it may permanently forgo paper circulation and move from a daily to a weekly online publication, something akin to a blog.

The possible demise of *El Espectador* is not a uniquely Colombian phenomenon. Other flagship Spanish-language newspapers, like *El Pais* in Spain, have moved online, with somewhat lackluster results. Of course, there are plenty of explanations for why newspapers everywhere are disappearing. I believe one of them is that they remain attached to the "objectivity" dogma that has governed traditional media since the first modern newspapers emerged in Europe during the Enlightenment.

Later, as I majored in Communications & Journalism at Javeriana University in Bogota, the same "objectivity" mantra was relentlessly hammered into my head for five years. It turned out to be wrong, and I dare submit the death of so many newspapers as Exhibit A. There is no such thing as objectivity in this world, there is only a complex, ever-adapting sum of subjectivities. If you can boil these down into narratives that bring about positive change for human collectives, then there is hope for humanity. The rest is just random, mindless, heartless storytelling.

My college professors insisted on this "objectivity" mantra, but I was never able to swallow it entirely. It seemed tasteless, generalizing, pertaining to no one. Three decades later, I finally understood that "objectivity" is the main culprit behind the mainstream media's current crisis. The idea of readers, listeners, or followers as a sanitized collective is a postmodern illusion; the likeness of nobody, the furthest most expression of the Spirit of Untruth. Dismissing what motivates individuals and force-feeding them into binary or polarized pre-packaged ideological structures remains hypocritical hubris, and the media has paid a considerable price for embracing these sirens' songs.

The internet and social media have given voice to the masses. Federico Mayor Zaragoza, former head of UNESCO, once told me, "Since the advent of the internet, no one is obliged to accept the inexorable." Yet a cacophony of voices leads only to chaos because it restricts our capacity to find meaning amidst complexity. This entails a huge opportunity for the media, which could stop feeding the chaos by listening deeply to multiple perspectives from audiences and present true meaning and insight for these challenging times. This is why Cynefin's potential for media and communications is revolutionary. Cynefin is the appropriate framework, and the media should start paying attention.

As I was choosing a specialization, I was weighing traditional journalism, internal corporate communications, and strategic communications/education through audio/visual channels. Although I loved writing, and held fond memories of my years at *El Espectador*, I could not follow this path. It seemed absurd, unimaginably dull, shallow, and soulless. Thank God I chose the latter. The toxic, politically correct, highly pasteurized "objective" narratives offered by the mainstream media, breed populism, polarization and ultimately lead to chaos. They have brought about a rebellious need for texture, granularity, and bluntness amongst the masses.

MAKING SENSE OF IT ALL

My challenge, once I met Dave Snowden in Bogota during his 2014 New Narrative for Colombia stint, after the Peace Process with the FARC guerrillas was finally announced, was figuring out a way to further use the Cynefin Framework for beneficial, sustainable, real change.

In 2017 the 'United Way Colombia/Secretary of Education - Live Education Innovation Laboratory' was born. Its aim was activating a living laboratory within public school classrooms by providing an ongoing feedforward between teachers and students. This would allow for adjustments to improve the quality of the education experience. Over four years, we engaged close to 10,000 students across the municipalities of Bogota, Medellin, and Cali, the country's three largest cities.

We co-designed feedback and feedforward studies to capture assessments of the Future of Education from educators and students. We developed an approach that comprised a robust human-centered design thinking element. We trained teachers to make sense of the data and to develop small experiments in their classrooms in response to student needs. We created a supporting kit that included "playing cards" to buttress the ongoing use of data while keeping a finger on the pulse of educational innovations.

The work was done in collaboration with two master's degree students of Information Engineering at Bogota's University of Los Andes, using machine learning and visual analytics methodology designed by

Tamara Munzner, University of British Columbia computer science professor. The challenge was to make sense of 10,000 stories from both students and teachers, while gaining a deeper level of sense-making from an outsized volume of data by natural language processing applied to text, drawings, and stories captured through SenseMaker. By creating language processing libraries, it prioritized children's emotional tone, and was capable of identifying – for example – a pattern of sadness in a student's narrative even when the child self-referenced as happy.

Two significant findings emerged in terms of public policy design and implementation: 1) Teachers are not there to transfer information, they are no longer teachers in a traditional sense. They are most effective when they see themselves, and are seen as mentors, counselors, guides and/or facilitators; 2) The two words most associated with happy children are "Life" and "Play." These two elements are particularly relevant during this time of COVID-19, given all public and private schools in the country have been "virtual-only" since March 31, 2020. It's been announced that by August 2020, schools should start to partially reopen, combining physical attendance with some work time at home (as of the closing of this text, Colombia was reaching an epidemiological curve peak).

Through these investigations, we identified that students see school as the central axis in their community and that the strongest motivation for attending, is the emotional connection with other children and their teachers. While the ministry had assumed that students are motivated to go to school to cultivate a stronger sense of competition, the data provided evidence that what's really wanted, and what would be more beneficial, is a stronger collegial environment that supports developing teamwork and upholds the importance of understanding others. The appropriate vectors were developed and are currently being implemented. The teachers involved in the study have also been trained in sense-making methods, design thinking approaches, and how to apply these to create more organic motivational strategies inside their classrooms.

This is another example of how multiperspective collective witnessing is a much better guide for enhancing strength-building and resilience, than steering from "objective" top-down truth.

CHASING EL DORADO

Another significant challenge faced by Colombia was accurately portrayed in a recent article: "Proceeds from illegal gold mining in Colombia are estimated at approximately $2.4 billion, or three times the amount generated from Colombia's cocaine industry. Like cocaine, illegal mining poses a litany of challenges: undermining the rule of law, eroding security, and devastating the environment." [9]

Gran Colombia Gold, a large mining operation in Colombia, recently decided to use SenseMaker to tackle a particularly salient problem: illegal mining in its area of operations. In a part of the country that for at least 70 years has been under the influence of "informal" mining activities, an estimated 10,000 illegal miners in total were working. Before Gran Colombia Gold's arrival, most of the population in Segovia/Remedios (Antioquia Department) had little access to clean water, energy, paved roads, education, or telecommunications infrastructure. After several years of the company's operations, however, about 20% of mining activity in the region has been formalized. They have been contributing to local and national taxes, obtaining social security benefits and higher than minimum wages for their workers, and have been in compliance with work safety and environmental laws and regulations.

Yet, since the company arrived in the area, there have been eight armed blockades, effectively imposing de facto 45-day curfews, which have driven most local mom-and-pop businesses into bankruptcy. Regardless of as many as 1,500 police and army reinforcements being sent in by the Government of Colombia, it's been impossible to prevent blockade recurrences.

Gran Colombia Gold, a Canadian company listed on the Toronto Stock Exchange, assembled a group of anthropologists and social science experts to devise a comprehensive strategy with the local residents aimed at nudging illegal miners towards formalization. It included:

- Signing collective formalization agreements
- Investing in roads, recreation, education, and energy infrastructure
- Fostering organic cacao production by small farmers
- Training and certification for school headmasters from several public schools
- Aqueduct and water treatment plant construction
- Reforestation schemes with native trees alongside river decontamination
- Cultural activity sponsorship

Still, resistance to change prevails among members of the community who consider "the way things used to operate" to be preferable. The company decided to use SenseMaker to assess the way their initiatives work and determine the level and quality of their impact. The goal was to map out which of the initiatives under implementation had had the most positive (or negative) impact, and have been more successful in nudging miners towards formalization, reducing violence, building social trust, and ultimately improving people's lives.

The challenge meant identifying specific vectors aimed at beneficial, sustainable change in terms of violence prevention and mining activity formalization. This would be done by designing and building an interactive dashboard with specific measurable vector parameters for real-time monitoring of past, present, and future actions. In terms of Media & Strategic Communications, one aim is to use the resulting vectors to provide content to local, national, and international media. Like the Live Education Innovation Laboratory, this is an ongoing project, and the whole industry – not just in Colombia but throughout the region – is eyeing it carefully.

The Colombian Mining Association (ACM in Spanish) closely monitors the 17 Sustainable Development Goals (SDGs) in all large mining municipalities in Colombia. As recently as June 2020, it issued a report analyzing SDG compliance in the aforementioned territory. Of course, goals expressed as numbers are the bread and butter of the universal call to action for mass human endeavors like ending poverty, protecting the planet, and ensuring that all people enjoy peace and prosperity by 2030. But in deciding how and where to invest, Gran Colombia Gold is increasingly paying attention to Dave Snowden's body of scientific evidence. Evidence that when humans pursue specific measurable goals, and particularly when that goal is expressed as a number, intrinsic motivation is all but destroyed. In contrast, SenseMaker supports a co-productive, citizen-centered approach to monitoring, evaluating, and acting based on 'moving' narratives, not 'objective' numbers.

It's safe to say that few tools are better adapted to the complexity media and communications are mired in, and deal with every day, than those afforded by "sense-making a la Cynefin." This area of human endeavor is perhaps more in need than ever of such groundbreaking innovation since the Spirit of Truth visited our young Frenchman in his dreams 401 years ago. It is easy to foresee the enormous impact Cynefin can have on human rights, public health, education, responsible governance, environmental awareness, and sustainable economic development for millions of people around the world. I celebrate the Cynefin Revolution on its 21st anniversary!

References

1. "La Vie de M. Descartes - Wikisource." 30 dic.. 2019, https://fr.wikisource.org/wiki/La_Vie_de_M._Descartes.

2. "Math and Mathematicians: The History of Math Discoveries ...." https://books.google.com/books/about/Math_and_Mathematicians.html?id=ALHF7hEdO5IC.

3. "Somnio Ergo Sum: Descartes's Three Dreams - Project MUSE." https://muse.jhu.edu/article/415709.

4. "Dreaming, Philosophy of | Internet Encyclopedia of Philosophy." https://www.iep.utm.edu/dreaming/.

5. "The Metaphysical Foundations of Newtonian Science ...." https://link.springer.com/chapter/10.1007/978-94-009-4730-6_2

6. "The Structure of Scientific Revolutions." https://www.lri.fr/~mbl/Stanford/CS477/papers/Kuhn-SSR-2ndEd.pdf. p.41.

7. "Complexity, citizen engagement in a Post-Social Media time ...." 14 Feb.. 2018, Complexity, citizen engagement in a Post-Social Media time | David Snowden | TEDx University of Nicosia.

8. "Information Space (RLE: Organizations). Max Boisot https://books.google.com/books?id=Oa4w-wRD6Sf8C&pg=PA22&lpg=PA22&dq=data+itself+can+be+thought+of+as+an+energetic+phenome-non+that+links+us+in+our+capacity+as+knowing+subjects+to+an+external+physical+world&source=bl&ots=x-eEckJ6R3W&sig=ACfU3U20O3pGpvVmdYzDQkCN7qXKphe-aA&hl=es.

9. "Already a Scourge, Illegal Gold Mining in Colombia Is Getting ...." 27 Jul.. 2018, https://www.worldpoliticsreview.com/insights/25266/already-a-scourge-illegal-gold-mining-in-colombia-is-getting-worse.

What to read next

 Next Full Chapter: A Cynefin Approach to Leading Safety in Organizations, Gary Wong..., p.357

 Next Chronological: Cynefin's Influence on The Flow System, John R. Turner and Nigel Thurlow, p.320

 Next Theoretical: A Cynefin Approach to Leading Safety in Organizations, Gary Wong..., p.357

 More on Cynefin Principle 2: When Disease Requires a Complexity Framework, Riva Greenberg..., p.153

 More on Cynefin Principle 2.2: Weaving Well-being into the Fabric of our Organizations..., Marion Kiely..., p.227

SHALLOW DIPS INTO CHAOS AT THE THEATRE

JESKO VON DEN STEINEN

ABOUT THE AUTHOR

Jesko von den Steinen is formerly a principal solo artist with Cirque du Soleil. He is also a co-creator with Franco Dragone of 'The House Of Dancing Water,' the world's largest water-based theatrical experience at the City of Dreams in Macau. Currently helping organizations confront digital, strategic, and cultural 'change' in times of uncertainty, Jesko is the lead facilitator and designer for 'The Difference', a complex problem solution hub for experience consulting with PwC in Hong Kong. Jesko served as associate director of Strategic HR, leading an Innovation & Transformation hub for an industry-leading fortune 500 company in Asia. In Montreal, Jesko has worked with SIDLEE, as a creative strategist and experience designer.

ABOUT THIS CHAPTER

 Vignette    Narrative

 Chronology: Piece 29 of 33

SHALLOW DIPS INTO CHAOS AT THE THEATRE

JESKO VON DEN STEINEN

What do theatre, opera and the natural sciences have to do with each other? Or, how Cynefin and complexity theory have helped me maintain my sanity in the creative process.

In 2010, in Macau, China, in a large multi-stage purpose-built theatre, I was on stage at the end of a long day of rehearsal. It was around 10 p.m. The entire cast and crew were mentally and physically exhausted. The theatre director Franco Dragone, one of the world's most eminent directors from Cirque du Soleil and numerous operas, was watching the action on stage and had hit a mental block. No one knew how to get a significantly large prop off the stage without disrupting the story, flow, and pace of the show. [1]

Franco was getting increasingly agitated. We'd been at it for over three hours. I too was tired, frustrated, and wet from being in and out of the water all day. Suddenly, Franco starts yelling:

"Christian, run across the stage! Luke, change the lighting to the scene we worked on last week! Pat, I want different images on the screen! No, you idiot! I have seen these too often! Jean, shut-up! Don't move! Not until I tell you! OK, fountains go… I don't care, anything, give me something, now!"

What the director was doing, in our language, was 'shaking the stage.' Franco was pushing the cast and crew into a 'shallow liminal dip of Chaos.' He was hunting for a novel moment, or to make one or more new, unexpected connections. More importantly, he was trying to crack the mold that had been formed by the cast and crew around a seemingly intractable problem.

When creating theatre that is not text-based, the technical elements on stage speak just as much as the performers. The set pieces, projections, lighting, props all help to tell the story. Intentional juxtapositioning components on stage in unexpected ways can reveal themselves to tell a part of a tale that we hadn't seen previously. Therefore, when we are stuck in the creative process, and do not see a way out, a way to find resolution is to 'shake the stage.' We intentionally shake the 'snow globe' of our current perspective to see whether we discover something new. This is a sort of 'safe-to-fail' experiment that allows us the opportunity to find novelty. It is a shallow contained dip into Chaos.

It is important to note that activity is not executed gratuitously. It requires a leader's sensitivity, to wait long enough so that enough pressure has built up among the participants, so that a break into Chaos is necessary. If and when we found something, the director would seize on it (act, sense, respond) and then begin to develop coherence around it. Franco would continue:

"Yes! this! OK now, Jean move... slowly slowly. OK Guards! Come stage left! Stage lifts down... Let's try, OK no, let's try Pyramid boys... on stage, NOW!"

Eventually, we were no longer shaking the stage. Franco had found something new and we were building again.

Franco had the automation team sink the stage lifts into the water while the fountains were engaged. The water jet fountains, along with LED lights are embedded into the stage lift. As soon as the stage lifts began to lower into the water of the pool, the fountains lost their amplitude. Suddenly, they no longer looked as they were engineered to look. Rather the fountains "became" tea candles floating on the water. It is simple moments like these that aren't engineered or planned that often become the most engaging for the audience.

Figure 1. An image from "The House of Dancing Water" rehearsals. A Theatrical large scale acrobatic performance in Macau at the "City of Dreams," Melco Resorts Entertainment with Medhy Nasser

To clarify, the creative process when building a new show is a unique time where everything is possible. Everything is percolating with potential and ideas. It is very different once you are performing the show ten times a week. When you are performing ten times a week, you focus on refining the performance, joining breath to action, sculpting the rhythms of the scenic action for the audience trying to reach a union between action and self-reflective observation. In opposition, when you are creating, you are often trying to get out of your own way. You want to dialogue with the subconscious, allowing collisions to occur, and experiment.

The type of creative behavior required depends on the context and context matters. An attempt to apply the same behavioral modality in operations, as in creation, may end up with an injured performer, or as we've recently experienced in the industry, a fatality on stage.

As performers and creatives, we are acutely aware that innovation and exaptation generally only occur when the conscious mind is out of the way. This usually happens in moments of fatigue, necessity, or state of playfulness. (Starvation, Pressure, Perspective shift). Theatre directors do this consciously by forcing a shallow dip into Chaos. For example Jerzy Grotowski, the influential 20th-century director, would famously work his actors to exhaustion in rehearsal. He assumed that only once the actors were out of energy, would they be able to drop the artifice of social behavior and enter the more profound truth of their performance. [2] It is not just creatives who play in the zone of exhaustion either. In religious rituals and ceremonies like the Sufi Sema of the Mevlevi order, more commonly known as the whirling dervishes, they often seek divine moments of insight and breakthrough at the threshold between a conscious state of mind and the unconscious. [3]

Dave often points out that the Chaotic domain requires an immense amount of energy and resources to sustain if done intentionally. Working actors or dancers to exhaustion is unsustainable in the long run, especially when you have shows to sell. Nor should intentionally seeking chaos be considered as a normal means of operation in the creative process. But, when you are stuck looking to break a pattern, find something new, taking a shallow dive into Chaos to 'shake the stage' can be very helpful. It allows us the opportunity to discover something genuinely novel.

I have always understood Franco's 'madness' to be uniquely his own. It is an accepted cliché of any director or famous Chef de Cuisine to be temperamental and demanding of his team. I thought I understood what Franco was trying to achieve. It wasn't until eight years later, once discovering the sense-making Framework of Cynefin and the Cynefin dynamics that I was able to reframe my experience and understand the creative process in a different light. My time in theatre and circus have given me an intrinsic understanding of working within complex adaptive systems. I have only realized that after being introduced to Cynefin.

PICKING UP PEBBLES ON THE PATH

I have worked in and created theatre and circus for over 25 years. I have performed over 5,000 times on stage. About six years ago, from the time of writing, I became creatively restless and curious to explore other areas of interest. I wanted to understand the business side of show business. This led me to pursue an MBA, subsequently landing a job in strategic Human Resources. I ran an innovation and organizational transformation hub within a Fortune 500 firm in Asia. It was here, in an office working in Human Resources, where I first learned of the Cynefin Framework.

One day, a colleague of mine was watching YouTube videos in his office. I kept hearing him laugh when viewing the same particular videos. He would often watch them repeatedly. I began to recognize these videos because of the distinctive voice I heard. Eventually, out of curiosity, I mustered up the effort to walk into his office to see what my colleague was watching. I saw an older gentleman with a mischievous grin and considerable intellectual parry, explaining complexity theory and a framework. It was Dave Snowden.

I began watching Dave's videos myself. I immediately saw the storytelling capability of a seasoned 'raconteur.' Dave would use similar themes in each talk, but by shifting ever so slightly, the tone, language, or emphasis depending on the audience, would elicit an entirely different talk. In addition, I noticed that Dave would drop these little concept pebbles along the way in his talks. It was up to us, the audience, to either know his reference already or, by letting our curiosity get the better of us, research and explore what was said.

When you start to pick up the pebbles, especially Dave's pebbles, you do so at your peril. There are whole other worlds of knowledge to unpack, connect, and synthesize. You need time, patience, and love for an ambiguity that becomes very specific. I often curse Dave for his mischievous oratorical skill.

But of course more than that, I'm grateful. The Cynefin Framework has helped me ground my previous experiences in the theatre by placing them within the context of complex adaptive systems theory. Along with the discipline of the natural sciences as a rigorous check against various cognitive biases, I am able to use the creative tools of art and theatre to support organizations to 'manage' uncertainty and complexity.

Standing cold and wet on the stage in Macau over ten years ago, being yelled at by an irate Italian director, I never dreamed that I would see the utility in the pattern of knowledge management and entirely understand.

Being part of the Cynefin community is central to this. Robed in the armor of the pragmatic, cynical curmudgeon, Dave's immense humanism often disarms me. His sense of care and intellectually rigorous curiosity is contagious. I am happy to walk along this Cynefin path and continue to pick up pebbles – thank you.

References

1. "Dragone · Spectators are our passion. Creation is our core.," Dragone. http://dragone.com/en (accessed Aug. 12, 2020).

2. Grotowski, J., & Barba, E. (2002). Towards a poor theatre (1st Routledge ed. ed.). New York.

3. "UNESCO - Mevlevi Sema ceremony." https://ich.unesco.org/en/lists (accessed Aug. 12, 2020).

What to read next

 Next Vignette: An Accidental Journey, Simon Wardley, p.354

 Next Chronological: An Accidental Journey, Simon Wardley, p.354

 Next Narrative: An Accidental Journey, Simon Wardley, p.354

AN ACCIDENTAL JOURNEY

SIMON WARDLEY

ABOUT THE AUTHOR

Simon Wardley is a researcher for the Leading Edge Forum, focused on the intersection of business strategy and new technologies. As a geneticist with a love of mathematics and a fascination in economics, Simon has always found himself dealing with complex, complicated and evolving systems, whether it's in behavioral patterns, environmental risks of chemical pollution, developing novel computer systems or managing companies.

ABOUT THIS CHAPTER

 Vignette   Narrative

 Chronology: Piece 30 of 33

AN ACCIDENTAL JOURNEY

SIMON WARDLEY

If anyone were to ask me when I first encountered Cynefin, my honest answer would be I don't know, and I probably never will. There is a simple reason for this; my interest mapping competitive spaces requires, among other things, my textual analysis of many publications. Before I'd even heard of Cynefin, I am sure several of the publications associated with it, would have doubtless been caught up in my analysis net. Of course, when I finally became consciously aware of Cynefin, it was apparent that the techniques of Wardley mapping and Cynefin were complimentary. And once I met Dave, we quickly found additional shared connections in the work of Max Henri Boisot and Ralph Douglas Stacey.

My first meeting with Dave was a result of 'gravitational attraction.' I speak at numerous conferences and have a bit of a reputation for dismantling ideas that lack context like the use of "agile" everywhere, the use of "six sigma" everywhere, and the use of just about any management approach irrespective of the context. As I moved in my orbit of open-source, government, and technology fields, I often found myself arguing on the same side as this Snowden chap. I probably hadn't made the connection to Cynefin at the time, but that rapidly followed. We bumped into each other frequently, especially online, and eventually shared a stage.

Dave and I are kindred spirits in many things, although we walk a slightly different path. While Wardley mapping is about understanding a landscape, it does not tell you what to do and how to do it. For that you need to apply thought and patterns. Using patterns comes from experience. The tricky bit is how to apply thought, how to think about a space. As Cat Swetel – a third member of our epistemic justice league – would say, it's not the maps but the mapping that matters i.e., the act of thinking about the space. The maps are simply a vehicle for communication.

So how do we, and how should we, think about a space? As a broader decision-making framework, Cynefin tackles that question. While Wardley maps show you the landscape, Cynefin will teach you how to think about that landscape. Of course like most of life it's not a simple translation. The map can be complicated, simultaneously containing elements that are obvious and others that are chaotic. So you have to decide how broad or narrow a picture you wish to take before applying thought (in this case Cynefin) to it. The practice of doing this is evolving, we're still learning how to do this. But then all things evolve – activities, practices, data, knowledge, even ethical values – through use and competition.

Has my work been influenced by Dave Snowden's thinking and the Cynefin Framework? Of course, and almost certainly long before I was aware of this. Our association may have started by a fortuitous conceptual collision, but it's been a beneficial collision for the entire mapping community, and I hope we can return the favor to the Cynefin community. Many are members of both collectives.

I'm delighted to have been asked to write this short vignette on my experience of Cynefin and meeting Dave. For me, it has helped provide a systematic way of thinking about a landscape. Something that I was missing, and for that I will be forever grateful. Thank you Dave, thank you Cynefin, and thank you Cynefin community.

What to read next

 Next Vignette: Walk With Me: Reflections on a Decade's Journey..., Jules Yim, p.370

 Next Chronological: Not all Those who Wander through Complexity are Lost, Anna Panagiotou, p.276

 Next Narrative: Walk With Me: Reflections on a Decade's Journey..., Jules Yim, p.370

A CYNEFIN APPROACH TO LEADING SAFETY IN ORGANIZATIONS

GARY WONG AND MICHAEL CHEVELDAVE

ABOUT THE AUTHORS

Gary Wong has over 45 years experience starting with his career at BC Hydro where he worked in engineering, line operations, business consulting and training roles. He later joined Ernst & Young Consulting (now Capgemini Consulting) as a Senior Manager in Strategy & Transformation. Gary has operated his own independent consulting practice for the past 15 years focusing on complexity thinking and safety. Gary has an engineering degree from UBC and an MBA from SFU. He is also a certified FranklinCovey 7 Habits facilitator and an Edward de Bono Six Thinking Hats and Lateral Thinking instructor.

Michael Cheveldave is a global trainer, facilitator, and senior consultant with Cognitive Edge. With a background in engineering, Michael strives to enhance organizational performance by delivering a pragmatic understanding of complex human dynamics. His work with Cynefin started in 2005 and his experience includes engagements worldwide. Michael has a B. Eng. degree from the University of Victoria and a Knowledge Management Certificate from Royal Roads University.

ABOUT THIS CHAPTER

 Full Chapter

 Theoretical

 Chronology: Piece 14 of 33

 Cynefin Principles

A CYNEFIN APPROACH TO LEADING SAFETY IN ORGANIZATIONS

GARY WONG AND MICHAEL CHEVELDAVE

Most leaders see safety issues as ordered, existing in the Cynefin Framework domains of Clear and Complicated, where best practices are valued. Yet while some safety solutions live here most safety issues do not. We will introduce you to an eye-opening mapping exercise, seeing safety as an emergent property of a complex adaptive system, and why you should manage a mixed portfolio of safety practices to increase both robustness and resilience.

All of us want to live in safe, danger-free environments. We want the places where we work, the public parks where we walk, the roads upon which we drive, and the airspace in which we fly to be safe. As citizens, we expect our cities to be safe. Yet, as we write this chapter, a major explosion has just caused catastrophic devastation in Beirut, Lebanon. For years ammonium nitrate was stored unsafely in a warehouse at the port. Why were these untenable conditions permitted to exist for so long? Why were warnings communicated to authorities and yet no action taken?

As a safety leader, either high above in the C-suite or down on the front lines, you want your organization to be safe. In this chapter we will explain that the way you perceive safety may be blinding you from detecting potential catastrophes and preventing you from taking decisive action. The Cynefin Framework can help you see safety challenges in an entirely new way.

We see safety not as a product or service, nor something to be created. Rather, we see safety as an emergent property of a complex adaptive system. Safety emerges from the relationships and interactions among people, machines, events (e.g., COVID-19), and ideas (e.g., Zero Harm). Holding this view, you can shape interactions and the environment to be opportunities for safety to emerge.

A complex adaptive system, according to the Cynefin Framework, includes the ordered Clear and Complicated domains, as well as the unordered Complex and Chaotic domains. Beside regarding various operating and environmental contexts, we now add the entanglement of human beings who need psychological safety to perform well.

According to Amy Edmundson, Novartis Professor of Leadership at Harvard Business School, "Psychological safety is the belief that the environment is safe for interpersonal risk-taking. People feel able to speak up when needed – with relevant ideas, questions, or concerns – without being shut down gratuitously. Psychological safety is present when colleagues trust and respect each other and feel able, even obligated, to be candid." [1] In this complex system of human behavior and relationships, with our state of being always changing, what is safe one moment may be unsafe the next.

A BRIEF REFLECTION ON HOW SAFETY HAS EVOLVED

Safety has predominantly been focused on what goes wrong, a perspective that Erik Hollnagel, an internationally recognized safety expert, has called Safety-I. [2] For the past century, Safety-I has emphasized training, eliminating errors, imposing compliance rules, reprimanding undesirable behaviors, assessing known hazards/risks, setting accident targets, and assigning blame. Practices such as these, although valid for some aspects of safety, remain narrow and are unable to deal with the growing level of complexity and uncertainty in the whole environment from which safety emerges.

The need to relook at safety has prompted responses from academics and consultants, bringing about new approaches like Safety-II, Safety Differently, New View, and Human & Organization Principles (HOP). [3] [4] [5] [6] Unfortunately, the plethora of approaches has mostly led to increased confusion, from regulators to workers. Todd Conklin's "Safety Spear," (see Figure 1) highlights the disconnect that often occurs between those at high risk (workers at the sharp end of the stick) and regulators who are far removed at the other end, but have the most authority. Workers at the sharp end are often acutely aware of the complex realities of safety in the field as they live it daily. The Cynefin Framework acknowledges this reality and offers the opportunity to bridge the awareness gap.

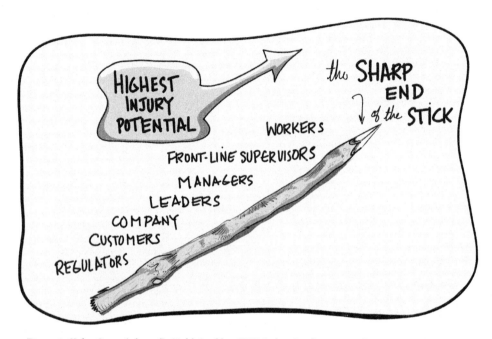

Figure 1. Safety Spear (adapted). Todd Conklin. TFZ Safety Conference 2016.

Before the 1979 accident at Three Mile Island, the human role in the safe operation of civilian nuclear power plants received little attention. *The Kemeny Report* on the Three Mile Island accident did not use the term 'safety culture,' however, it fully identified all relevant aspects of safety culture. It was only after the 1986 accident at Chernobyl that the term 'safety culture' came into widespread use. [7]

One definition of safety culture that resonates with us is Richter & Koch's. It appreciates human aspects – stories, myths, rituals, heroes. These provide context in terms of perspectives, feelings, and emotions. [8]

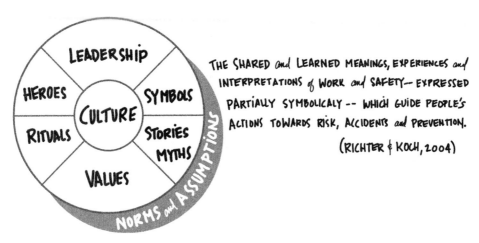

Figure 2. Safety Culture definition

Unfortunately, over the years 'safety culture' has become a catch-all when an investigation cannot locate a root cause. However, as noted by Erik Hollnagel, "We must face the fact that the world cannot be explained by cause-effect models. Incidents and accidents do not only happen in a linear way, but include emergent phenomena stemming from the complexity of the overall system." [9] Safety culture undeniably resides in the Cynefin Complex domain.

APPLYING CYNEFIN IN SAFETY

Safety leaders experience that Safety-I serves users well in maintaining the number of accidents at an acceptable level. The key to success here is identifying known risks. However, Erik Hollnagel points out that this is also Safety-I's weakness, "We can guard against everything that we can imagine. But we cannot imagine everything. Therefore, we cannot guard against everything." [9] Paradigms like Safety-II attempt to stay open relying on human judgment and experience to adjust for behavior in the absence of explicit risk procedures, or when rules get in the way, or when unexpected changes in working conditions signal danger emerging.

Taking a complexity-based approach to safety, we can better understand the impact of more frequent catastrophic surprises and why early detection capability to prevent failures from happening is paramount. Using Cyenfin we can reap valuable lessons from past and current experiences in mining, aerospace, oil & gas, electric utilities, healthcare, and construction, and military and police forces.

Following, we highlight three key points that can assist you in applying Cynefin to your safety environments.

KEY-POINT #1: WORK WITH THE SYSTEM AS A WHOLE

An excessive focus on the avoidance of accidents has resulted in our dominant mindset that safety is an ordered system. Safety professionals typically take a Complicated approach to safety using their expertise to interpret safety acts, laws and regulations passed down the Safety Spear (see Figure 1 earlier). They then turn them into governing policies, standards, systems, rules and procedures. Rigid ones, like Golden Safety Rules, are in the Clear domain and join highly constrained procedures called Best Practices. [10] Like best practices, they are appropriate when clear and obvious order characterizes the space or practice. (i.e., surgeon scrub-down procedures, confined space entry check-lists. etc.)

Workarounds and rule bending, or breaking to get the job done, are "weak signals" that at least some of your safety rules are not up to the variability and diversity of daily work. When deviations are discovered, the Safety-I response is to add more rules to fix the previously unknown, but now identified, risk. Yet an excessively constrained work environment puts workers and the organization at risk in several ways:

1. Too many rules to remember cause cognitive overload and can lead to anger and frustration, which leads to worker distraction.

2. Questionable workarounds are often passed down from masters to apprentices as tacit knowledge, and become dubious generational heuristics.

3. Workarounds become habits and start becoming part of the culture. "Normalization of deviance" is a term used by sociologist Diane Vaughan to describe the process where a clearly unsafe practice comes to be considered normal if it does not immediately cause a catastrophe, "a long incubation period [before a final disaster] with early warning signs that were either misinterpreted, ignored or missed completely." [11] (The original example cited by Vaughn was the events leading to the Space Shuttle Challenger disaster.) [12] For fear of upsetting senior executives, management may refuse to change an extreme rule despite workers pleas. An example is the forced wearing of hard hats under open skies in extremely hot weather. Todd Conklin spoke about the danger, "Workers don't cause failures. They trigger latent conditions that lie dormant in organizations waiting for a specific moment in time." [13]

4. A culture of fear builds when workers experience "can't win" dilemmas. If they bend the rule, then they will be punished. If they bend the work to comply, then the job doesn't get done and they may be punished.

5.   Safety incentives which are meant to improve safety, like bonuses and rewards, often compromise safety performance and result in unintended consequences. For example, an "All incidents must be reported" policy runs up against an incentive where a bonus is paid for the frequency and severity of accidents occurring below a certain threshold. Workers may game the system by not reporting incidents.

During a series of Cynefin and Safety training workshops we delivered, participants mapped their way to a startling understanding. One exercise we ran finished with the participants creating two mappings: (1) a mapping of safety solutions, and (2) a mapping of safety issues they identified as needing resolution. Figure 3 below reveals the pattern of how the most common safety solutions were mapped onto the Cynefin Framework. These included: safety rules, standard operating procedures, checklists, personal protective equipment (PPE), vehicles, tools, and equipment manuals. They were placed in the Clear (previously Obvious and Simple) domain. Root cause analysis, behavior-based safety programs, safety management systems, and Bowtie risk analysis were placed in the Complicated domain. These cause and effect solutions are based on Systems Thinking and a reductionistic engineering model design mindset.

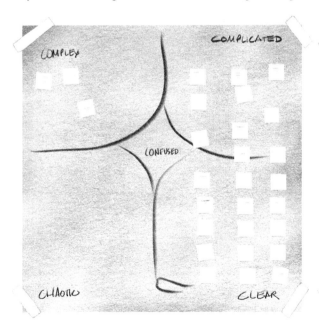

Figure 3. Cynefin mapping of safety solutions

Figure 4. Cynefin mapping of safety issues

Not surprisingly, the safety issues cover all the Cynefin domains (Figure 4). The contrast between the two maps always stuns workshop attendees. While there are plenty of ordered Clear and Complicated issues to be resolved, few acknowledge Complex domain issues. The key takeaway from the exercise was that despite the Safety-I mindset's efforts to improve safety, it falls short of tackling intractable safety issues when cause and effect relationships are either unknown, unknowable, or non-existing since the conditions are complex.

A similar finding emerged in a Deloitte Mining Safety case from 2009. [14] Figure 5 identifies the results from that engagement showing how many of the safety issues for this company's South African mining operations were complex. Yet the tools most commonly deployed to this day have been created with an assumption that the context is predominantly ordered.

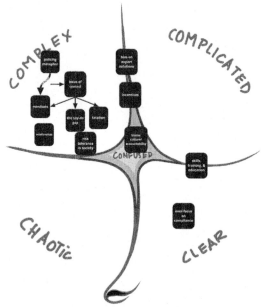

Figure 5. Unaddressed safety issues reside in the Complex domain

This narrow view of safety often omits complex aspects of safety – culture, attitudes, group behavior patterns, etc. In a personal communication with a manager during a Cynefin Safety workshop he stated, "We're really good at using a hammer. So good that we see everything as a nail. We blindly start hammering away even if it's a screw. And when we don't get the results we want, we still keep pounding away to the point of damaging the wood."

KEY-POINT #2: WORK FROM YOUR PRESENT STATE

Every company's safety environment will vary depending on the nature of the sector, its business history, and its unique operating culture. What is almost uniform, however, is that most safety executives (at the blunt end of the Safety Spear) focus on the idealized state and not sufficiently on the present state. In their expected role as company visionaries, they focus on creating future-oriented visions such as "Safety Excellence," "Zero Harm," "Incident Free," "Safety is Priority 1" with far-reaching statements and posters. Indoctrinated with these idealized states, leaders and managers believe that they can achieve it through an engineering-like approach. Guided by "what gets measured gets done," safety leaders set targets using Safety-I measures often mandated by regulatory bodies like the Occupational Safety and Health Administration (OSHA). The output is a "work-as-imagined" three to five-year corporate top-down safety plan with minimal input from front-line workers.

Annual operating plans serve to manage the implementation of the corporate plan – deviations from the plan is non-compliance. When safety performance does not improve, faults are found in the plans typically with finger-pointing attached. The reaction is to create a brand new safety vision based on the latest fad and start the cycle all over again. If you have lamented about this cycle (some have called it a downward spiral), what can you do differently? You can't change the past, and, you can't predict an idealistic future. What you can do is disrupt this pattern by staying in the present and evolving its potential.

By mapping your operating environment and comparing your safety tools as suggested in key-point #1, you can take the first step in understanding the present. Realize, however, that different operating units, functions, and management levels likely will have diverse views of your environment. Part of the work is recognizing the different perspectives and arriving at a wider agreement across the organization.

As shown, Cynefin mapping identifies how many safety issues fall into the Complex domain. A major mistake far too many leaders make is applying ordered safety solutions to "fix" complex issues (i.e., hammering a screw), which then creates false expectations. Working from your present state to handle complex issues means viewing the safety vision as directional instead of an end-state: there is no gap to close. Managing the evolutionary potential of your present, and taking action in a way appropriate to the nature of your system, leads us to key-point #3.

KEY-POINT #3: WORK WITH SMALL ACTIONS TO CREATE CONDITIONS FOR BIG IMPROVEMENTS

"Managing the present to create a new direction of travel is more important than creating false expectations about how things could be in the future." Dave Snowden

Besides uncertainty and unpredictability, another phenomenon of the Complex domain is how small initial changes can result in significant changes. That said, not all interventions will have impacts; some will have no effect at all. Consequently, since the impacts cannot be predicted or assured, we develop a portfolio of trial and error projects. Trial and error is synonymous with safe-to-fail experiments, probes, perturbations, safe-to-try, and pilots.

Developing a trial and error portfolio is not randomly choosing to try anything. Rather it feeds off the complex issues identified on the Cynefin maps. The disciplined process focuses on addressing immediate safety concerns (e.g., close to the Clear/Chaotic boundary) and facilitating learning. One practical approach is to assemble learning teams, each running a small project from start to finish. Teams are intentionally kept small, with three to five members. A recommended composition is a trio with an experienced field worker bringing first-hand knowledge of safety heuristics, a recent college graduate with fresh ideas, and a safety leader who has the authority to make things happen.

We believe an overarching safety strategy is managing a mixed portfolio of ordered and complex projects to strengthen robustness (Safety-I) and build resilience (Safety-II). As you might imagine, there is an ongoing debate between safety practitioners who promote Safety-II and those who defend Safety-I. We side with researchers who have concluded that combining Safety-I and Safety-II perspectives broaden understanding of safety management. [15]

Robustness is taking a Safety-I approach to prevent something from going wrong in the Clear domain and falling into the Chaotic domain. This is the primary intent of "fail-safe" ordered engineering projects and programs. Resilience is associated with Safety-II because "everyone at the sharp end knows that it is only possible to get work done by continually adjusting what they do under expected and unexpected conditions." [16] The main intent behind trial and error is to shape the safety culture by stimulating change towards the safety vision while on an emergent pathway forward. We monitor for impact, not measure for the outcome.

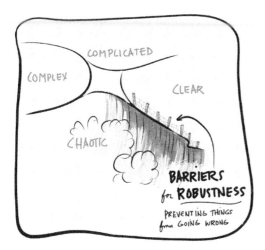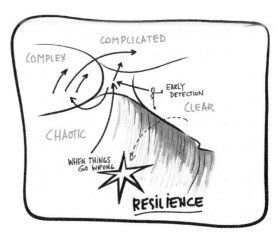

Figure 6. Cynefin guided safety strategies

From the operational aspect of people working in a system, robustness, as the left illustration in Figure 6 shows, is the appropriate application of rigid constraints (safety rules, standard operating procedures, best practices). Resilience, shown in the right illustration, is recovering from failure. In safety, a fall into the Chaotic domain relates to human accidents and failures – machines, equipment, tools, vehicles, facilities. Both minor scrapes and disasters show up as surprises and people are always caught off guard.

In the Chaotic domain you 'Act-Sense-Respond' to stabilize the bad situation and move to the Confused domain. Why confused? Because you still don't know why the accident occurred. So the next step is to analyze, either with causal experts in the Complicated domain, or seek to understand in the Complex domain. It's highly conceivable that an investigation will involve a move to both Complicated and Complex domains.

In his book *Drift into Failure*, [17] Sidney Dekker warns against assuming that the entirety of the accident must be investigated in the Complicated domain, "The search for the 'broken part or person' that underpins linear models, where risk is considered in terms of – energy-to-be-contained, barriers and layers of defense, or cause and effect – are misleading – because they assume rational decision-making." His point is that we need to make sense of the conditions the worker faced when a fateful decision was made. This is accomplished by discovering in the Complex domain what system constraints influenced the decision.

As shown in Figure 6, resilience also includes early detection of weak signals (e.g., workarounds, psychological fear). As previously mentioned, Dianne Vaughan calls this behavior the "normalization of deviance." The early detection pathway is through the Confused domain to the Complex domain to make sense of the system as a whole, work with the present state, and work with small actions to create conditions for significant improvements.

NEXT STEPS

Our hope is that safety leaders use the Cynefin Framework to expand their view of safety to include the complexity lens. By doing so you will equip yourself with a significant approach, with rich tools, to crack the proverbial "safety nut."

Safety culture is a messy, constantly changing entanglement of human factors interrelated with organizational systems, processes, and structures. Shaping safety culture requires feedback from everyone on the Safety Spear, in particular, front-line supervisors and workers. The next logical step would be introducing narrative tools powered by Cynefin's SenseMaker to collect feedback and narratives in real-time to assess and monitor the changes that enable safety to emerge.

References

1. Edmondson, Amy. How fearless organizations succeed. Strategy & Business, 2018. https://www.strategy-business.com/article/How-Fearless-Organizations-Succeed

2. Hollnagel, Erik. Safety-I and safety-II: the past and future of safety management. Farnham: Ashgate, 2014. Print.

3. Hollnagel, Erik. Safety-I and safety-II: the past and future of safety management. Farnham: Ashgate, 2014. Print.

4. https://safetydifferently.com/what-we-do/

5. https://safetydifferently.com/the-new-view-of-safety-with-todd-conklin

6. Conklin, Todd. The 5 Principles of Human Performance: a contemporary update of the building blocks of human performance for the new view of safety. Santa Fe, New Mexico: Pre-Accident Investigation Media, 2019. Print.

7. Van Erp, Jan. Safety Culture and the Accident at Three Mile Island. https://inis.iaea.org/collection/NCLCollectionStore/_Public/34/007/34007188.pdf?r=1&r=1

8. Choudhry et al. The Nature of Safety Culture: A survey of the state-of-the-art. ScienceDirect: Volume 45, Issue 10, December 2007, pp.993-1012.

9. Hollnagel, Erik. Safety-I and safety-II : the past and future of safety management. Farnham: Ashgate, 2014.

10. https://safetyrisk.net/golden-safety-rules/

11. https://en.wikipedia.org/wiki/Normalization_of_deviance

12. https://en.wikipedia.org/wiki/Space_Shuttle_Challenger_disaster

13. Conklin, Todd. TFZ Safety Conference, 2016.

14. Deloitte & Touche. Mining Safety: A Business Imperative. 2009. https://bit.ly/3dQ4ROb

15. Jones et al. Understanding procedural violations using Safety-I and Safety-II: The case of community pharmacies. ScienceDirect: Volume 105, June 2018, pp.114-120.

16. Hollnagel et al. From Safety-I to Safety-II: A White Paper. The Resilient Health Care Net: Published simultaneously by the University of Southern Denmark, University of Florida, USA, and Macquarie University, Australia. 2015.

17. Dekker, Sidney. Drift into failure: from hunting broken components to understanding complex systems. Farnham, Surrey, England Burlington, Vt: Ashgate, 2011.

What to read next

 Next Full Chapter: The Story of Cynefin 'Coming Home' to Welsh Public Services, Chris Bolton, p.98

 Next Chronological: Walk With Me: Reflections on a Decade's Journey with Cynefin, Jules Yim, p.370

 Next Theoretical: Cynefin and Delivery, Greg Brougham, p.113

 More on Cynefin Principle 1.3: The Story of Cynefin 'Coming Home' to Welsh Public Services, Chris Bolton, p.98

 More on Cynefin Principle 2.1: Cynefin and Delivery, Greg Brougham, p.113

WALK WITH ME: REFLECTIONS ON A DECADE'S JOURNEY WITH CYNEFIN

JULES YIM

ABOUT THE AUTHOR

Jules Yim has been associated with Cognitive Edge and Dave Snowden since 2009, when she was brought on board to participate in the delivery of government projects in Singapore. Since then, she has worked to apply anthro-complexity to organizations around the world. Jules's background in linguistics and literature has proven to be fortuitous and invaluable. Other interests include computational linguistics, urban planning and governance, futures and foresight, and climate change and narrative.

ABOUT THIS CHAPTER

 Vignette   Narrative

 Chronology: Piece 15 of 33

WALK WITH ME: REFLECTIONS ON A DECADE'S JOURNEY WITH CYNEFIN

JULES YIM

It has been a full ten years and a bit since I first came in contact with the Cynefin Framework. Both personally and professionally, I've been privileged to witness its evolution, and by extension, the development of its creator's thinking.

I never consciously stopped to reflect on how this journey influenced my intellectual development, but this occasion of its twenty-first birthday is a perfect moment to do so.

I am grateful for the timely meeting back in 2009 with Dave Snowden. It brought me into the intellectual orbit of a man who articulated the world of 'anthro-complexity,' a world I never thought available in the corporate world.

Non-linearity. Interacting agents. Emergence. Dynamics. The flow of movement. Liminality. These words pass easily from our lips now, and they articulate what I've always observed about the universe. I cannot, in all honesty say that discovering the Cynefin Framework was life-altering, rather it was life-affirming. I had rediscovered my ethnolinguistic heritage and put myself through a rigorous course of study in my teenage years. Hearing Dave reference Taoism a dozen times in his blog, and many more times on stage and in private, was deeply satisfying to me.

It was the first time I heard a Westerner speak of non-linearity as a positive thing. It was the first time I could connect 無為 Wu-Wei (action through inaction) to strategy. It was also the first time I'd ever considered that the embodied cultural philosophy I grew up in was so directly relevant and related to my professional life.

The Cynefin Framework is a philosophic tapestry of Dave's profoundly humanistic and sympathetic ideals. It pleasingly articulates his world-view in a way that invites others to make sense of theirs too. It is intrinsically collaborative and collectivist, communitarian and coherent.

Interestingly enough, I believe the Complex domain's Probe-Sense-Respond action framework is articulated in the 鬼谷子 Sage of Ghost Valley's treatise, based on Taoist thinking. [1] The first chapter of the treatise, 捭闔 "Opening and closing the gate," stresses the importance of continually surveying the permanently changing 形勢 (landscape) for its actual conditions, in order to act in it.

I've seen the bottom-right domain renamed from Simple to Obvious to Clear as Dave sought to express his thinking better. Perhaps the most overlooked but immensely important Disorder domain – now A/C 'Aporetic / Confused,' and links to 無為 Wu-Wei, is a domain I hope to study throughout my life.

In this respect I am reminded of Dreyfus and Dorrance Kelly in *All Things Shining*. I believe that Dave, being a craftsman himself, will appreciate the sentiment: "The task of the craftsman is not to generate the meaning, but rather to cultivate in himself the skill for discerning the meanings that are already there." [2]

I believe the Cynefin Framework helped me and countless others over the past twenty one years articulate what we have always known or believed to be true about the world. The Framework helps us discern meanings that already exist, and create meanings both for ourselves and in collaboration with others. I have used the framework countless times with clients and several times to resolve conflicts in non-professional settings.

The Cynefin Framework's legacy, I believe, will be its power of collective sense-making and meaning-making that future generations will discover and benefit from. I look forward to seeing what the next decade brings.

References

1. https://en.wikipedia.org/wiki/Guiguzi

2. Dreyfus, Hubert L, and Sean Kelly. All Things Shining: Reading the Western Classics to Find Meaning in a Secular Age. New York: Free Press, 2011, p.209.

What to read next

 Next Vignette: How the Cynefin Framework Changed my Take on Research, Milica Begovic, p.90

 Next Chronological: How the Cynefin Framework Changed my Take on Research, Milica Begovic, p.90

 Next Narrative: How the Cynefin Framework Changed my Take on Research, Milica Begovic, p.90

SUE BORCHARDT

ILLUSTRATOR OF THIS BOOK

ABOUT THE ARTIST

Sue Borchardt is a research artist whose work weaves ideas, story-telling, art, and user experience into animated videos and visual artifacts that aid sense-making. She holds a Bachelors Degree in Electrical Engineering from the University of Maryland and a Masters in Human Development and Psychology from Harvard's Graduate School of Education. A fascination with the complexity of individual, group, and organizational change efforts, motivates her to continue to learn about learning, bringing an ever-expanding set of lenses to her inquiry. Among these disciplinary lenses are neuroscience, biology, adult development, cognitive science, social psychology, and qualitative research.